ASTROLOGER'S
APPRENTICE

Book One of the
Astrotheologian Series

DAVID JOHN JAEGERS

ISBN: 978-0-692-66211-3
Library of Congress: 2016912983

For Information, Address:

    Shimmering Water Productions, LLC
    HC 2 Box 5090
    Hiram, MO 63944

LIFE IS NOT A TRAGEDY WE NEED TO ESCAPE
ON THE WINGS OF COMIC RELIEF.
LIFE IS A COMEDY, ALL TOO OFTEN BROUGHT
CRASHING DOWN
BY OUR OWN TRAGIC CHOICES.

Table of Contents

Chapter 1. Change

The cloud forming on Robert's horizon did indeed
have a silver lining, in the form of a pleasant vision, one in
which he could see himself spending time with Rufus.
This young man would soon discover the true basis for his
irrational fascination with his eccentric uncle. He could
never have guessed that it would be about Rufus teaching
him an ancient language, one that that would put his life
on a new path.

Robert was an excellent student, able to absorb and
process anything his very capable, private school teachers
could deliver. With no particular athletic interests or
abilities, he prioritized succeeding academically. At
seventeen, however, it was just beginning to worry him
that he hadn't the vaguest notion what he wanted to
pursue after high school, and he couldn't imagine how
starting over in a new school was going to help.

Of course, Robert respected his mother's need to
move back to the country. But he shuddered at the
thought of leaving the security of his friends and his high
school at such a critical time, the end of his junior year.
Ginny had seldom seriously mentioned moving back to
the area where she was raised. But when her own mother
suffered a massive stroke, she experienced the absolute

anguish of being forced to cope from a distance. As her mother's life slowly faded, the stoic loneliness displayed by her father Samuel gripped her heart and would not let go. Ginny had begun six months earlier to ask Robert's father James if there were any chance of moving back to the country so she could be closer to her father.

When James was able to secure a position with the rural electric cooperative in the county next to where Grandpa Samuel lived, what had been a latent, constant yearning quickly morphed into an action plan for the family. Consummate provider, James could now satisfy his wife's need without having to give up anything financially. James was the breadwinner, the rock, the dutiful husband, but hardly a role model for his son. Robert did not see himself following in his father's footsteps. He couldn't escape the inference that his father's dreams, if there were any, seemed to be locked away somewhere, without the faintest hint that they would ever see the light of day.

Why were some people content with the secure life of family and adequate material provisions, while others seemed to be driven by an internal compass pointing them towards more inspirational, less practical concerns? At seventeen, Robert couldn't possibly know what would come of these feelings, but they worked him constantly, like strong hands on the wheel of a ship sailing through a storm.

Why did people chase the dreams they chase? Better yet, why did some people appear to not chase dreams at all? Seeming resigned to a singular fate, they ceased to question. Robert's curiosity about the whys and wherefores of people's choices flavored all his dealings with classmates, friends, family, and even strangers. His analytical skills were so far ahead of his intuitive abilities, that he often found himself spinning his mental wheels with little or nothing to show for it. The only person he had ever met whose eyes signaled the possibility of answers was his Uncle Rufus, a man he barely knew.

Robert was struggling with how to tell his best friends at school. The opportunity presented itself one day in the lunchroom when Andrew snuck up behind him, and shook his chair.

"You're not going to believe this."

"Try me."

"Cindy said she'd hang out with me Saturday."

Robert gave away his distracted state when he dryly muttered.

"That's nice."

Andrew jumped into the seat across from Robert and fired again.

"I can't believe you're not more excited for me. Maybe even for yourself, because you know that she has so many sweet looking girl friends. What's going on with you?"

Robert pulled out his phone and read the latest text to Andrew.

"Robert, they accepted the offer. I hope you're still OK with moving to the country."

"So that's really going to happen?"

"Yeah. Even though I've known for six months that it might happen, the reality is pretty weird for me right now."

Robert put his head down, closed his eyes and took a deep breath. He held it for the longest time, finally letting it out ever so slowly. After a while, he raised his head and mustered a forced smile.

"But, yeah, about Cindy, you're a lucky son of a bitch! Is that better? You're a stud muffin for sure. No holding you back now."

Suddenly grasping the gravity of Robert's emotions, Andrew tried to make it right.

"I'm sorry Robert. I know this is big deal."

Robert tried to convince his friend that he was simply jealous about Cindy, and that it wasn't about the move at all. But Andrew knew better. He cooled the girl talk.

Andrew was 6 foot, 170 pounds, adept at all sports, handsome at seventeen, and got along with everyone, especially girls. Given his prowess on court and field, people would have allowed Andrew a certain amount of arrogance. But he was actually quite humble. He had a way of going along with people's wishes without seeming like a follower. Once the mood of the crowd seemed set, he was the one who would be able to just say, in so many words, or with just a smile, "well, OK, sounds good, let's do it." Andrew was one of the few people at the prestigious private school who managed to be a 'regular guy' in spite of his family's great wealth.

Robert, on the other hand, was all too often a step off the sidewalk, appearing to miss the flow of the social process. Constantly analyzing people's words and actions, he reacted too slowly to the consensus to be perceived as part of it. Everyone liked Robert, but had grown to expect few social moves or personal gestures. They accepted him as the little intellectual, and learned to appreciate his contributions, which tended to come in the form of overly succinct analyses, often ill-timed and easily misunderstood.

It was ironic that this 5' 10", 150 pound, gangly boy with sandy blond hair was the one who often intimidated people. Robert came off as "smart", in a way that made people wary. Well aware of how people perceived him, he tried very hard to control his penchant for awkward, reductionist observations. Feeling insecure as a person, and trying too hard to fit in, at the same time, was a dangerous combination. Robert applied scientific reasoning to everyday human experience. His attempts at jest, or whim, or idle comment sounded more like well-constructed logic. If there were a problem to solve, ask

Robert. If you found yourself wondering how to deal with a social situation, look to Andrew. They had each other's back.

As they left the cafeteria, Robert was glad that his next class was World Religions. His favorite class by far, it allowed him to override his thoughts about the move, not to mention his fears about the upcoming Junior Prom. He could consider that there was more to life than chemistry, calculus, and physics, all the things people pushed him toward, just because he was so good at them.

His school was of Catholic affiliation, manned mostly by Jesuit priests. Growing up Catholic, his mother having converted when she married his father James, Robert had an excellent grasp of this one theology. But when he was allowed to embrace the subtleties of the other religions of the world, he became very excited. He was learning that the effort to discern the spiritual meaning of life was important for all people, and that any belief was better than no belief at all. World Religion class opened his eyes to the difference between religion, theology, and philosophy, exposing him to the incredible number of possible approaches to this ultimate question of God.

He remembered his Uncle Rufus at Thanksgiving dinner, going on and on, after too much wine, about the importance of liberal education, and how it was so crucial for the individual to chart his own course. Robert was just beginning to understand, that for most people, God was part of the equation. Unlike the fixed bodies of knowledge, like calculus and physics, religion required each individual's subjective input. Robert was so impressed that the priest was not just selling Catholicism, but was more than willing to share knowledge about all religions, confident that he wouldn't lose any followers.

As he went about his student routine that week, Robert made a concerted effort to put a positive spin on the move. There was nothing he could do about it. His favorite little worry, whether he should succumb to the constant pressure to ask someone to the Junior Prom, had been suddenly replaced by a whole bucket full of worries.

On the Friday night after he received the news, he arrived home to find his parents on the phone with the realtor. Feeling fortunate to be barely noticed, he skipped up the steps to his bedroom, and zoned out in his recliner. Closing his eyes, he settled into streams of speculation about what moving to the country would really mean for him. If it didn't feel good, he steered around it. All he knew of the country was what he'd heard at the dinner table growing up and what he'd experienced at family re-unions and visits with his grandparents. What there actually was to do on a daily basis, or what the small public school was really going to be like, was impossible to know.

To survive in that moment, Robert reached deep into his imagination. As he dreamed about being on the farm with his Uncle Rufus, he experienced the genesis of a new power. He was discovering the ability to spin a tale of a fantasy in his mind, and use its magic threads to weave a new reality.

Robert's Aunt Katie had married an intriguing man. He went by Rufus, but his real name was Evan, after his grandfather. Rufus conducted himself with a subtle sense of fearlessness and personal courage. He embraced his eccentric nature with a quiet confidence, as if he would be surprised if people thought otherwise. Marching to the beat of a drummer that few people could even hear, he was effortlessly kind and thoughtful. The proverbial taxi driver with the PHD, Rufus had pre-disposed Robert to question the conventional. Robert remembered how his ears would perk up when Rufus spoke at family gatherings.

While he waited for the call to dinner, Robert wallowed in soothing fantasy.

At the dinner table, there was no shortage of talk about the effect of the move on the children. But Robert and his sister Angela weren't fooled. It was obvious that James and Ginny were totally pre-occupied with closing on the house they had found in the country. It was only about two miles from school, and five miles from Grandpa Samuel's cattle farm.

Robert's sister Angela was just finishing eighth grade. When the move was announced, she tried to appear disappointed about missing out on the private school education she had been promised. But as far as Robert could tell, she was actually excited about the move to the country. She and Robert had discussed the prospect of attending an all girl high school on more than one occasion. Even though she wouldn't admit it to her parents, Angela wasn't quite sure she wanted the uniform and all that went with it, in particular, life without boys.

The attitude of Robert's father was clear. Whatever made Ginny happy was what was going to happen. The kids would just have to adapt.

When they had finished the blessing, Ginny delivered some news.

"Oh, by the way, I almost forgot. I was actually able to talk with Gary today. His commanders made an exception. They let him talk on the phone even though he is preparing for a covert mission! He said to tell you that he loves you very much. He said he is very happy for me, and congratulated your father on his new job. I hope you all get to talk to him soon."

Gary was Robert's older brother. He was Army Special Operations. James and Ginny were super proud of their first born. Having already left home, he would be the one of their children least affected by the move. When they talked about Gary, they didn't have to feel guilty. Robert could hear it in their voices.

It was settled on that first day of spring. Ginny called

her father Samuel to tell him the news. James would leave in the morning to close on the house. When school was out, the family would move.

James and Ginny had always prioritized the evening meal, but this one was special.   They shared many thoughts and feelings about the good times they had experienced in the country growing up, as if to encourage happy expectations in their children. Robert and Angela mostly just listened, sensing how important it was for their parents to convince themselves that they were doing the right thing.

Chapter 2. Goin' Up to Country

As Easter break approached, Robert and Andrew decided to take advantage of the last remnants of parental guilt. They cooked up a scheme to get permission for a road trip. They proposed to check out Robert's new stomping grounds, visit Rufus and Katie's farm, and then spend the night at Grandpa Samuel's. To legitimize their going it alone, they chose a couple of days that Robert's parents had to work. When asked why they had to go on those particular days, instead of waiting to go with the family, they claimed that those were the only days that Andrew didn't have a baseball game. It worked. James and Ginny agreed to the trip on the condition that the boys spend the night at Samuel's.

The two young men talked non-stop on the way down. Excited to be free and on the road, they shared ideas and feelings like never before. Andrew's favorite topics were Cindy and baseball. Robert would begin with his sense of anticipation about his new school and his new life in the country, but would always end up on his Uncle Rufus. Andrew couldn't deny the pattern.

"Why do you like your uncle so much? You hardly know him."

"Maybe it's because Rufus was a teacher, and I like

learning. Maybe it's because he's 'different'. Maybe it's because he's a thinker like me. Maybe it's because ....."

"Maybe it's because you're desperately trying to find something to be happy about, considering you're moving to East Jesus!"

Andrew seemed fine with keeping the focus on Rufus.

"Why do they call him Rufus anyway? That's not really his name, is it?"

"Apparently, when he was a teacher, he would surprise the kids with different funny names and disguises to stimulate their imagination. One of his favorite characters was Professor Rufus T. Schicklgruber. With a German accent, he would use the Rufus T. Schicklgruber character to talk about Einstein and various physics topics. To show off, or just for laughs, the students would call him Rufus outside of class. They knew that if they called him by his real first name, Evan, they'd be in big trouble. But if they called him Rufus, or Rufus T. Schicklgruber, he would let it slide, anything to win them over to a greater appreciation of science. After a while, everyone just started calling him Rufus."

"You said he was into astrology?"

"As long as I can remember, people in my family have whispered about that, and apparently it's way beyond what you read in the newspaper or some app you can access on your smart phone. Something about charts. I really don't know, but I am curious. I think Rufus has his shit together, so maybe he's onto something. You know what I mean? I've overheard him talking at family get-togethers, something about learning astrology when he was young. I'm not sure anyone takes him seriously."

Andrew just shrugged and then offered the obvious.

"Maybe we can get him talking about it."

As they approached Robert's new home from the west, they noticed more and more signs indicating road improvements were underway. The state highway dated back to the days when roads followed the natural ridges and valleys. Now, after much planning and patience, and a few too many fatal accidents, the highway into the small town was getting its share of highway funds. They were taking the steepness out of the hills and softening the extremes in the curves.

In fact, the improvements planned for one of the sharpest curves accounted for why Robert's new family home was on the market. In order to straighten out the curve, the highway engineers had to eliminate the beautiful, steep, forested hollow that had been the resident's view for over fifty years. Passing traffic would no longer be slowing to a crawl, forced to admire the magnificent slope and the lake below. Instead, when the road was straightened, the traffic would be whizzing by at 55 mph. This new front yard view did not please the owners, so they put the property up for sale.

Robert liked what he saw immediately upon approaching the house. His parents had done well with all those suburban real estate equity dollars. A story and a half design, with two friendly yellow-sided dormers poking out toward the road, this brown brick house seemed solid and comfortable. There was a long porch across the front and the west side was graced with a greenhouse extension. The property was forested on the south and the west, having been managed over the years to leave only majestic hardwood trees. The natural understory of vines and brushy trees was all gone, replaced by grasses.

As Andrew pulled into the circular driveway, Robert couldn't take his eyes off the huge hollow to the east that was being prepared for tens of thousands of cubic yards of fill. He regretted the loss of the forest, but as a fledgling engineer, he was excited about the opportunity to witness such a massive undertaking. He suddenly had a twinge of allegory. What did the project before him portend about his own path?

For a second, mesmerized by the construction site, he was lost in a daydream about how cool it would be to watch the project unfold. He thought how strange it was that one man's road improvement was another man's eyesore. Robert looked all around his new home and perceived an atmosphere that was unique, natural, and wholesome, with no immediate neighbors, only passersby.

Andrew shook him out of his mind space and dragged him toward the key waiting under the mat. They checked out the house, admiring the huge stone fireplace, the massive country kitchen, the spacious back patio that overlooked the lake, and the toasty greenhouse off the master bedroom on the west. Robert made his claim on the east-side upstairs bedroom because it overlooked the construction. He felt good about the new place and silently thanked his parents. Even Andrew, who lived in a mansion, was impressed.

But it was still just a vacant house. They saw no reason to linger. Besides, they were hungry. It was time to head to Grandpa Samuels's for lunch. The sooner they got that out of the way, the sooner they could see Rufus and Katie.

Getting to Grandpa Samuel's farm meant continuing eastward. They soon arrived at Robert's new school.

"This is where Rufus used to teach?"

"Yeah. I don't remember exactly why he quit teaching science and became a nurse, but I know that he had a really good reputation as a teacher. I remember my Mom always saying how proud Katie was of Rufus. The students really liked him."

Next was the small town. It was drab in comparison to the suburban landscape they were used to. Andrew was the first to comment.

"Not much going on here. I see stores and churches

and gas stations, and that's about it."

Before they knew it, they were through the town.

A few miles east, they turned off the state highway and onto a long gravel drive that proceeded uphill between two gently sloping cow pastures, arriving at a house and series of barns on the top of the hill. Robert's Grandpa Samuel greeted them with a brief smile and a "howdy". He removed his cap to reveal a head of thick grey hair. His weathered face of seventy-four years featured wrinkles that all seemed to be in the right place. He was a handsome, strong, country man that Robert loved and respected, but did not know very well.

Once in the back door of the large farm house, they went right for the kitchen table. Samuel seemed as hungry as the boys, having been up since dawn messing with his cattle. Lunch consisted of ham and cheese on homemade bread, potato chips, dill pickles, and a coconut cream pie from Ginny. She didn't have time to make her father a pie, but she wanted to send something. So she had Robert pick one up from the bakery on the way out of town. It seemed kind of backwards, taking a pie to the country, but Samuel wasn't complaining.

In an attempt to bridge the generational, cultural gap that lay before him, Samuel focused on the boy's school experiences, their parents, and things they liked to do. But Robert had a better idea. He skillfully steered his grandfather toward more provocative subjects, like politics, taxes, government, and of course, guns. He was pretty sure Andrew had never met anyone like Samuel. Robert didn't want his friend to miss out on the opportunity to feel the conservative heat.

But eventually it was fidget time. The boys began clearing the table and washing the dishes. Although Samuel enjoyed observing such dutiful behavior, he knew the boys wanted to run along and enjoy the April weather. So he made them stop. Besides, he just wanted to get back to his cattle.

Samuel had political and religious differences with Rufus, but never uttered one regret about him marrying his daughter Katie. Cut from the original bolt of conservative cloth, Samuel couldn't get past Rufus's ponytail, much less understand his political philosophy. Samuel would always say Rufus was just "fiddle-fartin' around", implying that he wasn't a real farmer because he raised sheep instead of cattle. The two of them playfully sniped at each other whenever they were together, but Samuel never questioned Rufus's love for his daughter, and that's what really mattered.

Knowing where they were headed, and certain that the boys would repeat everything he had said, Samuel laid it on the line.

"I know you young men won't buy into Rufus's bullshit. I know you're smarter than that. Don't let that sheepherder get you all confused."

"Yes Grandpa. We'll see you later, OK Grandpa?"

Chapter 3. Uncle Rufus

The boys were happy for the experience with Samuel, and for the lunch, but were ecstatic about their escape. After passing back through the small town and by the new house, they had only a twenty minute cruise westward to their true destination.

In no time, Robert was directing Andrew down a narrow gravel road. After only a quarter mile, they crossed over a large creek on the concrete "low water bridge", and then proceeded up the creek bottom. It was obvious from the debris along the road that it was subject to flash flooding. Rufus claimed it was part of the mystique of "living on the other side of the creek", and that the occasional inconvenience of high water limiting access was well worth it. Thirty years before, when the country folk didn't pay much attention to such properties, Rufus had bought a hundred acres, as he liked to say, "for the price of a pickup truck". Now the local people envied Rufus's place and what he had done with it.

They came up out of the bottom and started up a hill. As the road leveled off, at the beginning of Rufus and Katie's farm, they could see the sheep in the field on the left. They soon came to the long driveway that led uphill to the house. The dogs greeted them with joyful barking while Katie came out on the back porch to motion them to continue around to the back part of the house.

Robert jumped out of the passenger side and greeted his Aunt Katie while Andrew showed a little bit of hesitation with regard to the big dogs. Katie walked right over to Andrew and assured him that they were just excited to have visitors and that there was nothing to fear. The dogs were large, protective of Katie, but were never aggressive with people. Their main purpose in life, other than being spoiled by Katie, was to guard the sheep from predators, wide awake and working at night and lazing around the yard during the day.

"C'mon into the house."

As they entered the kitchen and sat down, Robert and Andrew were visibly nervous. After only a glimpse of the back yard area and the forest that surrounded it, it felt a little weird to be coming inside so quickly. After a few rounds of small talk, Katie sensed their discomfort.

"You all should go find Rufus. It's such a beautiful day. Look at you. Two energetic boys. You don't want to be sittin' around the table talkin' with me. You need to get out and do somethin'."

"Actually, Aunt Katie, sitting around the table and talking was most of what we did at Grandpa Samuel's. Between that and sitting in the car half the day so far, it would be great to go for a walk."

"Well then, take Andrew down the road to the lambin' barn. The dogs'll go with you, and I'm sure you'll find Rufus. Do you want something to drink? I made some tea, or how about some lemonade?"

"No that's OK Aunt Katie. We're fine."

As they walked out the back door, across the porch and into the back yard, April's vibrance refreshed their mood. Birds were singing. The sun was bright. It was all good.

The back yard environment consisted of a concrete

driveway/patio, a swimming pool area up in the back accessible by a series of stone steps, a small lawn area to the west that gave way to a couple of raised-bed gardens, and a huge porch on the west side of the house that was surrounded by large trees just beginning to fill out with leaves. The natural beauty of the place was accentuated by the gentle breeze and warm sunshine. They were just standing there on the driveway, taking it all in, when Robert felt compelled to brag.

"Rufus built all this, the house, and even the swimming pool."

"No way! I remember when they built our pool. There were ten guys!"

Andrew knew absolutely nothing about construction, lived in a mansion, and had never done a day of physical labor in his life.

"Yeah, I think it's pretty neat. Rufus designed it all, and built it all himself. Speaking of Rufus, let's go find him."

They headed down the long driveway toward the gravel road, with the dogs on their heels.

Showing off his admittedly meager knowledge of all things country, Robert reminded Andrew to watch out for snakes, and to periodically check his pant legs for ticks. Andrew could see right away that the environment was a wild one. For Rufus, yard was yard and forest was forest. There was a distinct line of demarcation between the two. His yard rivaled any in suburbia. But where the woods started, the landscaping stopped.

Along the narrow gravel road, there were large trees, small trees, vines, shrubby plants, briars, and various wildflowers just starting to bloom. They saw a rabbit, several squirrels, a couple of doves, and many other song birds in the first couple hundred feet. The dogs suddenly, confidently ran ahead, to show off the fact that they knew exactly where the boys were going.

After a while they turned to the right, down a less-travelled gravel road. Robert explained why the lambing barn was down the hill so far from the house. When Rufus originally built the barn, he lived in an old house on the adjacent property. Thinking he and Katie would stay there longer than they did, he had built the lambing barn to suit their situation at the time. The location of the lambing barn relative to the house on the hill would always serve to ensure plenty of exercise.

As they entered through the gate to the barnyard, they could hear him. Whenever he spoke, some of the sheep would 'baaa' in refrain. It sounded very natural and peaceful.

Rufus apparently saw them through one of the windows of the barn, so he came out into the barnyard to greet them. His slender, muscular six-foot frame sported a Henley and jeans. His graying blond hair was tied back in a ponytail that stuck out from under his stocking cap. He wiped his hands on his pants as he smiled and proclaimed his satisfaction.

"Just had a set of twins."

He looked squarely at Andrew, kind of waving his hand in the air instead of offering to shake. It took Andrew a second to process. Rufus may very well have been probing intimate places.

"It's so nice to meet a friend of Robert's. I don't know if you've been around animals much, but you should come in the barn and see my new lambs."

He patted Robert on the back, and ushered the two young men into the barn.

"Don't worry. I won't put you to work. I just have to observe these new ones for a while. I used to ask my students over and over, 'what's the key to science?' Eventually, they learned to answer without hesitation: 'Observation!'"

The three of them stood back about fifteen feet away

from a ewe and her newborn lambs. Rufus talked casually about this and that, seeming very confident that the lambs would get what they needed from their mama. Already on their feet, they noodled around the side of the mama in search of the teat. They had to get that first milk, that colostrum, in order to survive. The mama expertly licked and baaa'd and nudged and maneuvered her body until each of them found a teat. Audible suckling and wagging tails confirmed success. The ewe stared straight ahead and chewed her cud as she let her milk down, oblivious to the visitors. After this first milk dance was completed, her behavior would become much more protective, especially with strangers present. But for now, she just did her part instinctively, with post-partum lactation hormones completely in charge of her behavior.

All of a sudden, Rufus decided it was time to go, and walked through the main door into the barnyard, holding it open for the boys to follow. Rufus explained that all the chores were done. He pointed over toward the field behind the barn, remarked that all the mamas and lambs were doing fine and that he would come back to check on the newborns later.

"Let's go back to the house another way, so I can show you around a bit."

He looked over the boys' foot wear, silently nodded approval, and led them toward a large wooden gate that opened to a field to the west. They walked in silence for five minutes or so, like they were just out for exercise. After passing through another gate into yet another field, Rufus cautioned them to watch where they stepped as they passed through a low lying area that tended to be a little mucky. The boys followed his lead, stepping on the higher places, eventually arriving at yet another gate. It accessed a small clearing near the creek.

Robert was getting excited.

"Oh, good, we're going to the creek."

Hearing the word "creek", the dogs pushed to the front, wanting to be the first ones through the gate. "Go to creek" was an important part of Rufus's dogs training.

"Yeah, it's such a nice day. I wanted you to see what the beavers have been up to."

As they approached the spring branch that ran through the farm, it became obvious to Robert that things had changed a lot since he was there many years before. The beavers had raised the translucent green blue water to the very top of the banks. A great blue heron rose majestically into the air. Spring peepers, oblivious to the presence of the men, offered their own version of a background instrumental. The dogs ran upstream to find a shallower spot to cross the creek, anticipating the opportunity to chase a deer or two in the forest on the other side.

The sheep farmer talked about how the creek was when he first came there, and chronicled all the changes the beavers' voracious appetite and dam-building lifestyle had imposed. Rufus seemed just as excited to show off his beavers as he had the newborn lambs. For him, animal husbandry and wildlife protection were merely different manifestations of the same naturalistic philosophy.

As Robert and Andrew listened to Rufus's ramblings of appreciation for being able to live his version of a natural life, there was no way they could know the rest of the story. For Rufus, it wasn't just about the countless hours of peace and quiet, and the deep reflection they enabled. The man was convinced that his choice of this isolated, rural environment had enabled him to discover his truth, that astrology was simply another form of naturalism. Believing he had achieved the ability to dance in step with the rhythms of the universe, Rufus was on the verge of dropping everything to pursue a grand quest, to prove to the world that astrological energies are as natural as life itself. But he firmly believed that it was not yet the time to reveal this to anyone, not even to his wife.

When thirst induced a departure from the lowlands, they made the long, steady upslope grind northward, through two fields and then across the county road. They hopped up a short trail through the pines, entered the basement door, and trumpeted up the stairs to Katie's kitchen.

The boys were thrilled with the fresh-squeezed lemonade. Rufus grabbed a beer from the refrigerator and declared it was the perfect time to adjourn to the west-side porch. He had designed it for just such a day. The late afternoon sunshine was pouring in under the raised-beam roof. The dogs, eager for the company, but still wearing their winter coats, declined the invitation, and left the April Sun worship to the humans.

After what seemed like an eternity, the boys were saved from Katie's polite inquisition. It was Robert's mother Ginny on the phone. Rufus politely excused himself, eager to shower off the barn dust. Robert and Andrew headed up to the swimming pool area, on the excuse that Katie might want privacy.

Rufus had not opened the pool yet, but the large concrete deck, cabana on the east, and pool bar on the west, made for an interesting tour. Having grown up with a swimming pool, Andrew had to admit, that except for the lack of a fancy wrought iron fence around the perimeter, the pool environment that Rufus had designed was every bit as nice as his parent's. The large oak trees on the east and west provided morning and evening shade, as well as an attractive surround. There were no neighbors, just forest, and it made for a sense of privacy that was more warm and genuine than any fence could ever provide.

Robert was happy to see Rufus emerge from the house and join them at the pool. He was smiling as he drank another beer, and asked the boys if they wanted to see his garden. He loved his garden. Rufus loved to brag about how he was manning the hoe in the garden with his father when he was only five years old. It was one of his earliest memories. Not only was he the only one of the six kids in his family to become an avid gardener, he was also the only one who had chosen a path to the country life. He had listened intently at the family dinner table, to all the talk of the "good old days". While the other kids surmised from their parent's stories that country life must have been hard, Rufus was soaking up the knowledge, and charging his batteries, preparing to become the modern day homesteader that he was.

The garden tour didn't mean much to the boys, as they were not really interested in learning all the details about how to raise peas, or spinach, or shallots, or potatoes. But they could see how happy it made Rufus to share his knowledge. There was a strawberry patch, long rows of raspberry plants, and fertile asparagus beds, all carefully constructed and tended. Rufus didn't try to grow large quantities of each individual crop, but he loved the idea of 'fresh'. The emphasis was on variety and quality. Robert did show some genuine interest in the difference between the early stuff, like peas and spinach, that could germinate and thrive in the cooler weather, and the late stuff, like tomatoes and green beans that had to wait until after the last frost to be sowed or planted. Each man, from his own dramatically different perspective, truly appreciated the experience.

As they came back up on the porch, Katie brought the boys back to reality.

"You're mother says hello and she's glad that you're having a good time. She left a message for Grandpa Samuel that you would be there with dinner by six o'clock."

"I wish we didn't have to leave so soon. But I understand that Grandpa is expecting us. How can we help with the dinner stuff?"

"I have everything ready. Thanks to Rufus, we are all going to feast on chicken and dumplings. Andrew, would you like to help me load the dinner into your car? I know that Rufus wants to speak with Robert about something before you guys get going."

Andrew joyfully followed Katie to the kitchen, leaving Rufus and Robert alone.

"That isn't how I thought you'd find out I wanted to speak with you privately before you left, but it doesn't really matter. I just wanted to let you know that you are always welcome here, and I'm excited about the prospect of you being closer. I know that Samuel and I differ on a few things, and that I am just your uncle-in-law, but I just wanted to tell you, man to man, that you are welcome here anytime."

Rufus and Katie had no children. When they were married, Katie's mother and father were not so thrilled. They knew Rufus was a good man, but they sensed that he was not their ticket to a houseful of grandchildren. The fact that Samuel and Rufus were miles apart, politically and philosophically, had never resulted in any serious friction, but the adoption of a "no religion and politics" protocol at family gatherings always seemed to be a good idea. Indeed, the fact that Robert and Andrew were not spending the night with Rufus and Katie, as they would have preferred, and were essentially required to head back to Samuel's place, was clear testimony to how sensitive certain people were about the Rufus influence.

Robert didn't know what to say. He really liked Rufus and Katie and the farm, but had applied only an optimistic, youthful assumption that he would be seeing more of them after the move. He did not expect such a willful, heartfelt invitation. He could do nothing more than say "OK", while his mind raced over the possibilities, and his heart told him that he may have found a different kind of friend.

"I'm so glad you feel that way, Uncle Rufus, because I really am looking forward to visiting."

"Good. Then it's settled. This summer, after you move, you and I can do some country stuff. Hey, I bet you'd like to go on a float trip. Have you ever been canoeing?"

"No, but it sounds great. Thanks."

Katie and Andrew returned to the porch to remind Robert that it was time to go.

Rufus reached to shake Andrew's hand.

"So when's your birthday Andrew? You and Robert seem very different, but are obviously good friends."

Rufus blushed, suddenly self-conscious about his question.

Andrew sensed his discomfort.

"Oh, that's OK. I'm a Capricorn, if that's what you mean. I was born on January 18th."

"Oh, that's great. Pardon me for asking. I'm kind of an amateur astrologer, especially when it comes to gaining insight into relationships that seem to work."

Andrew said nothing, kind and gracious as always, and unaware of the intense curiosity that was welling up in his friend Robert.

Katie steered the whole group back to the kitchen. She called Grandpa Samuel to let him know about the dinner that was headed his way. All he had to do was heat it up.

Chapter 4. Suburban Soiree

As the word spread about Robert moving, he got a lot of extra attention at school, especially from the counselor. Mr. Dempsey had always taken an interest in Robert's future. He saw a young man with an unselfish spirit whose God-given intelligence could take him anywhere he wanted to go. Mr. Dempsey knew that Robert had not come from wealth, or even from a family tradition of higher learning. Perhaps for this reason, or just because of a personal connection, he paid him special attention.

One day, they talked about achievement test scores, potential majors, and college applications. Personality and learning style inventory results led the counselor to suggest a path oriented to math and science. It was true that Robert's favorite course was physics, so he listened intently and acknowledged that such a direction was logical.

Mr. Dempsey admitted his concern that Robert may be at risk of under-achieving in the small, rural, public school environment. He also wanted Robert to realize that the choice of college was important, and that financial aid would be available. So he suggested some things Robert could work on during the summer.

Andrew continued to excel at baseball. He was

leading the team in hitting and played a mean third base. When it came to college, even though he didn't need the financial support, he held out hope for an athletic scholarship. His father didn't have any problem with baseball, but he insisted that Andrew pick a major that would allow him to pursue his family tradition, making a lot of money.

The spring social scene was heating up for everyone except Robert. But with the prospect of his moving, the pressure to get him to the prom was intensifying. As it turned out, active encouragement was not the answer. All Robert needed was to be in the right place at the right time. One day, as he watched Andrew play baseball, he was spotted by Cindy, who insisted that he join her.

Cindy was flanked by two friends who often accompanied her to such events. Robert found one of them, a girl named Michelle, to be totally intimidating. Slender, athletic, and always sporting low-cut tank tops and tight jeans, she was his fantasy girl. When he was in her presence, he was so overwhelmed sensually that he could barely function. Robert still hadn't relaxed into the realization that every seventeen year old boy had a Michelle, and that it was OK.

On the other side of Cindy was Samantha, a pretty brunette who was more tomboy than goddess, more serious than sexy. Robert had competed against her in academic contests. He could enjoy her feminine form but still find his way to her brain.

After some chit chat, Samantha invited Robert to the concession stand and gave it her best shot.

"What's this about you leaving us? You can't do that."

Robert stopped, and without thinking for once, made a gesture unusual for him. He reached out and touched her on the shoulder as if he wanted to put his arm around her, as if to say "that's so sweet of you to say." He quickly returned to a position facing her but couldn't help notice how much that gesture had pleased her.

Smiling at him, hands on hips, Samantha just let it out.

"Robert, I realize that we don't know each other very well, but I have to be honest with you. For several weeks now, Cindy and I have been trying to figure out how to get you to ask me to your prom. We've strictly prohibited Andrew from bringing up the idea with you because we thought that approach might backfire. We know he's always trying to fix you up with girls and that you get tired of that. You need to be your own man."

She paused, hoping he would say something. When he didn't, she reached out to him and playfully pushed at his chest.

"So what'd you think Robert? Do you want to go to the prom with me or not? This is the place where you're supposed to say something. You know you might actually have fun!"

Robert just stood there trembling for a moment, waiting for a bonafide sense of happiness to take hold. When it didn't, he resorted to super-rational mode, his default self. How could he say no to this person? She was so brave and so nice, and he did like her. Robert had no desire to go to the prom, but his analytical brain told him that it made sense to the prom. This was vintage Robert.

"Of course, I'll go with you."

When the ball game was over, as Andrew joined the group, the news of the prom date came out. Michelle offered Robert and Samantha her congratulations and took off with one of the boys from the opposing team. That's when Robert discovered, that for Andrew, it was more about the post-prom pool party than it was about the actual junior prom. It would be 'invitation only' on the following day, starting about noon. Andrew wasn't looking for a big blow-out party. Stealing some private time with Cindy was his priority. He even begged Cindy not to invite Michelle. He was all too familiar with the public school crowd Michelle hung out with.

When the big night finally arrived, Samantha made Robert's prom experience as painless as her invitation. She made it about Robert having a good time with his friends, and not about her personal romantic desires. As the affair came to a close, drowning in Robert's vociferous thanks, Samantha admitted that she was consciously paying it forward. As a military brat, she was all too familiar with saying goodbye to friends and having to start over when her family moved to the next base. But altruism aside, she did exact a payment, in the way she handled the good night kiss.

Robert awakened the next day feeling frisky, confident, and ready for a pool party. Andrew's parents not only condoned such events at their home, but they shelled out for the food, drink, and party favors. The housekeeper Millie was to keep everyone happy. She approached the affair like any other she managed for Andrew's parents, with a few caveats: no alcohol and no free run of the house. If it couldn't happen in the yard, in the rose garden, in the pool, on the pool deck, or in the cabana, it wasn't allowed. There was a bathroom and changing room just inside the rear entrance to the house, on the way into the kitchen, and that was the only exception. The guests knew the routine.

It was a win for everyone, including Andrew's parents, who had no desire to chaperon one of these events. The young people were fine with Millie, because not only did she wait on them hand and foot, but they were confident in her neutrality. As long as the behavior wasn't outrageous, and nothing got broken, she was fine with 'see no evil, speak no evil, hear no evil'.

It was the first week of May. The pool was perfect as always, and the weather wasn't bad. By one o'clock the party was on. It was all couples, except for Robert and Andrew's friend Petey. Everything was going according to plan until Michelle showed up with a guy named Todd. Their entrance was met with raised eyebrows all around, but Andrew took no action. When another half a dozen boys and girls showed up, alarm bells sounded. Presumably Todd's friends from the local public school, and not very well known to Andrew, their presence transformed a perfect day into something tense. A couple of Andrew's baseball friends decided to take Todd aside and grill him, while Cindy and Michelle disappeared into the bathroom. Assurances were accepted that it was not a crash. There would be no more surprise guests.

Thankfully, a happy, relaxed atmosphere returned. As the afternoon wore on, there was some sneaking to the cars for a sip of wine that had found its way out of a parent's cellar. But the kids were discrete. Just as many of the "private-schoolers", also known as preps, were hitting the bottle as the "public-schoolers". All in the range of seventeen to eighteen, these upper middle class suburban kids knew how to handle the alcohol scene. Bending the rules at a place like Andrew's was easy. Access to the huge property was by way of a long, tortuous driveway lined with trees and shrubs. As long as they didn't linger at the vehicles for too long or in too great a number, it was pretty easy to conceal their actions.

It didn't take long for Todd to locate Petey to inquire about a little smoke. Petey was a confirmed hacker and pothead. He looked like Billy Mummy from Lost in Space. Raised by a couple of computer scientists, he was the prototypical computer nerd. What wasn't so obvious was that he really liked to smoke marijuana. Managing to stay in school because he was just plain brilliant, Petey was the proverbial cat with nine lives, always managing to get out of trouble as easily as he got into it.

Michelle talked Samantha and Robert into coming

along when it was time to step behind the garage. Robert, who had only tried pot a few times, was surprised how comfortable Samantha was. She explained that her older brothers were all stoners, and even though she didn't join them very often, she was used to hanging around with people who liked to get high. After peer pressure propelled even Robert to take a couple of hits, they returned to the pool area, some more self-conscious than others.

Robert and Samantha had some quiet time together, tried making out in the pool, but the awkwardness of it propelled them quickly back to the cerebral plane. Robert really liked her, told her so, and asked if he could see her again before he moved to the country. She was in agreement with the idea, but it was clear that neither of them really knew what it meant. They were on a high, in more ways than one, but knew deep down that the demands of school year's end and Robert's departure would probably put the kibosh on any kind of meaningful relationship.

Andrew and Cindy did disappear into the house while Millie was occupied at the barbeque pit, with everyone whispering that they probably went well past the kitchen. When the two lovebirds returned, everyone played it cool. The gorgeous, vivacious Cindy really had it bad for Andrew, and he wasn't exactly protesting.

About five o'clock, Robert's twenty-four hour romance came to a close. He walked Samantha down the long driveway so she could intercept her father. She had a prior commitment with her family for that evening. Robert once again may have overdone his gratitude, but Samantha really didn't mind. She felt good about having taken the initiative. With the good night kiss already in the bank, they settled for a long warm hug as her father beckoned.

Relieved to return to bachelor status, Robert sought

out his friend Petey. It didn't take long to find him. He had drawn a crowd in a shady corner of the rose garden. Undeterred by the curious scrutiny of strangers, Petey was going on and on about his latest fantasy cybercrimes. Robert thought it possible that the cyber groupies were less interested in Petey's hacking strategies than they were in his reputation for being generous with the ganga. In any case, Robert's arrival induced the crowd's departure, leaving the two friends to settle into a place that was familiar, a close friendship solidly grounded in a cognitive conjunction. They talked science until dark.

Chapter 5. Transition Day

Moving day was there before they knew it. James did the big rental truck thing, and had plenty of help loading the family's possessions, thanks to work friends, church friends, and his own children's friends. Rufus and Katie brought their pickup truck to haul delicate items, a gesture that Ginny really appreciated.

Andrew came over to help. When the packing was finished, neither he nor Robert was quite prepared to say goodbye. Robert had never actually left anything or anyone. In that moment, the enormity of the change he was facing was becoming more apparent. Boys don't hug, and shed tears, he thought, or do they? As the one leaving the scene first, Andrew put his best foot forward.

"I'm not sure when I'll see you, but we'll figure something out. I'm going to California with my folks for two weeks, and then to baseball camp. After that, maybe we could do one of those canoe trips Rufus talked about."

Robert was slow to respond, as he tried not to seem overwhelmed. He managed only a brave, firm handshake. Neither of the boys had any desire to mark their parting with a gesture more outwardly emotional.

"Let's just stay in touch any way we can. I have no idea what this move is going to be like, but I will be sure to keep you posted. You are my best friend, and I think I'm about to find out what that really means."

At that point, Andrew made his exit, so Robert could be with his family during the short time that remained before their departure. The family gathered in the kitchen of the house and said a prayer of thanks for all the blessings that had come to the family while they lived in the house. There were hugs all around, and a few tears, mostly Angela's. At fourteen, she was intensely focused on everything she was leaving behind and not so much on what lie ahead. Her understanding mother hugged her and promised her that it was going to be alright.

Robert was lucky enough to ride with Rufus. Katie rode with Ginny and Angela. James wanted to fly solo in the moving van, and wouldn't let anyone convince him otherwise.

As they caravanned to Robert's new home in the country, Rufus and his nephew spoke of many things: global warming, religion, the school Robert would be attending, and education in general. About half way to their destination, Rufus made a comment that gave Robert the excuse he needed. He said something about it being a "good time of year for him".

"You mean a good time of year for you astrologically?"

"As a matter of fact, that's exactly what I meant. It's kind of hard to explain in a few words, but I can try, if you want. In fact I'll just come out and say it, as if you had some training. The Sun is moving into my tenth house, where I have three beneficent planets, Mercury, Venus, and Jupiter."

"I know about the planets, and what the signs of the Zodiac are. I've played around with some of those smart phone apps. It's a good way to get the girls talking, and I need all the help I can get with that. But you just said something about your tenth house."

"Well Robert, it goes something like this. A long time ago, in a galaxy far, far away. . . . . Sorry, just kidding. A long time ago, as the ancient people watched the sky, they realized they could divide the universe up in to twelve sections based on early theories of geometry. They noticed that twelve constellations coincided with each of the twelve thirty-degree sections, for a total circle of 360 degrees. Imagine slicing through an orange with twelve sections, each one with its own namesake constellation. They are called Aires, Taurus, Gemini, and so on. When astrologers need to describe the different parts of a person's horoscope, which they depict on paper as a circle, they call each one of these thirty-degree segments a "house". There are twelve "houses" that make up the sphere. Each of the twelve signs 'rules', or corresponds, with each of these twelve houses."

Rufus turned to Robert for a second to see if he was getting through to him. As an experienced teacher, he had mastered that crucial intuitive power essential for making a quick comprehension check. Deciding that Robert was with him so far, he forged ahead.

"At night, as ancient people watched the sky . . . . because, after all, they didn't have anything better to do, they noticed that each of the constellations was moving across the sky one after the other. Each season, and even each night, they noticed that the positions changed. Some of the wisest amongst them probably realized that the same thing was happening during the day, but we don't know that for sure. They just knew that there was a flow. Later on, closer to modern times, when astronomers were able to demonstrate that the Earth was spinning on its axis, this cyclic, perpetual motion of the celestial bodies was confirmed."

"From their vantage point on Earth, they could see that the Sun passes through each and every one of the background sections in a year's time. Places like

Stonehenge and all the other ancient monuments that were used to track astronomical phenomenon shed a lot of light on the movements of the universe relative to our vantage point on Earth. Many observers noticed this pattern, of night sky background constellations changing through the seasons, repeating itself year after year with great precision, and they began to question if it had any significance for human behavior and events."

Rufus could tell that Robert was capable of a high level of mental engagement, so he pressed on by asking a challenging question.

"How do we reconcile the revolution of the Earth through the twelve sections, in a year's time, with rotation of the Earth through the twelve sections in one day?"

Rufus couldn't help but look over to judge whether Robert even understood the question.

"So there's more to it than just having a birthday every year?"

"Yes. Your birthday is when the Sun is at the same degree of the 360 degree circle as it was on the day you were born. For me it was 28 degrees of Taurus, otherwise known as May 19th, and for you it was 18 degrees of Sagittarius, otherwise known as December 10th. It repeats every year, obviously. The Earth's journey around the Sun is predicable."

"OK, I'm totally with you."

"But if we look at things on a short term basis, the Earth spinning on its axis means we are travelling through all the signs of zodiac in only twenty four hours. So how do we reconcile the revolutions with the rotations, so we can make some sense out it? One happens every year and the other happens every day. Is there any significance to that daily journey through the zodiac, or is it just about the annual journey?"

Robert confided that he was a little bit vague about what Rufus was saying, but promised he was trying.

Rufus sympathized and encouraged him to stay focused on what he knew about astronomy and geometry. The rest would sink in later.

"Imagine that we are at the center pole of a merry-go-round looking out in one direction, watching the painted ponies go round and round. If the merry-go-round takes a whole year to go all the way around, we would observe the slow passage of each one of the twelve ponies through each of the twelve different backgrounds, one at a time. But if the merry go round takes only one day to go around, we would observe the ponies passing rather quickly through each of the twelve backgrounds. That's quite a different perspective."

"Ok, that helps."

"But in reality, my dear Robert, each of these two events is happening simultaneously, and continuously, and that is what makes an honest approach to astrology so complicated. If it were just about the time of year, like when the Sun is in each of those sections of the universe, it would be easy to understand. But when you consider that the earth rotates through all of those backgrounds in only twenty-four hours, and the Moon in twenty-eight days, it's far from simple. Astrologers recognized a long time ago that they would have to agree on a reference point."

Rufus made another quick comprehension check. Robert said he was fine, and begged his uncle to proceed.

"From our point of view on earth, looking out in all directions, what do we keep track of the most? The Sun, right? You could make an argument for the Moon, but most people would say it's the Sun?"

"I agree."

"The Sun is that familiar heavenly body that helps us keep track of the day and the hour. It has a profound effect on the way life on Earth is conducted. But to astrologers, it is much more, because it offers us a reference point for viewing the universe beyond. For us, it moves in the foreground. We take it for granted: sunrise, sunset, sunrise, sunset. But in the background, in that magical 360 degree universe are all the stars and constellations, as well as all the other planets. We're spinning through all that during every twenty-four hour day. So how do we find our place, how do we know where we are, at any given time?

"I'm not sure what you mean. It's confusing. You're asking me to visualize a 360 degree universe that's in constant motion."

"Right, but that'll make your head spin. Astrologers had to come up with a way to get everyone on the same page, so they could communicate what was going on without going crazy. They knew they had to agree on a certain time of day to freeze-frame that background view. In order to reconcile what we are seeing as we spin on our axis, with what we see as we revolve around the Sun, astrologers realized they had to agree on a certain time of day to take a reading."

"So what is that certain time?"

"Sunrise! At sunrise every day, we hit the pause button. It offers us a chance to stop spinning, so we can reference the positions of the moon, the planets, and all the constellations. The snapshot at sunrise allows us to reconcile the rotation with the revolutions, and agree on what we see against the background, you know, so we can talk about it."

Robert surprised Rufus.

"I think I get what you're saying. I just had this vision of some guy, sitting in front of his tent in the desert watching the constellations on the horizon fade from view as the Sun rose. It actually makes sense that they would to take their reading at dawn each day. Very cool, Rufus."

"Yes, very cool, Robert. So, if we need to chart an exact view of that background we keep talking about, at any time of day or night, all we have to do is extrapolate.

It's just math."

"So when my guy in the desert got together with the astronomers and the mathematicians, astrology kind of became a science."

Robert seemed very confident in his comprehension, which made Rufus wonder how capable this young man's processor really was. Very few people were able to visualize complex three-dimensional motion models without the help of a visual aid.

"Now, let's get back to the sections, keeping in mind that you really are 'the center of the universe'. So what makes you a Sagittarius? The background of the sunrise, on the day you were born, was the constellation Sagittarius. From November 21 to December 22, that section, or sign we call Sagittarius, appeared on the eastern horizon at dawn. When the Sun rose on December 10th, otherwise known as your birthday, it rose at the 18 degree mark within that thirty degree section of the universe. That's your 'Sun sign'. You can determine the exact degree and minute and second of Sagittarius just by looking it up in a table, and doing a little math to adjust for the actual time of day you were born.

"I understand logically what you're saying. I like astronomy and can visualize three dimensions pretty well, but I'm still a little unclear about the house thing? That's where we started, you know."

"OK, here's the deal. There are twelve houses, and the beginning of the first one, your own personal first house, down to the exact degree, minute and second, is the sign that was noted on the eastern horizon at the exact moment of your birth. Few people are born at exactly dawn. If they were, then the person's Sun sign and the beginning of their first house would be the same. But people are born all different times of the day and night, so the Sun sign and the 'rising sign', also called the 'ascendant', are rarely going to be the same. Whatever sign is on your first house cusp determines which signs are on the cusps of the houses, all the way around the circle. Your 'ascendant' is the exact degree of a sign that was on the eastern horizon at the time of your birth. Just like the Sun 'rises' as the Earth rotates on its axis, so does your own personal "rising sign". It is extremely important. The easiest way to determine if a person is actually familiar with true scientific astrology is to mention 'rising sign'. If they don't recognize the term, well . . . . you get the idea."

"Rufus, this is so hard to visualize. Let's see if I'm making any progress. So, at the exact moment I took my first breath, if I could have looked to the eastern horizon, out into the universe, the constellation I would have seen would have been. . . . .? Something other than Sagittarius, like any of the other signs, but we don't have enough information right now? We need my time of birth?"

"Yeah, that's it, Robert."

Having vigorously stressed the actual physical, geometric, and astronomical aspects, Rufus was comfortable with the scientific character of the lesson. But he realized he was being a bit unfair to his protégé. There was no opportunity for visual aids, not even paper and pencil illustrations, while driving down the highway in a pickup truck. He was asking Robert to grasp complex, esoteric concepts and geometric constructs with nothing more than his mind's eye.

"Houses are a bit more difficult to explain fully without drawing a picture, but the simple answer is, and where we'll leave it for now, is that, houses are your own personal way of dividing your horoscope into twelve areas of emphasis. Everyone's horoscope, or chart, is graphically represented as twelve houses, or thirty degree sections of the circle. At the moment of your birth, the Sun, the Moon, and the planets, each one independent of the other, are located within those personalized twelve houses, and that's your horoscope. Throughout your life, these heavenly bodies continuously transit through your twelve houses at different rates. The Moon visits each house in thirty days, the Sun visits each one every year, Mars in six years, Saturn in thirty years, and so on, depending on the planets revolution time. The reason everyone's horoscope is so completely different from everyone else's, even if they are born on the same day, is that everyone's birth TIME is so different. Another factor is that people are born in different parts of the world. The location is very important. The Sun doesn't rise at the same time everywhere on the planet, you know."

As they turned off of the four-lane highway and proceeded eastward on the state highway, both men were feeling pretty good.

"We'll give it another try soon, Robert. That is, if you're interested in learning more."

"So that's what astrology is really about, continuous cycles, only with a lot of different players that move at a lot of different speeds."

Knowing that their private time was soon coming to an end, and happy for the experience, Rufus acknowledged the truth of where astrology had led him.

"It's not clear whether the events of your life have anything to do with these cycles, and I admit it's extremely complicated. It's tedious to demonstrate, frustrating to model, difficult to explain, and presumably impossible to prove."

Although he was happy with his effort, Rufus was still convinced that he was being unfair to Robert. But he knew that true learning often started with a challenge. The creation of mental disequilibrium in the mind of the student could be an important first step towards authentic learning. Anyway, Robert didn't exactly appear upset.

"So let's just call this the first lesson, and we'll go

forward on another day. I was about a year older than you are now when my sister talked me into taking an astrology class. We learned how to construct and interpret horoscopes, with no help from computers. These are things you are capable of learning at your age, but it's going to take more than one lesson, even for a 'brainiac' like you."

"I don't know where you get that 'brainiac' idea, but I'll take it as a compliment.   Astrology might be just the brain food I need. I knew it was about a person being born in a certain sign, and that it had to do with the Sun being in a certain part of the sky. But that's about all I knew. Now I realize there are a million more variables."

"That's right. There's more to it than just the position of the Sun when you're born. As you have learned studying science, some things are very complicated, especially dynamic systems. Some things never stop. Some things can't be easily examined under a microscope, observed in a petri dish, or even in a particle accelerator. Because the phenomena are in constant, ever changing states, examining them in a given moment requires sophisticated modeling and experimentation. That's the way it is with astrology."

"Like the weather."

"You are exactly right. That's an excellent example. You really are a brainiac."

Rufus began laughing out loud, amused by the fact that Robert was getting kind of perturbed at his overuse of "brainiac". He apologized for being such a wise ass. Rufus knew that his nephew was capable of understanding the astrological model, but he had no idea how badly the young man wanted to learn it. There was no time to pursue the question, as they were about to pull into the driveway of Robert's new home.

Grandpa Samuel was ready to assist James with the task of backing the truck up to the front entrance. It had been decided that the front was the best off-loading point for the big stuff, while the small items could be carried in through the kitchen. There was plenty of help and plenty of incentives. Aunt Louise had provided a wonderful variety of refreshments. The new furniture had already been delivered and there were no appliances to mess with, as they had come with the house. The only problem was the impending thunderstorm, because it forced them to move a little faster than they would have liked.

Rufus and Katie took off as soon as the unloading was finished. Rufus had chores to do before dark and Katie had to work early the following day. Ginny was reluctant to let Grandpa Samuel drive himself home, but finally consented, as long as he promised to call as soon as he got there. She sent him with a plate of food and promised him that she would be over to see him in the morning. No matter how much work there was ahead of her, getting settled in her new home, Ginny was not about to forget the reason she was imposing this crazy dislocation on her family. It was the well-being of her dear father.

As night fell, James and Ginny signaled the need for privacy, maybe to make plans for the coming week, or just to relish in the accomplishments of the day. Robert used the time before dark to walk around the property and just breathe. His mind was racing with thoughts of the time he had with Rufus. He was happy and nervous at the same time. He definitely didn't feel like sleeping. After texting Samantha and Andrew, Robert lay down on the grassy slope behind the house to gaze at the lake below. The sun was at his back, lending a surreal appearance to the lake surface as the light faded rapidly through the trees up the hill behind him.

Chapter 6. Dutiful Son

During the first few weeks of June, Robert was satisfied with helping his mother. Cleaning, painting, yard work, and running errands, was his new life. Several days a week, Ginny farmed him out to Grandpa Samuel, who taught him how to drive a tractor and help in the hay. Robert's father was putting in long days as the supervisor of a three county line crew.

Rufus came up with a plan to provide some relief. Enlisting Katie as the messenger, they requested that Robert be allowed to help them on the farm. Considering Robert's unselfish contributions to her cause, Ginny could hardly refuse.

Bright and early on a Tuesday, Robert's father dropped him off, to spend three whole days with Rufus. As he got out of the rural electric coop truck, barely able to contain his excitement, he thanked his Dad for the ride and headed for the back porch. Rufus came running out the back door in his stocking feet. James, who had started backing up, finally noticed him and stopped. Rufus approached the truck.

"Thanks for letting me borrow your boy. We're hopin' to make some hay."

"That's fine, Rufus, but I have to get going."

"I know. I'm sorry. But I have to ask you if it's OK to take Robert on the river, if we can get all the hay put up."

Robert, who overheard the question and the answer, was beaming with pleasure. He had become so programmed to daily work and was so glad to be away from home that he had forgotten all about this little thing called fun. As his father pulled away, Rufus's words were music to his ears.

"Why don't you go ahead and get into your swimming suit while I finish up at the computer. I'll be out in a little bit to talk about what we need to get done today. I'm so glad you came."

Robert had been swimming in the pool before, but was really excited to have it all to himself. Intermittent birdsong was all he could hear over the subtle, low pitch hum of the pool pump and the water rippling from the jets. Peaking between the tall trees, the morning sun was just warm enough to induce a dive into the deep end.

When Rufus joined him after about thirty minutes, dressed in boots and jeans, he offered Robert hot tea.

"Have you had a proper breakfast?"

"No sir."

"Well, we will rectify that situation very soon. You're going to need some fuel in your tank."

"Yes sir."

"We'll start out with some raspberry picking and then get ready to put up some hay. The neighbor will be over about noon to make square bales of the wheat and clover. We'll start raking it about 10:30. It's a great day for putting up hay because it's not quite as hot and humid as it could be this time of the summer."

"So, what do I need to do?"

"It's all about boots and jeans."

The raspberry picking was fun for Robert, but the learning curve was steep. Picking the berries and avoiding the thorns required a distinct digital dexterity and a keen eye. Rufus could follow right behind him and quickly come up with another handful every time. He would just laugh and remind Robert that some things take a lot of practice. Robert was encouraged to sample as many of the plump black fruits as he desired on his way to a breakfast of eggs, bacon, biscuits, and gravy.

Hay hauling wasn't quite as much fun. As the bales came off the baler, Robert and Rufus would pick them up, load them on the pickup truck in a precise arrangement, and then transport them to the barn to be stacked. Quickly learning the routine, Robert was thankful that his mother and his grandfather had worked him so hard over the previous several weeks. He could never have gone from laying around after school to this kind of demanding physical labor out in the hot sun.

The two of them took a brief break to drink water when each load was in the barn. It was all about sweating and grunting, and it actually made Robert feel really good. Rufus would alternatively whistle and tell silly stories. Having performed the task so many times by himself, he was extremely happy to have help. Every once in a while, just when Robert was really struggling, Rufus would shout out: "Are we not men?", or "We're havin' fun now!"

Two hundred and forty-one square bales took them six trips and the better part of the afternoon. Robert discovered how wonderful it felt to have the hay in the barn. But self-satisfaction aside, they couldn't get their boots and jeans off fast enough when they returned to the house. After what they'd experienced, the rush of the chilly pool water was indescribable.

They pulled up a chair in the shade. Rufus grabbed a couple beers from the cabana frig and joked about how weird it was to step out of the hayfield and into what looked like a resort. He told Robert that "back in the day", they would get so hot hauling hay that they'd have to jump in the creek with their clothes on several times before they were finished.

Cool and content after a few beers by the pool, they retired to the house, where Rufus cooked and entertained. Mentally massaged by sun stroke or alcohol, or both, Robert had the look of a loose cannon, eager to fire questions about the one subject that was on his now very supple mind.

Rufus was easy. Katie wouldn't be home until late, and he was perfectly comfortable peeling potatoes, frying chicken, and talking astrology. Robert had done a little research since his first lesson on moving day. He didn't need Rufus to teach him about the signs, planets, and aspects. He wanted to know WHY Rufus thought there was any validity to astrology.

"After our discussion in the truck that day, I've been dying to ask you one question, and I think now is the time. WHY do you believe in astrology?"

Rufus was a little bit surprised, but was not one to back away from a challenge.

"You can believe in God, or you can believe in America as the greatest country on Earth, but you can't believe in astrology. Astrology is like mathematics or physics or language. It's a tool, an organized system of thought that can be used to investigate or discover something. Believing is an act of faith. I believe in God, but I don't believe in astrology. I can only make observations that either uphold or refute astrological theory."

Realizing that his answer to Robert was a bit metaphysical for a seventeen year old, he decided to pause and reflect. Feeling responsible for the integrity of Robert's indoctrination, he wanted to be careful.

Rufus bore the scars of arguments with skeptics who tried to paint him into the "believe in astrology" corner, and had learned to actively resist becoming defensive.

Not only that, but just underneath the surface was a built in, knee jerk, animosity for people who automatically assumed that studying astrology meant that he was some kind of atheist. He knew that Robert was pure of heart, and reminded himself to respect that. He also knew that Robert had the kind of analytical mind that was actually capable of rising above the common misconception that astrology was nothing more than a silly daily prediction in the newspaper.

He took a deep breath and offered his best guidance.

"From my observations, there are correlations that are beyond coincidence. Relationships I've had, as well as many of the significant events of my life, have induced me to examine the astrological data. Having accumulated many, many observations over a long enough period of time, I am able to postulate that the aspects formed by the Sun, Moon, and planets, as they move through my natal chart, do in fact positively correlate with these relationships and events. The observations are most often retrospective, and cannot be proven by any objective measure. That's the point when a person begins to appear that he or she believes in astrology. They have seen enough to be driven to continue their observations, all the while being able to prove nothing. Just like a person trying to prove something about God, or heaven, or hell. Make sense?"

Robert seemed to grasp the distinction.

"What made you want to learn about it, you know, in the first place?"

"Back when I was about your age, my sister and I took a class at a local Junior College, one of those evening, continuing education kind of things. It was presented as a self-knowledge technique. We were taught how to construct natal horoscopes, using the exact date, time, and location of our birth. Once we had generated that graphic illustration of where the Sun, Moon, and all the planets were positioned at the time of our birth, we researched what the positions of the Sun, Moon, and the planets supposedly meant for us."

"What about my natal horoscope. Can you do me one?"

"Oh, I'd have to get all the books off the shelf and it would probably take me hours, assuming I can remember how to do all the calculations."

Robert seemed disappointed, and actually became a bit anxious. Rufus let him suffer while he grabbed another beer from the frig, and then laughed his way back to honesty.

"I'm just kidding, Robert. Luckily, in the age of computers, it's quite simple. You go to a website, put in your birth date, along with the exact time and location, click to generate a natal horoscope, and then hit print. The only problem is, unless you know how to interpret it, it will be about as useful to you as a pirate's treasure map drawn with unfamiliar symbols, and in a foreign language."

"But you can do that part."

"Not so fast young fella'. That has to be up to you. I speak French with people who can speak French. I'm not a French translator."

"Just as getting to know yourself as a human being is a personal task that takes a lot of time and effort, so is using your birth chart to gain insight into your natural tendencies. No one can, or should, do it for you. "

"But you can help me get started, right?"

"I guess so. But we can't afford any trouble with your folks. Astrology isn't exactly mainstream, especially in this part of the world. This is what they call the Bible belt, you know. Even though I fervently believe in God, read the Bible, and go to church, as soon I say astrology to a person like your grandfather, or even your mother, red flags start popping up in their little brains. You see what I mean?"

As Rufus served the fried chicken, mashed potatoes, and green beans, he assured Robert that he would help him, if that's what he really wanted. Then he changed the subject completely.

"Robert, I think we should go on the river tomorrow."

"I thought we were going to shear sheep."

"Believe me, I'd rather get the chores done first, but they're calling for a chance of thunderstorms. We can't go on the river Thursday if there's gonna be rough weather."

Robert didn't argue. He had never experienced either activity, but going canoeing sounded like a lot more fun than shearing sheep.

Chapter 7. Independence Day

During the run up to the Fourth of July, Robert was content, but beginning to worry that he was losing sight of his own future. He spent most days helping his mother with home improvements or supporting her efforts to look after Grandpa Samuel. He didn't have a summer job and had little opportunity to meet new people. Memories of the three days with Rufus were his primary sustenance when he found himself starving for something beyond the mundane. At least he had his beginner astrology book, which he kept under his mattress.

One day, he was helping his mother wash the upstairs windows.

"Is it OK if I take the car one day and go to town? Maybe I can even find a job."

"Of course it would be OK, honey. I realize that this summer is getting a little tedious for you."

"I have no money except for my allowance. You pay my cell phone bill. I don't even let myself think about having my own car."

"I know. If we hadn't moved down here, you would have had a good shot at a summer job. Instead, you're just helping me all the time. But, give your father and I some credit. We know that your adjustment to a new school is going to be hard enough without having to ride the bus, especially considering you'll be a senior. Robert, you are brave and resilient, but even that would be a little much. Give your father and I some credit."

As he washed the window in his own bedroom, Robert was bubbling with excitement about the idea of a car. As his scrubbing cleared the window, his focus shifted beyond the glass, to the highway. The workers were getting closer to opening up the new section. He imagined what it would be like to be the first one to drive his car on the new stretch of road.

At dinner that very evening, James was enthusiastically supportive of the car initiative, with only one qualification. He insisted that Robert be responsible for the search. Robert listened very carefully and respectfully to his father's stipulations. But as soon as the family finished eating, he asked if he could be excused. Once out on his civil engineer fantasy walk, he called Andrew. He shared his excitement about the car, the upcoming Fourth of July party, and of course, his hottest burning desire, to make his way up to the City for a visit.

Independence Day finally arrived, adorned in some of the most beautiful weather of the summer. No rain chances, an expected high temperature in the mid-eighties, and reasonable relative humidity. The Holiday was to serve as the family's house warming.

The attendees were an interesting mix of local country relatives, old friends from their previous life in the suburbs, and relatives of James from the western part of the state. A meat lover's menu of chicken, pulled pork, pork ribs, and beef brisket was catered by the local restaurant. Ginny, Katie, and Aunt Louise supplemented the barbecue with a cornucopia of family-favorite side dishes and desserts.

Shaded by large oak trees, the patio in the back of the house off the kitchen served as the main gathering place for the guests. A fireworks area was designated down the hill from the patio toward the lake. Ginny felt she had to ask Robert yet another favor, to be in charge of firework safety. She was well aware of her relatives' propensity for irresponsible pyrotechnics.

After a while, with all the guests arranged into kind of a matrix on the patio, the socially correct exchange of trivial pleasantries began to sputter, inducing Grandpa Samuel to send a poke Rufus's way.

"Haven't seen you in church for a good long while Evan."

Rufus accepted being addressed by his real name at gatherings of this sort.   It saved him the trouble of explaining why people called him Rufus. Grandpa Samuel called him Evan because he thought the whole idea of a grown man going by a nickname was ridiculous.

"But Samuel, I sincerely believe that Jesus Christ is my one, true Lord and Savior, and I do good works."

"It's important to do good works Evan, but you're missin' out on God's words from the Bible. You need to go to Church and let the preacher keep you up on what the Bible says, especially in these times, you know."

Rufus had learned over the years that avoidance of religion and politics at family gatherings was a wise policy. He tried to listen to that little voice that was suggesting polite agreement with Samuel, but he just couldn't manage it. People close to him on the patio were raising their antennae to this young conversation, eager to see it grow. With interest piqued, Rufus decided to throw out a line.

"The Bible is the good book. I've read it front to back several times. But it's not the only book. For thousands of years, many, many truly holy men, and women, have offered wisdom and advice for living, advice that is totally consistent with Christ's teachings, just not stated the same way as in the Bible. I can interpret the Bible for myself. I think the preacher is a good man, but when I don't exactly agree with his interpretation, what am I supposed to do? Samuel, I probably should go to Church, and I don't mind you suggesting that I do. I think you are a very wise man."

As he digested that, Samuel appeared a little bit disarmed by the gratuitous nature of Rufus's final comment. As one may, or may not, have expected, another voice joined the conversation. It was James, Robert's father, someone who usually stayed out of such entanglements.

"Rufus has his own way. We all know that. But I'd like to tell you both what I think. You not only need to go to church, but you might want to consider that the one true, holy and apostolic church is the Catholic Church."

James was uncharacteristically bold in his statement, perhaps because he was on home turf. He raised his beer in a quick toast, smiled big, and walked into the kitchen. As a confirmed Protestant, Samuel was deeply affected by that comment. What he had intended as a casual cock fight, was now feeling a bit too serious.

"I got nothin' more to say about it. One of my daughters has become a Catholic, and the other one doesn't come to church as often as she used to because of you, Evan. I hope you all know what you're doin'. Eternity's a long time, either way, if you know what I mean."

Just when everyone thought it was done, another cock crowed.

"I used to think that James was right. I was raised Catholic and I don't regret a minute of it. But I'm becoming more and more convinced that religion alone cannot save us."

This comment came from Thomas, James' brother. Actually, he was one of those people Rufus had in mind when he cast his bait.

Robert and the rest of the passive crowd waited to see where this was going to go. Many of them probably wondered if Thomas would have said the same thing if James were still present on the patio. Rufus turned his lawn chair toward Thomas, took a swig from his beer, and invited him to go on.

"Things have happened to me, particularly as a parent, to make me realize that what organized religion is offering is becoming less effective. It doesn't seem to account enough for individual differences in people."

Rufus cried out "Bingo!", and jumped out of his chair to click beer bottles with Thomas.

"Tell me more, mon frère. Tell me more."

"OK, let's put it this way. In this day and age, it just isn't enough for people, especially young people, to accept advice about how to live based on prospective roads to heaven and hell, or God and Satan. These kids are getting hit from all sides by way too many, often conflicting, voices, and they're mostly secular voices. Religion just isn't able to compete any more. Religion alone just cannot help them interpret right and wrong the way it did when we were kids."

Rufus interrupted.

"You mean they just don't really have the tools to cope with all the stuff life throws at them?"

"Right."

Body language revealed that Grandpa Samuel was folding his hand. They could have his ante and his opening bet. He was out. Rufus wanted to raise the stakes.

"You can't give it to 'em', that's for sure. But you're still obliged to help them figure it out. Those are two different things. To a lot of young people, the Bible seems to be offering a 'yellow brick road'. But they're more sophisticated than that."

Their conversation was interrupted by Ginny and

family bursting through the kitchen door with food, food, food. Robert immediately silenced the firecracker kids, which brought a welcome quiet, allowing Ginny to speak to all the guests.

"I'm so happy you all could come to bless our new home. I want you all to remember Gary on this day, as he fights for our freedom. I'm hoping he'll get to call us, but I really don't know."

The crowd let out a series of "woo hoos" and "booyaa's" and "here here's" as they raised their glasses to Gary.

Aunt Louise cried out from the serving table, "come and get it!", and the feast was underway. The cessation of firework activity allowed Robert to join his uncles in line. as they continued their conversation. Rufus was picking up where he had left off.

"We all have experiences in this life that lead us to certain beliefs. It's the beliefs that we generate through a lot of effort, through active, conscious reflection that help us develop the tools to cope. Religion, and faith in God, can help you along the way. But it's dangerous to leave too much up to the preacher. You have to know yourself, your own personal strengths and limitations. It's hard work. So how do we help a young person to get to know himself or herself. That's the question. Because of so much technology at their fingertips, they're drowning in a virtual world of limitless information. Where do they find the time to get to know their own thoughts and feelings? How can we help them structure their search to discover what is uniquely true about themselves?"

All of a sudden, Thomas seemed reluctant to continue the discussion, causing Rufus to fear he was talking too much. When the topic was one of his liking, he tended to get carried away, especially after a few bottles of beer. But the change in Thomas was only due to the fact that his wife and daughter were beckoning him to join them further up in the line.

The two men shook hands, confirming their mutual admiration and desire to speak later. Turning his attention to his nephew, Rufus asked Robert how he was getting along with all his country cousins. The answer didn't surprise him. Whether it was the cultural differences or the scarcity of relatives his age, Robert was feeling socially awkward and lonely. But that was nothing new for him. He intimated that what he had overheard impressed him very much, and pointed to his World Religions class as his own personal hotbed of formative growth. As he made his plate, Rufus promised they would talk more, and then apologized for having to go and join Katie and some other relatives.

Robert's sister Angela was having a much better time than he was. One of her best friends from back in the suburbs had made the trip with her parents. For Angela, having her there made relating to her country cousins so much easier. It was a girl thing.

Thomas and his wife Ellen happened to be seated near Rufus and Katie during dinner. Katie asked how their family was getting along. She politely squelched her concern when the answer came back superficial and somewhat evasive. It was apparent to Katie that Ellen was actively trying to suppress her emotions.

When the ladies headed into the kitchen to help with the after dinner clean up, Thomas and Rufus had a chance to talk. Rufus shared his wife's inkling that something was not quite right, so instead of making small talk, he offered his support.

"Thomas, maybe the thoughts you shared before dinner have something to do with your own family? If there is any way I can help. . . . . . "

"Rufus, you are a fascinating character. I hardly know you, but for some reason I trust you. The fact is, my son John is in jail right now. I know it's just a bump in the road, but it's killing my wife. As she says, this isn't how it was supposed to be."

Rufus had just enough time, before the women returned, to convince Thomas that even a cursory reading of John's horoscope would offer some clues that could guide Thomas's effort to help him. He explained the importance of having an accurate birth time. Thomas promised to email the necessary information. He was clearly a father that would do anything for his son.

Most of the people that had come from the City departed within a short time after eating. Ginny and James spent a lot of time saying goodbye, forced to face the uneasy queasiness of profound change, as they felt themselves drifting away from their old life and friendships toward the inevitable tying of new knots. Along with the promises to stay in touch, there were tears, as well as fears, that the distance would erode the strength of so many of the old ties.

The local family members settled into various activities. The kids went back to shooting fireworks and playing. The men played horseshoes. The women swapped recipes and told stories of loved ones' escapades. Robert was happy to be a part of it all, but didn't feel particularly connected to any one group more than any other. Once again, Robert was the observer, the analyst. It was his nature. As he absorbed the scene, his thoughts turned to how much he loved his mother and father. He knew they were extremely happy on this day, and that was all that really mattered.

Having been partnered with his father to pitch horseshoes, it was finally their turn to compete. He would pitch against Rufus, who, along with his partner, had been winning most of the games. This gave Robert a valuable opportunity to spend socially sanctioned time with his uncle. As they watched the other pair of competitors pitch the horseshoes towards their end, they had a chance to talk

"Have you been studying the astrology book I gave you?"

"You bet I have. I think I've mastered the signs, the planets, and the houses pretty well, but I still have a lot of questions."

"Come out to the farm whenever you can. Just call first because I'll be leaving the area for a while next week."

"Where are you going?"

"I'm going up north to attend a little get-together. Let's just leave it at that for now."

Rufus acted like he either could not, or did not want to, tell Robert the purpose of the trip. As he stepped up to pitch his two shoes, Robert couldn't help but wonder why.

As dusk fell upon the Fourth of July, the local relatives headed for the fireworks show in town. Relatives of James, like Thomas and his family, who had come a long way, would be spending the night. Rufus and Katie offered to take Grandpa Samuel home.

Robert was a little surprised when Rufus cornered him while Katie was saying her goodbyes and helping Samuel to the car.

"Robert. Now that you have studied, you're ready take a look at your own chart. You will have to have the exact time of the day, and the location where you were born. It's on your birth certificate."

"OK. I understand. Without that information, there's no way to determine my 'rising sign,' which means there's no way to know the precise position of the planets in the houses. Right?"

"That's exactly right. Without the rising sign, you're plotting a course without a sextant."

Chapter 8. The Ride

He felt awful about invading his parent's privacy, but Robert finally found his birth certificate. Rufus's admonition about people's perception of astrology often being negative had effectively prepared him to rationalize his sneaky behavior. No need to explain why he needed the information.

In the meantime, Andrew was texting often, encouraging Robert to make a trip to the City. With no progress finding a car, Robert approached his mother one morning on their way to help Grandpa Samuel.

"Andrew wants to know if I can come up there for a visit next week."

"How are you going to get there? I have no problem with you going, but neither your father nor I have time to take you. Even if you managed to find a car that quickly, I don't think your father would let you take it to the City."

"I think I can catch a ride with Rufus. He told me he was going that way. He said something about going up north."

"Well, that's funny. Katie didn't say anything about them going on a vacation or anything. Where's he going?"

"I don't know, but if I can get a ride there and back, may I go?"

"Well sure, honey, but I think we'll need to get more information from Rufus."

Rufus acknowledged receipt of Robert's birth time in a return email, and verified a Thursday through Sunday trip north of the City, still without divulging his destination. He would bring a copy of Robert's horoscope with him, so they could discuss it on the way up to Andrew's.

Robert was so relieved that he could tell Andrew he had a ride. Andrew had been so insistent that Robert come on that particular weekend.

With firm plans for fun, his attitude improved about some of the things he had been putting off. He researched colleges and shopped for a car. He worked long days painting his grandfather's house, for which he earned a much better rate of pay than he did for farm chores. He was regaining control of his life.

At noon Thursday, he was ready. Robert was at the truck with his things before Rufus could even think about coming to the door.

"Good morning young fella'. How goes it?"

"I'm so excited about seeing my friends, I can't even tell ya'."

"You'll have lots of friends in your life, but I can understand that the ones you have now probably seem irreplaceable. Let's go."

As they started up the road, when he was finished pondering that strange comment, Robert noticed that Rufus was kind of dressed up, which reminded him that he still didn't know the true purpose of his uncle's journey. Katie had told Ginny that it was something about a conference, leaving Ginny to assume it had to do with nursing.

"Are you going to some kind of conference?"

Rufus apologized for keeping Robert in the dark. He wanted to avoid the raised eyebrows and wisecracks that would surely come if people knew the truth.

"I'm attending an astrology conference. I haven't been to this particular one for several years, and I want to run my latest ideas by some of the people who will be in attendance."

"Does Aunt Katie know where you're going?"

"Oh yeah. Katie tolerates my fascination with all things astrological, but because she has never become a student of the art herself, she isn't a very good sounding board. Every so often, I need to flock with birds of the same feather to keep my sanity. Katie strongly supports me getting out on my own to pursue my interests. Besides, it's the perfect time of the year to get away from the farm. The sheep and horses don't need me this time of the year, the garden is on autopilot, and you can only spend so much time by the pool. Living in the middle of nowhere has one major downside, insufficient face to face contact with other people."

Excited by the thought of talking astrology with Rufus, Robert didn't waste any time before he asked Rufus if he could see his horoscope. Rufus handed him a multi-colored circular diagram that showed the Sun, the Moon, and the planets as they were positioned on the day of Robert's birth. Each of these important celestial players was listed in a table that specified exact location down to the geometric degree, minute, and second that corresponded with Robert's exact birth time. Another table summarized the important aspects, including the conjunctions, sextiles, trines, squares, and oppositions that were formed between the players. Each aspect that was within three degrees of being exactly zero, sixty, one hundred twenty, ninety, or one hundred eighty degrees, was also depicted on the chart itself with red and blue lines. With only symbols, numbers, and lines, it looked like hieroglyphics.

"This is so cool, Rufus."

"Yes it is. There's only one Robert, and this chart represents a three dimensional snapshot of the universe at the very moment he came into this world."

Rufus then reached into the back seat, retrieved a large book, and handed it to Robert.

"But we're not ready for the computer generated chart. It may give the wrong impression. We need to start at the beginning."

Robert looked at the book. The American Ephemeris for the 20th Century, 1900 to 2000, at Noon. As he paged through it, he found few words. Each page was nothing but tables of dates, symbols, and numbers.

Rufus asked him to turn to his birth year and find the data for his particular day, December 10th. When he had found it, Rufus handed him a highlighter.

"Now, highlight your line of data and let's talk. You Sun sign is Sagittarius. So now we know that you are one of twelve different kinds of people. So, where was the moon when you were born?"

Having learned the symbols for the signs of the zodiac as well as the symbols for the Sun, Moon, and planets, Robert replied quickly and proudly.

"My Moon sign is Cancer."

"OK, if we combine one of twelve Sun signs with one of twelve Moon signs, we know you are one of one-hundred and forty-four different kinds of people, because twelve times twelve is one hundred forty-four. Sagittarius Sun, Cancer Moon. Are you with me so far?"

"Yes sir."

"Now look to the sign on your first house cusp in your chart."

"My Ascendant is nineteen degrees, forty three minutes of Pisces."

"Sun in Sagittarius. One out of twelve chance. Moon in Cancer. One out of twelve chance. Rising sign, Pisces. One out of twelve chance. We have now determined that you are one of 1,728 different kinds of people."

"Now, just for grins, let's say that the exact degree of each of these matters, that it's not just about the sign. All of a sudden we're really talking about 360 X 360 X 360, or 466,560,000 possibilities."

Robert, a lover of all things mathematical, was so impressed.

"Now throw in the exact degrees of all the planets, the aspects between them, and which house they occupy."

"Sounds like an infinite number of possibilities!"

Taking his hands completely off the steering wheel, Rufus raised his arms in a celebratory "ta da".

"That's right Robert, meaning that true scientific astrology could be construed as a proof that all people are completely unique from one another. The popular 'newspaper' interpretation implies that there are only twelve different kinds of people. Nothing could be more ridiculous. People can share certain traits, but traits in different unique combinations are what account for human diversity.

"So what good is astrology?"

"Other than for you to get to know yourself a little better, I'm not sure, Robert. You'll have to decide for yourself."

Rufus handed him another book, The Astrologer's Handbook.

"Now that you have your own chart, look up your planets, the houses they occupy, and note the meaning of any significant aspects. Learn about rulers-ships, when the planets are exalted, and when they are in detriment. See if you agree with what the books tell you. Again, I say, do the work, and decide for yourself whether the conclusions reached by astrologers over many centuries fit your own perception of yourself."

"What if I don't agree?"

"That's fine. Just keep in mind the two most

important things a person has to remember when delving into his or her own astrological profile. First, one planet or sign does not define you. One piece of the puzzle does not depict the scene. One or two notes of the song do not reveal the melody. You are a product of the interplay amongst all the components of the chart. As the proverbial center of the universe, to gain enlightenment, you must always be willing to gravitate to the center. That's where you will find your ultimate self, if you're being honest about it."

"Number two: Free will is paramount. A person may be born with definite tendencies, God-given talents, and even regrettable faults, but it is the whole person's exercise of free will that leads them to discover their destiny. You can, and must, choose who you are, with each and every decision you make."

"It's complicated."

"Too complicated for most. Just have fun with it. Don't take it too seriously. Just look for helpful clues, and always resist the temptation to make predictions. That's not what it's for. You can't base decisions on it. This planet you're riding on is constantly rotating within a field of the twelve segments of the zodiac. It is simultaneously revolving around our Sun. Someone is being born somewhere right now, at this very instant, to add their uniqueness to this mix we call humanity. Just try to learn a little bit about your own strengths and weaknesses, so you can be better prepared to make a contribution."

"Thanks, Rufus."

"For what? Talking about something I love? I should be thanking you."

"Thanks for considering me worthy, is what I mean."

"Robert, you have a great mind, and I am a great teacher. By the way, if you ever want to talk about college choices or anything related to your future, you know you can count on me to listen."

"I may very well do that, because I have no idea what I'm going to do. Mom and Dad aren't much help. Not only do they have no experience with the kinds of choices I'm faced with, they assume I'm trying to make a lot of money and raise a family. For them, it's cut and dried. But I'm not so sure about all that."

"Maybe you will take a less conventional path, but only you can decide."

"Mr. Dempsey says science or engineering."

"Yeah, but what do you say? Just because a person CAN do something, doesn't mean they necessarily WANT to do something. With greater talent comes a wider range of choices, and thus a more difficult decision."

Rufus sensed Robert's uncertainty. As he recalled all the twists and turns in his own path, he sympathized with Robert's dilemma. Rufus was the first person to go out of his way to help a person identify their own path, but the last person to choose it for them.

As they approached their destination, Robert changed the subject. In a most light-hearted, joyful way, he turned to observations about the differences between city and country life. Having spent a fair amount of time living in cities, Rufus could relate. He encouraged Robert to actively appreciate the opportunity he had, to see life from both sides.

There was one important thing that Rufus did not share with his nephew at that time. Even with all the wisdom of all the observations down through the ages, there was actually no easy way to verify that astrology had any validity whatsoever. Rufus's fascination with this supposition was the principal reason he was attending the conference. He appreciated the fact, that over an extremely long period of time, very sincere, capable people had generated a complex body of correlations between celestial movements and people's lives. But he was fascinated with the thought that in this more modern era, technology might enable a more sophisticated way of collecting data on these correlations, real or imagined. Why not pursue some kind of "proof", some kind of validation?

"There's one more thing, Robert. Why do you think I insisted that you look up your data in the Ephemeris, instead of the just looking at your chart?"

"To show the astronomical basis for the chart?"

"Yes, but more than that."

"To show how easy it is for one person's chart to be different from another's?"

"Also true. It was to make the point that there's nothing static about you, or your horoscope. There is constant motion. Time marches on. If the celestial bodies do have some kind of inexplicable influence because of their positions when you are born, wouldn't it make sense that they continue to have an influence as their positions change throughout your life? My interest in astrology expanded exponentially when I began to view it in that light. Instead of just focusing on the strengths and weaknesses encrypted in my natal chart, I began to feel an overwhelming sense of awe about how I was constantly changing throughout my life. I give astrology some credence, not simply because I agree with my own individuality being Taurus-like, or my own Moon energies feeling Sagittarian, but because the changes I have been through seem to correlate with the celestial flow."

"I sort of understand, Rufus, but I don't think I'm quite ready for all that."

"Just have fun with it. Life's too mysterious. Don't take it so serious."

When they finally arrived, Rufus lingered just long enough to greet Andrew and remind him of his open invitation to go canoeing.

Robert was so happy to see Andrew, and it was so obvious that the feeling was mutual. Andrew looked good as usual. Playing baseball most days, and exempt from even the thought of a summer job, Andrew spent most evenings with his darling Cindy. She was going to be attending a school on the west coast, meaning Andrew was about to be in for a real shock.

"Robert, I can see that the country bumpkin lifestyle has had one advantage. You must have gained at least ten pounds of muscle. But we've got to work on the tan. This redneck, working-man tan isn't going to fly at the pool party on Saturday. Yes Mister, I'm throwing you a party. You'll be the guest of honor."

Robert didn't know what to say. He wasn't really surprised about Andrew hosting a party. He just hadn't considered being the reason for the party.

They headed into the house to listen to music in the family rec room. They played some games and made some calls, as they effortlessly fell back into their old routine. Seventeen was feeling really, really, good.

When the call to dinner came, Andrew invited Robert upstairs so he could drop off his bags and freshen up. When Andrew opened the door to the spacious guest room, Robert questioned whether he was making some kind of mistake. Normally, this luxurious room that overlooked the pool area was strictly off limits. But Andrew gleefully insisted that it was his mother who had made the selection.   Robert was overcome by a sense of celebrity like he had never before felt.

The room was so nicely furnished that it just screamed "take off your shoes". White plush carpet gave way to a king-sized bed adorned with a frilly lace bedspread that was so exquisite that Robert looked around for an alternate place to set his bags. Huge white-mullioned wood windows bordered by long satin drapes extended almost to the ceiling. The bathroom, as big as Robert's bedroom at home, included a Jacuzzi tub and separate shower.

"I'm afraid to touch anything."

"Oh, you'll get used to it. All you have to remember is that it's your room. Just don't bring people up here and you'll be fine. My mom just wanted you to have a special time while you're here. She was just trying to be nice."

Andrew's mother was a beautiful, happy, middle-aged socialite whose days revolved around charity work, tennis, and planning trips for her and her family. His father was an attorney by education, but spent most his time at the family brokerage firm or attending board meetings of the companies in which the family had a major stake.

After dinner, Andrew provided Robert with what he really needed, an extended cruise of all the old hangouts. In spite of becoming a little bit tired of explaining to people where he had moved, and why, Robert had an excellent time. On the road, in between stops, he shared his excitement about his time with Rufus, and confessed his growing interest in astrology

"Since you texted me about how you were studying that stuff, I've downloaded a few astrology apps to my phone. But I must say, it seems kind of hokey."

"Rufus is teaching me how to go beyond Sun signs."

"Well, when you get it all figured out, just let me know. I don't know if I have time for all that. Hey, maybe on Saturday, you can put on a turban and dress up in a robe and tell people their fortunes."

Robert didn't think that was very funny, but it did remind him of his supposition, that astrology might be an excellent way to impress the girls.

Before they turned in for the night, with Andrew standing at the door of Robert's little luxury suite, Andrew reminded his friend that he had early baseball practice, followed by a lunch date with Cindy. He insisted that Robert sleep in, as if, in his words, he was "on vacation".

Chapter 9. Robert's Day

Robert was awakened on Friday morning by the sound of Millie setting up chairs and tables by the pool. After checking out the huge walk-in shower, he headed down to the kitchen. Andrew was long gone, and so were his parents. When he'd finished the wonderful breakfast that Millie prepared, he settled in as lord of the manor, studying the astrology books that Rufus had lent him, as he peacefully, and diligently, set about trying to figure out just who he really was.

Andrew arrived home late in the afternoon, accompanied by Cindy and Samantha. The plan was to take Robert out for some fun, first to the mall, and then to an evening concert in the park. Samantha was leaving the next morning to go on vacation with her parents. It worked out perfectly for Robert, because he got to see her during his visit, but could still avoid the prospect of being her date for the pool party. Nothing against Samantha, but Robert was feeling "available" for the first time in his life.

When the guests began arriving about noon on Saturday, Robert realized Andrew wasn't kidding about throwing him a real party. His best friend had invited all factions of people who had played a part in Robert's life in the suburbs: people that he had gone to grade school with, science club types from high school, old neighbors, and of course, Cindy's numerous girl friends, some of the finest looking young ladies around.

Andrew's mother and father were actively hosting the party. They were sensitive to Andrew's regret that he had not thrown Robert a party at the end of the school year before he moved to the country, and were now sparing no expense. Not only was there food and drink of every description, but there was a band stage and dance area set up on the tennis court adjacent to the pool area.

Robert suspected that it wasn't all about him. He knew that Andrew's parents were sensitive to the fact that their dear son's girlfriend was about to leave for college on the west coast. But such considerations hardly mattered to the attendees. They could see immediately that they were walking into the party of the summer.

Playing on Robert's legendary status as a genius, or his newfound tawny brown muscular body, or his burgeoning astrological knowledge, Andrew actively showed him off to the girls at the party. At first, Robert welcomed all the attention, but as he was forced to field more and more inane, superficial astrology questions, he recalled Rufus's caveats about any public defense of the art.

But when one particular person questioned him, it didn't bother him at all. Suddenly, there was Kristin, his grade school sweetheart. She had blossomed into a young lady that was now making him blush. In seventh and eighth grade, the age when a boy like Robert had no idea how to act, she had a terrible crush on him. In that singular moment, standing there by the pool, Robert was compelled by this one girl's presence to finally confront his ultimate insecurity, the fear of desiring someone so much that rationality would simply disappear.

"Aren't you going to ask me my birthday Robert? So

you can peer into the depths of my very soul?"

Robert took a deep breath, and marshaled all his confidence.

"Yes as a matter of fact, I can generate your horoscope right here on my smart phone and given a few minutes to analyze it, I can tell you all about your future. What is your birthday young lady? Please include the exact time of the day, as well as the exact location!"

He couldn't believe what had just come out of his mouth.

When she stopped giggling, Kristin playfully conceded .

"Yes Master. Who am I to question your great powers?"

Robert's success so far made him wonder if he wasn't actually becoming someone other than the speechless dork he had been so many times before. In that very moment, he decided that portraying an acceptable social self required no analysis. But he couldn't help but wonder if it were not more about Kristin's magic than it was about his own enlightenment. Looking in every direction more than once, as if he were questioning whether he was dreaming, he managed to will himself back onto the sidewalk.

"Seriously, Kristin. Oh my God! Ummm. . . . . . Are you here with anyone? Ummm. . . . It's so good to see you. . . . . . . It's been such a long time."

"I received an invitation from Andrew's mother, based on a list that Andrew had put together. I asked a girlfriend of mine to come along, and here we are."

Her friend walked up, as if on cue. She had been hanging out with one of Todd's friends, a boy named Steve, who was a member of the band that was to play music on the tennis court area later that evening. The four of them grabbed some pool time and then headed off to the lawn area past the tennis courts where people were playing croquet.

Robert found out that croquet was really just the perfect excuse to be as far away from the house as possible. Arriving at the peg at the far end of the course, they were invited behind the junipers for a few hits. As it turned out, most of the croquet people were stoners. Robert just feigned a hit on the joint to be sociable. He didn't want his inexperience with marijuana to screw things up with Kristin.

She was about 5' 6", ashy blond, with straight full-bodied hair beautifully framing her face and neck, but well off of her tanned shoulders. Her greenish blue eyes were wide set above magical cheekbones that highlighted a permanent smile. A flexible, athletic frame portrayed a very active person. To Robert, she looked better than fantastic.

He fought off thoughts of 'why is she being so nice to me?' and just tried to have a good time. He couldn't have predicted that his happiest moments of the day would be the result of re-uniting with an old grade school friend. She was good for him on this day because she was so naturally confident in herself that she made him feel confident. Kristin had managed to make him stop thinking.

The band did their best to entertain the group with what sounded like an attempt at modern punk rock rap reggae. It didn't really work, but that might have actually been the idea. The musicians were just trying to have a good time themselves. The people that "got it" really had fun with it, and the rest didn't seem to care. In any case, it didn't last very long. When the DJ took over, absolutely everyone was relieved.

Andrew's parents were understandably antsy. There were an awful lot of kids in one place, and many of them were unknown quantities. Fortunately, departures tended to accelerate as evening turned to night. Robert was very busy with goodbyes, trying to resist the thought that he would probably not see many of the people again, at least for such a meaningful experience.

As the crowd dwindled to a nucleus of Andrew and Cindy's close friends, Andrew's parents felt comfortable leaving for a late dinner date, leaving Millie in charge. Robert didn't have to ask Kristin and her friend to stay. Michelle and Todd were their transportation, and they were not in any hurry to leave a party that was becoming more intimate.

Cindy talked Andrew into the game room. Another group lingered at the swimming pool. Michelle and Todd joined their musician friends, who were jamming it up, reluctant to pack up their musical instruments for the night. Kristin's girlfriend decided to join them, leaving Robert alone with his old flame.

When Millie came outside to clean up, they wandered into the kitchen. Making sure to be out of Millie's line of sight through the back door glass, Kristin walked over to Robert, grasped the top of his swimming trucks with her right hand, pulled him close, and kissed him on the lips. Just as abruptly, she let go of his trunks and backed away.

"I've been wanting to do that since the seventh grade."

In unfamiliar territory, Robert could only manage a feeble "me too".

From then on, it was Kristin on the make. Robert was way off the sidewalk this time. All he could think of was, just don't say anything stupid.

Millie returned to the kitchen with a huge mess on a cart. Robert held the door for her and Kristin asked if she could help. Millie just smiled.

"Now you children just go on. I've got this."

Robert suggested that they join the others in the game room, so they made a polite exit from the kitchen. They hadn't gotten very far when Kristin grabbed him by the shirt from behind, stopping him in his tracks. Smiling an irresistibly playful smile, she asserted herself again.

"Rumor has it that you have this really cool room upstairs, and I want to see it."

Robert's idiotic first instinct was to check in with Andrew first, but when she kissed him for a second time, whatever he was thinking instantly evaporated. He found himself taking her by the hand and guiding her up the stairs to his room.

After a lot of ooh's and aah's about how beautiful the room was, she took him by the hand and led him over to the window. There were just a few couples still out by the pool. The water shimmered as the last photons of dusky light gave way to the lights around the pool. Watching at the window, they saw several young people leave the pool to come into the house, leaving one lone couple in the deep end to make out against the ladder.

Robert had no idea what to expect. He had never been alone with a hot girl in such a circumstance ever before. She led him over to the bed and sat him down. She walked over to the door and flipped the light off, leaving only the light from the windows. Returning to the bed she stood in front of him, not touching him, just smiling warmly. She then unceremoniously removed her bikini top, allowing him to stare directly at her beautiful breasts. His inexperience froze him solid.

After what seemed like an hour, with Robert feeling like he needed to do something, but was afraid to make a wrong move, she beckoned him to stand up and take off his shirt. She brought herself tightly up against his chest and began kissing him softly on the lips. Real physical passion with a female consumed Robert for the first time in his life. Kristin's reaction to his kisses made him feel a sense of masculinity that he had only known in a fantasy.

Kristin still in control, Robert felt his swimming trunks coming down. She pushed and pulled them down his legs and steadied him as he stepped out of them. Robert felt her gently push him back on the bed, where he sat and watched her step back to remove her own bottoms.

"Robert, I know you like what you see. But don't get any ideas. I'm not going to sleep with you."

She came closer, where he could caress her gorgeous young body. They embraced, and then as they fell back onto the bed together, Kristin took complete control, joyously opening a door for Robert that would never again be closed.

After laying there in the bed together for a while, she whispered to him.

"Robert, you need to understand. That was something I just really wanted to do. You're not in love with me, and you don't owe me."

Robert positioned himself to be able to see right into her eyes.

"I don't care what you say. Right now, I love you."

She hopped up off the bed, slipping quickly back into her bikini.

"Whatever you say. All I know is that was great. Let's go join the others. This little secret of ours might not be safe if we linger up here too long."

Kristin disappeared briefly into the bathroom, giving Robert a chance to put his suit and shirt on. As they headed for the door, he tried to stop her and kiss her again, but she wasn't having it. She tried one more time to make him understand.

"Robert, there'll be plenty of time for good night kisses, but right now it's time to party."

She empathized with him, as the one responsible for his crazy confusion, and kissed him ever so softly on the lips.

"There may be a day in the future where you and I will get together and talk about what happened here tonight. But now is not the time. So we stole a few minutes making out in the coat room, like we always wanted to do in eighth grade. No big deal, except it was really great, don't you think?"

Robert was just barely beginning to comprehend. Reverting to the Robert that just didn't want to make a mistake with Kristin, he squelched his love sickness. Kristin went into the bathroom one more time, and came out grinning. They proceeded to the game room holding hands without saying one more word.

Chapter 10. Senior Year

Rufus showed up at 5 PM Sunday, right on time. He could hardly watch as Robert said goodbye to Andrew once again. In spite of the usual promises to stay in touch, the boys felt themselves slipping into a new reality, like it or not, one that the summer had only hinted at.

Robert tried to imagine Andrew at school. Who would he have lunch with? Who would help him with his science homework and remind him about assignments? Robert didn't even want to think about his own senior year. He would not only be without his friends, but he would be in an educational environment that was totally foreign to him, a small town public school.

Robert found Rufus in good spirits, but seeming a bit tired. At first, conversation barely percolated. Poor Robert, on a high when it came to Kristin, and on a low when it came to Andrew, was reluctant to talk about either situation. He decided to press Rufus for some details about the conference.

"Did you get the answers that you were looking for?"

"I really can't say I did, Robert. It was a good conference. I re-connected with some people, and met some new people. I was reminded of how committed I am, but no one at the conference was able to help me.

Apparently, my fellow astrologers don't share my passion for improving the current state of data collection. They just want to talk about their own interpretive biases and share anecdotes about their clientele.

"What exactly do you mean by data collection? I've heard you use the term, but remember, I'm just a beginner."

"I'm sorry Robert. You're right. Let me explain it this way. Consider the handbook. Astrologers attempt to correlate the movements of the celestial bodies with the events of peoples' lives. Based on countless observations, they make inferences, and develop theories, just like we do in any science. Modern psychologists, sociologists, and anthropologists do the same thing. Data leads to inferences, hypotheses, testing, and theory refinement."

"But let's focus on our own science. Professional astrologers have constructed a lot of horoscopes, correlated them with actual peoples' lives, and used the information to perfect the science. It has taken centuries of effort. The person that wrote the book didn't just make it all up. He relied on the portfolios of chart interpretations generated by famous astrologers. That's what we mean by data collection. Just like Freud psycho-analyzed thousands of patients and came to certain conclusions, so have the best astrologers. But it always starts with data collection, generating horoscopes and interpreting them for real people. Does that help?"

Robert assured him that it did, but Rufus still seemed frustrated. He paused for a long while before he spoke again.

"I'm not a practicing astrologer. I'm just a man with a question. Can we come up with a better way to collect and analyze the data so we can bring astrology into the 21st century? Those people at the conference are still doing it the way they did two hundred years ago."

Rufus seemed to regret having delved into the subject

of data collection with Robert.

"I'm sorry, Robert. There's no way you can understand."

Rufus gripped the wheel tighter and sped up.

"I don't mean that as a put down. We'll talk about it some other time, if that's OK? I was trying to answer your question about the conference, but the answer feels complicated right now."

Robert said no more about it. As they got closer to home, each man kept his thoughts to himself. Robert recalled studying the book Rufus had given him. He actually had wondered how it was decided what the Sun or the Moon or a planet signified for a person. Who had made these rules? How often were the rules amended, and on what basis? OK, so gazillions of observations by astrologers over a long period of time have culminated in the currently accepted interpretive handbook. But how objective was the process? He was starting to understand what Rufus was getting at. There had to be a better way than just one chart interpretation at a time leading to piecemeal change.

Arriving home was kind of a shock. During his visit to his past life, Robert had essentially forgotten the quiet house out on the sharp curve of the highway. But now the party was over, both literally and figuratively. From this point forward, he had to put all his energies into preparing for his senior year in a new school.

He finally found a car, which enabled more frequent visits to Rufus and Katie's. They always seemed to have time for him, and he enjoyed the farm chores as much as he did spending time at the pool, talking astrology, or religion, or philosophy. Robert was gaining confidence.

When high school registration time came around, his father James accompanied him to see the counselor. James was very proud of his son's accomplishments and wasn't afraid to show it. Because the graduation requirements at

Robert's old school were so much more stringent than at his new school, Robert had already earned his high school credits for graduation. So they worked to find advanced placement courses and independent study to fill his days. They even finagled a position as a tutor by bending the work study rules just a bit. Officially he would be an intern at the Division of Family Services but he would spend all his time at school, tutoring "at risk" children.

Adapting to a new school was not easy, but Robert did his best. The most interesting adjustment came in the form of half the student body being female. Robert hadn't rubbed shoulders with girls at school since the eighth grade. The second most interesting feature was the general lack of academic enthusiasm, particularly among the seniors. Most of them talked more about being almost finished than they did about what they were actually learning. It was as if they were just trying to get it over with.

The teachers appeared to be well qualified, but few of them came across as leaders. The students seemed to be in charge. The authoritative atmosphere of the private school was just a memory for Robert.   A pseudo-academic atmosphere prevailed at his new school, with everyone going through the motions, moving things slowly forward. But for Robert, it was far too relaxed, almost country-clubbish.

Rufus had warned him about the work ethic of some of the tenured high school teachers. He called them "getalongs", meaning that they were well liked in the community and well liked by the students, and just plain "got along" with everyone. Unwilling to push the students, they appeared more subjective than objective, more complacent than progressive. They were not consciously, intentionally, lowering the standard. They just seemed to make lots of "exceptions" in order to, you know, "get along". The overall effect was institutionalized laissez-faire. Students who were pushed by their parents managed to get what they needed to succeed. But students who just wanted to slide through the system also seemed to get just what they were looking for, a comfortable ride.

All in all, Robert found it more amusing than worrisome. He had to remind himself not to judge too quickly or to paint with too broad a brush. There was a distinct minority who were highly motivated. But unlike his city school, where a combination of pressure from family and a rich academic tradition induced a collective push for high achievement, the majority at this public school unconsciously embraced only that which was "good enough".

For the first month, after the eye-popping experience he had with Kristin, he presumed that he was on his way to becoming some kind of ladies' man. He quickly decided otherwise when he learned the ways of the small town high school girl. Most of them valued the comfort level of associating with the boys they had grown up with, operated in tight-knit cliques, and disdained all things intellectual with a weird sense of bravado. Even some of the college-track girls in Robert's advance placement science classes seemed determined to be suspicious of the new guy. Not only that, but he was caught between his working class tan and his college prep self. When he opened his mouth, it was obvious that he was "not from there", and was therefore treated as a kind of curiosity. But he was fine with it. He just missed Andrew and Petey sometimes.

One day in computer technology class, he made a breakthrough. It wasn't a girl, which is what he thought he wanted. It was a guy.

The assignment was to work with a partner to develop a student survey. Robert's teacher had obtained permission for the middle school social studies classes to anonymously complete the surveys during a trip to the computer lab. The second part of the assignment was to prepare a presentation of the results for the computer tech class.

Robert was partnered with a fellow senior named Matthew. He was the son of a single mother who worked at the school as an aide. When he found out that Robert was Rufus's nephew, he just about screamed. His mother had been telling him all through elementary school about this wonderful eighth grade science teacher he would have one day. Unfortunately, Rufus left the profession when Matthew was in the sixth grade.

This new friend of Robert's was tall and strong, yet unassuming. He was slow to speak and appeared shy to those first meeting him. But when he did speak, he had one of those golden voices, projecting the carefully chosen words in a melodic way that got people's attention. He was more the country boy than the athlete, more a friend to the girls than a Romeo, more a dispassionate doer of good deeds than a show-off. His mother had raised him well. Like Robert, he had a keen mind for details. Unlike Robert, he fancied himself pursuing a career in the computer sciences.

After only a couple of weeks, they were carpooling. One day after school, as they worked on their survey assignment, the conversation turned to Rufus.

"I'm going out to see Rufus and Katie this Saturday. Do you want me to ask if you can come along? Rufus says it may be the last weekend the pool will be open."

"I'd love to, Robert, but I have to work all day Saturday. What about Sunday?"

"I'll find out and let you know."

Matthew's excitement about the possibility of finally making a connection with Rufus was obvious.

"I've never actually met the man, but I've always wanted to. I hope it works out. I don't care that much about swimming, but I'd love to get him talking physics."

The affable Matthew knew almost everyone at the school. He made Robert feel welcome. Robert's relationship with Andrew had been cooperative and supportive. Robert's relationship with Matthew was more direct and collaborative. For Robert, the eminently relatable Matthew was a godsend.

Chapter 11. Turkey Call

Having stayed in touch with Rufus, Robert's uncle Thomas, the fledgling turkey hunter, was planning to visit the farm for the fall season. Rufus talked him into coming on Sunday morning so he could have plenty of time to scout the hills before opening day on Monday. Thomas's desire to shoot a wild turkey gave Rufus and Katie a perfect excuse for a Sunday party. James and Ginny agreed to come. Robert's sister Angela was bringing a friend. Rufus invited the weekenders from up the valley and strongly encouraged Robert to bring his friend Matthew.

Using the now familiar excuse that Rufus and Katie needed his help, Robert drove out to the farm on Saturday morning. When he arrived he found Rufus out at the pool positioned to get the most out of the October sun. Leave it to Rufus to have a swimming pool open this far into the fall. Although Robert was not the polar bear that Rufus was, he did succumb to the pressure to go for a swim in the cold water. He didn't want Rufus to think he was a wimp. If Rufus thought freezing his ass off was a good idea, then so did Robert. As Robert fought to control his shivers, Rufus engaged him.

"I guess it's too soon to have heard from any

schools?"

"Right, but all the applications are either in the mail or in cyberspace. The counselor at my new school turned out to be a pretty good guy. He's no Mr. Dempsey, but he's helped me a lot. Actually, I've been meaning to ask you about the college thing. I know the subjects I COULD major in, but I don't know what I WANT to major in. You know what I mean?"

"I know exactly what you mean. Here's my advice. Tell them anything they want to hear. Get accepted. Get the scholarship money. Then, even if it takes until the end of your freshman year to make a final decision about your degree program, don't worry about it. My Dad used to make me listen to that Davy Crockett record, 'be sure you're right and then go ahead; be sure your right and then go ahead; it's up to you, to do, what Davy Crockett says'."

Rufus had a pretty good singing voice, and it obviously tickled him to reminisce about the song. He started laughing, presumably at himself.

"Look at me. I was terrible at deciding what I wanted to be when I grew up. With three degrees and a teacher's certificate, here I am, a med/surg nurse, and a sheep farmer."

"That is kind of funny. Everyone knows you're really smart, but look at you, yeah."

"Whatever floats your boat, that's what I say, Robert! I have no regrets about my circuitous journey. I have valued learning new things above all else, and that can mean you're always starting something new. My guiding principle has been the pursuit of knowledge for its own sake, and for what it allows me to experience. I've never tried to impress anyone, or get rich. Each time I felt myself descending into the bowels of the corporate world, I caught myself and quickly re-directed."

Robert admitted the truth that he had known for

years about his father, having watched him struggle diligently to be the perfect family man.

"I am trying to judge what I want to do by how happy people seem, you know, doing what they're doing. You can kind of tell the people who have made deliberate choices to do things that make them happy, as opposed to just fulfill responsibilities they perceive as important. Does that make any sense?"

"Yes it does. You keep looking at it that way, and you'll be fine. Learn as much as you can about everything you can, but mostly yourself. Study your chart. Identify your strengths and weaknesses. Get prepared for what life throws at you. You're beginning to notice that a lot of people operate on a premise no more sophisticated than 'it seemed like the thing to do at the time', or 'I just needed to make a living', or 'it must have been God's will'."

Not wanting to sound like he was being callous or poking fun at people, Rufus took a slightly different tack.

"Actually, we need to be sensitive to those that have been consumed by circumstance. Not all people have the opportunity to embark on a lifetime search for the perfect destiny. Not everyone can proceed through life independently. My father, and your father, had to make decisions that would lead to better outcomes for their spouse and their children, not just for themselves."

Rufus could tell he was sounding a little preachy, so he ended his soliloquy. Besides, he could tell that Robert wanted to talk astrology because he kept mentioning how much he'd been studying.

"I'm probably not ready for it, but now that I know my natal chart pretty well, I can't help but be more curious about transiting planets. I got online and found an Ephemeris for this year. But I'm not sure how to go about interpreting specific aspects I'm seeing between the planets and my own chart."

Rufus was impressed, but he felt some trepidation

about giving this young man yet another key, so early in his education.

"Oh, so you have decided that time didn't stop the moment you were born? That time marches on? That everything is constantly changing? Good for you. I will lend you a book that will help, as long as you promise not to take it too seriously. OK?"

Robert agreed. Rufus returned from the house with a book entitled Planets in Transit.

Robert didn't even get a chance to thank him or even open the book before Rufus broke into song again.

"And the seasons, they go round and round, and the painted ponies go up and down. We're captive on the carousel of time. We can't return, we can only look behind from where we came, and go round and round and round in the circle game."

Rufus had a little more trouble with Joni Mitchell than he did with Davy Crockett, but he got through it.

Robert was looking at Rufus and smiling. He had heard the song before, but was only now realizing the significance it had for Rufus. When Rufus had warned him about the temptation to use astrology as a predictive tool, he had definitely listened. But now, as Rufus repeated the words, "we can only look behind from where we came", Robert understood how serious his uncle really was about showing proper respect for the art, by making every attempt to keep the focus on the lessons of the past.

"You may search out the correlations to explain your experiences and your relationships. But don't try to plan, or predict. That's quicksand! OK?"

Rufus appeared to be quite serious, and it wasn't lost on Robert.

"I could get into big trouble with your parents by taking you too quickly down this path. But I trust you, and I figure you won't crash. Right, Robert?"

"Rufus, I've been thinking, as I consider what to take

up in college. . . . ."

The young man hesitated. He was having a lip biting moment.

"I just want to help other people. I can't really think of anything else I want to do for myself. If astrology makes me more able to figure out who I am, so I can help people, then I'm all for it. So thanks for trusting me with this knowledge. Your trust means a lot to me."

At that point, Rufus gave in to his thirst for beer, but he didn't offer one to his nephew. He enthusiastically drank about half the bottle, as if it were fuel for his coming tirade.

"It's like you're one of the starters on a baseball team. You can study the strengths and weaknesses of each of the players on the opposing team and prepare your game: your offense, your line up, your defense. But until the pitches are thrown and the bat meets the ball, you can't know the possible outcome of the game. Too many variables! Too much chance! All the preparation may increase your odds of success, but it doesn't guarantee it, or predict it. It's the same way with astrology. Even if you know that the Sun or the Moon or a certain planet is about to touch some aspect in your chart, you can't predict the outcome. You just have to play the game to the best of your ability."

"Then why have you been so fascinated with it your whole life, Rufus?"

"Because, like I said before, I've noticed things. I've noticed things about the movement of the Sun and the Moon and the planets through my chart. Relationships I've had and decisions I've made seem to make more sense. The bottom line is that my observations have made me a better person, more intuitive, and more tolerant. For me, that's been the goal, to notice the effects and to learn from them."

"Like Yoda, and the force! But in this case, it's many

forces, all swirling around us and trying to get our attention."

"That's an interesting way to put it, Robert. I like that. I guess that's what I've been doing, trying to get in touch with the force, or the forces. I guess that's what I've been doing."

Robert steered Rufus back to the subject of the decisions he had to make about his future.

"Well, anyway, I'm not sure what to take up in college. Right now, I'm just glad school is going OK. I feel useful at school, especially with the tutoring program. My advanced science classes are good, but strangely enough, I like the tutoring and the computer class more. And of course, I've been meaning to tell you, life is better since I met Matthew."

"Oh yes, Matthew. I really liked working with his mother at school. She's a good woman. Did Matthew say anything about her being done with her elementary education degree? She had been working hard to go from teacher's aide to certificated teacher."

"As a matter of fact, he said that she would be finished with her degree in the spring, and was most likely going to be hired to teach sixth grade next year."

"That's excellent. She'll make a great teacher."

After helping Rufus move the sheep in the afternoon, Robert went home for supper. Late into that night, he perused the book that Rufus had given him. Divided into chapters by Sun, Moon, Mercury, and so on, the author described the possible influences of each of these celestial players as they transit through the houses and form all the various aspects within the person's natal chart.

Robert used the current day's ephemeris data to identify the more significant transits in his chart. However fascinating, it was a bit overwhelming. He remembered Rufus's suggestion to learn the process by concentrating initially on the movement of the Moon, and then, later on, work up to some of the heavy hitting, slower moving, major planets. Robert found this newest brain food selection to be quite tasty.

Chapter 12. Astrologer Exposed

Considering the five hour drive, Thomas arrived at Rufus's farm quite early on Sunday morning. He could walk the turkey territory, enjoy the party, spend the night at the farm, and be prepared to enter the woods well before sunrise with plenty of rest and a solid plan.

The prospects for the hunt were good. Hunting turkeys in the fall depended on knowing where the flock was congregating. Unlike in spring, when the hunter relied primarily on sounding like a hen turkey desirous of a horny gobbler, the fall hunter's success depended on locating the flock in the early morning and scattering them, by any means possible. Then, playing on the hens' instinct to regroup, the hunter would use certain turkey calls to lure them back in. Rufus was pretty sure he knew where the turkeys were roosting at night, which would improve Thomas's chances of seeing them when they flew down out of the tall trees in the first hint of dawn light.

Thomas donned his new camouflage and the two men were in the woods within an hour. Their destination was a ridge that sloped upward to the southwest. They walked quietly, non-stop, single file. When they were close to the roost trees, Rufus signaled it was time for a break.

"I'm so glad that you could come, Thomas. I hope

you get a turkey. You seem like you need a victory of some sort. But mostly, I hope you enjoy the experience."

"Thanks, Rufus. This turkey hunting thing is important to me, but so is continuing to explore some of the ideas we shared on the Fourth of July. I want to know more about your approach. I'm desperately trying to reach my son, and I need an approach that is more contemporary than the Bible, something more effective than what I'm getting from the Church. I can't talk to James right now about my family struggles, even though I'd like to. When I mention alternative pathways, he thinks I'm abandoning my belief in God."

Those were magic words for Rufus, not only because he believed he had something to offer Thomas and his son John, but because he perceived Thomas as someone who might be in a position to return the favor.

"I think I might be able to help, but right now, let me show you some of the interesting features of this forest that may help you get your turkey."

Standing there in his own forest, Rufus was profoundly conflicted. He genuinely wanted to bring his expertise to bear on Thomas's family problem, but he also wanted to exploit an opportunity. Even though his plans for enhanced data collection were little more than fantasy, he couldn't help but consider what Thomas's employment at the U.S. Census Bureau might mean to his efforts in the future. Deciding, right then and there, that friendship was the most important consideration, he suppressed his usury thoughts, and concentrated on helping Thomas with the turkey hunt.

When they'd finished developing the morning plan, the two men left the woods. Soon after they reached the gravel road, they were overtaken by a pickup truck. It was Tim and Larry, the weekenders from up the valley. Rufus had invited them for "a few beers", and with introductions in place, Rufus and Thomas hitched a ride on the tailgate the rest of the way back to the house.

They were greeted by James and his family. Thomas hugged his brother James and pecked Ginny on the cheek. As Angela and her friend headed for the pool deck with their smart phones, Ginny playfully scolded Thomas for leaving his wife at home.

Katie invited everyone up onto the west-side porch to sample a wide variety of refreshment. It didn't take long for the men to start telling hunting stories and exhibit behaviors that treaded on the border of boisterous. Unimpressed with all the macho nonsense, Ginny and Katie escaped to the kitchen.

James, who had been the least talkative, suddenly directed a loaded question at Rufus, just as Robert and Matthew arrived on the porch.

"So do the stars indicate anything about my brother's chance of killing a turkey tomorrow? Robert says you're quite the astrologer. Can you use your powers to help Thomas?"

Rufus shook off his momentary discomfort with the unexpected question. It wasn't that he minded James asking. It was inevitable that the topic would come up at some point. He had never presumed that Robert would be able to keep it from his parents forever. But since Tim and Larry were largely unaware of how passionate he was about astrology, he had extra incentive to choose his words carefully. Even though evasion wasn't exactly his style, it was no time to poke at a hornet's nest.

"First of all, I regret to say, no predictions regarding turkeys. No light to shed there. But yes, James, I have been honest with Robert about my interest in astrology, and I guess I have kind of taken him on as my student. He knows not to take it too seriously, don't you Robert?"

"It's true Dad. It's just a hobby. It's not devil worship."

Robert couldn't believe that he had blurted out such a

ridiculous statement. As if the situation wasn't bad enough, he made the comments right when Ginny and Katie were returning to the porch, carrying trays loaded with appetizers: cucumber sandwiches, jalapeno poppers, and bacon-wrapped water chestnut/chicken livers. Ginny wasn't shy.

"So what's this about devil worship?"

"I was just calling Rufus out on this astrology thing, and Robert just may be feeling a bit defensive. He's the one that mentioned devil worship, not me."

Ginny smelled a chance to have some fun putting Rufus on the spot.

"Yeah, Rufus, what is going on with this astrology stuff? Don't you think he's a little young?"

Rufus was hearing the hornets buzzing, and he surely didn't want to feel their sting.

"Well, do you have anything to say for yourself, Rufus, teaching astrology to a seventeen year old boy?"

Ginny was forcing his hand, so he decided that the best defense was a good offense. He stood up, grabbed another beer from the cooler, and revealed himself to his in-laws and his guests.

"It's not like he's going to lose his religion, if that's what you're worried about. Astrology is totally compatible with Christianity. The Good Lord wants us to hone our God-given talents and avoid sin. Astrology can actually assist us in those efforts."

"Rufus, that's all fine and good, but Robert has enough on his plate. He doesn't need to be distracted by this nonsense."

"Nonsense? Oh, now Ginny, doesn't Samuel plant his garden and his crops by the moon?"

"Yes, but what's that got to do with it?"

At this point, James was just watching and listening, kind of glad that his wife was the one engaging Rufus.

"Everything. Just ask Samuel if he thinks it's

nonsense. The Farmer's Almanac talks about moon phases and barren signs and good times to kill weeds and so on and so forth. It's the same idea. People, right or wrong, attach significance to the movement of the heavenly bodies. Ask the Aztecs. Ask the Egyptians. Ask the Farmer's Almanac."

Thomas took a chance and jumped in.

"What Rufus means is that it's harmless to think that the phase of the moon has something to do with the sprouting of beans. There's no downside to it. It's harmless, as long as it doesn't become an obsession. Look at some of the things people do, and become obsessed with. I think Robert's probably level-headed enough to handle astrology, especially with such a great teacher."

Everyone had a good laugh at Rufus' expense on that one. Thomas re-gained their attention.

"If Rufus thinks the Moon passing through the constellation Taurus has some kind of significance for him because he's a Taurus, what's the harm?"
James decided to challenge his brother's support for Rufus.

"The Sun and the Moon can't have an effect on a person. The Sun warms the planet and the full moon's pretty to look at, but they don't influence our behavior. How could they do that? Our behavior is between us and Almighty God. That's how I've raised my son, and I pray that he doesn't lose sight of the truth."

Rufus was familiar with, and comfortable with, that line of reasoning.

"The point is that we don't really know if the celestial bodies influence our behavior. But we also don't know for sure that they don't. As I used to tell my students: there's so much more to know than what we already know."

Larry, usually quiet, unless directly addressed, all of a sudden jumped in.

"Rufus, what's that got to do with it? I say we just go

with what we know for sure, and all I know is, I'm ready for another cold one."

He got his beer, but he didn't get the laugh he was shooting for. People were becoming seriously intrigued by the discussion, and the teacher was just getting warmed up.

"Before Newton, and even after Newton, we knew that 'what goes up must come down'. It's true that Einstein's theory of relativity complicated our understanding of gravity a little bit, but not for the average person here on Earth. We just know that gravity exists. It's an attractive force between objects that is proportional to their size and the distance between them. But we don't know any more than that. We still don't know what causes it, and we don't really know how it works. It's just an extremely influential universal force, and we all notice its effect."

Katie was thinking Rufus was getting a little too preachy, so she stopped him.

"Honey, maybe our guests just want to relax and chat about less serious topics."

"You're right, darling. I'm sorry."

Rufus had learned to rely on Katie's instincts. He grabbed another beer, politely asked if anyone else needed anything to drink and sat down.

Tim, also a former teacher, had been the most frequent visitor to the beer cooler, and didn't want to see the discussion die.

"Oh, don't stop now. This is the best thing I've experienced in a long time. I remember teaching science to sixth-graders, and Rufus is right. There's so much more to be known than what we currently know."

He smiled when Rufus rewarded him with a quick private toast, and then he sought to revive the controversy by picking on Robert and Matthew.

"Pop quiz. Name another force in the universe

besides gravity."

Being the silly man that he could be after a few too many beers, he started humming the final jeopardy song. Matthew didn't let him get very far.

"What is electromagnetic force?"

"Very good, my friend. A force once undiscovered, then poorly understood, that we now know has a huge impact on our lives. Electromagnetic forces practically rule our modern existence. We rely on electromagnetic force to explain the chemical behavior of matter, electricity, computer technology, television, radio, smart phones, WiFi, spy satellites. . . . . . The force was always there. We just didn't understand it, or know how to use it."

Rufus was feeling the pressure as Katie tried to control her glare of disapproval. But he had mixed feelings, because many of the guests seemed to be enjoying the discussion, and even James didn't seem upset.

Suddenly, not wanting to be left out, or outdone by his friend Matthew, Robert blurted out another jeopardy answer.

"What is the nuclear force!"
Tim responded immediately. He was really enjoying taking the heat off of Rufus. It wasn't clear that he even remembered that astrology was the original topic.

"Oh, yes, the good old nuclear force, the ultimate source of all the energy in the universe. If you think about what is happening inside the Sun, and of course, inside all the trillions of stars, you realize that nuclear forces have an incredible influence on our lives. Once again, the force has always existed. We just didn't know how it worked."

James was looking a bit queasy, perhaps regretting his original decision to challenge Rufus, at least in this particular setting. He wasn't the drinker that Rufus and

Tim were, so he probably just wanted to put the worms back in the can and clamp the lid down tight.

Ginny, glass of wine in hand, came to her husband's rescue.

"Katie assures me that Rufus is harmless. If Rufus wants to do that astrology stuff, and Robert continues to be the perfect son, then what the hell?"

Ginny didn't expect a round of applause, but she got one. The breeze of tolerance had effectively lifted the fog of seriousness. The gentle, melodious rumbles of "how ya' doin'?" had been given new life.

Chapter 13. Heaven and Hell

The dinner was marvelous. Entertaining guests with their country idea of fine cuisine was Rufus and Katie's number one. Living in the middle of nowhere sometimes limited the social aspects of life, so they always went the extra mile when people came for dinner. Spinach/feta crostinies, Greek salad, leg of lamb, twice baked potatoes, broccoli, snow peas with scallions, and banana cream pie for dessert. Rufus served his famous wild grape wine with the dinner, even getting the nod from James that the young people could be included.

After dinner, James went for a walk with his brother Thomas, while Angela and her friend helped Ginny and Katie with the dishes. Robert and Matthew held Rufus to his promise to drive them down to the beaver pond. Rufus made sure they had working flashlights, gave them some tips about navigating the beaver pond with the small rowboat, reminded them about cottonmouths, and advised the best route back to the house. He made it clear that he would not be returning to pick them up.

By the time Rufus returned to the house, everyone had re-assembled on the porch. Larry's body language telegraphed the likelihood of 'thanks for everything, but we gotta go', just as Ginny and Katie were trying to get

everyone to consider playing a game. Carefully
noncommittal, Rufus headed straight for Thomas and Tim,
even if it meant a good chance of resurrecting the
astrology discussion.

"Great dinner, Rufus. I really enjoyed it. I'm all set
to skip breakfast and get up to my spot really early. Of
course, I just might have to take a piece of that banana pie
with me."

"You're quite welcome for dinner. As for the pie,
next time I'll make you your own private pie, just for the
hunt."

"I'm so glad you decided to join us, because Tim has
been asking a lot of questions about your 'astrology habit',
as he calls it, and I don't have the answers. I explained
that our relationship was energized on the Fourth of July,
and was based on a mutual interest in religion and
philosophy, not to mention your kind offer to help me
with John."

"So Rufus, do you really think there's something to
it? That whole discussion about forces in the universe,
previously unknown and mysterious, and then brought
into the realm of human understanding, really got me
going. It really made me think you might be serious. I
know you've forgotten more about science than I'll ever
know, but what is there about astrology that I'm missing?
I need all the help I can get!"

Rufus was actually flattered by Tim's interest, and
appreciated the non-judgmental spirit his friend conveyed.

"What do I know about astrology that you may need
to know? Only what I've read in books, and verified by
personal experience, that's all."

Rufus was used to dodging the question when it
came from a person whose astrological knowledge was
limited. But he obliged Tim's desire for a more complete
answer.

"I don't understand the exact nature of the forces,

but I think I have seen their effect. My comments earlier were not meant as a defense of astrology, but merely as an assurance that I didn't see astrology as being at odds with religion or morality. I actually see astrology and Christianity as quite compatible. Astrology can help a person be a better Christian."

Tim was unprepared for such a polished response. He actually seemed uncomfortable, and just looked around as if he was hoping for someone else to say something.

Ginny and Katie's efforts to get everyone to play cards or some other game were falling flat. Larry bowed out with a shrug and a "not tonight, thanks", while Angela and her friend made a move for the private confines of the basement to watch TV. Convinced that he too was off the hook, James wandered over to sit down with his brother.

It was extremely important to Rufus that James be a happy camper. Rufus desperately wanted to avoid anything that might complicate his relationship with Robert. Having no son of his own, and being so drawn to Robert, he was very mindful of the possibility that James could easily adopt the posture of the protective father.

"I'm so glad you and your family could come out today, and I assure you that I want only the best for Robert. You're his father, and I will always abide by whatever you say."

James's reaction to the gracious comment was one of relief and appreciation.

"I think Ginny had it right. Robert is a really good kid, with a bright future. I don't think we need to be worried about a little astrology. He goes to church on Sunday, and I'm proud of him. That's about it."

Thomas offered some icing for Rufus's conciliatory cake.

"I'm glad to hear you say that James. I haven't known Rufus for long, but I believe he really cares about people. He is a little different, but he doesn't push his beliefs on people. He calls it like he sees it, and is always ready to hear the other side. I'm sure he'd be the first one to tell you if he notices anything to be concerned about with Robert. I've really struggled with my faith since John has become so lost. I must say, in the brief time I've known him, Rufus has helped me a lot."

Thomas intimated, with a subtle gesture, that Tim was up to speed on his son John's recent difficulties with drugs and alcohol.

"I'm glad about that Thomas. I know it's been a bad deal."

"Thank you. Rufus was hardly the cause, although I have relied on him for validation, but I feel my attitudes changing . . . . I mean evolving . . . . . . about some of the teachings of the Church. You and I were both raised to put our faith in God and strictly adhere to what the Catholic Church tells us. Maybe I'm misguided, or bitter, because of my recent experience, but I just can't do that anymore."

James was shocked at Thomas's confession and seemed afraid to ask him to elaborate. He didn't have to, because Thomas was actually ready for something even more provocative.

"Tim, do you think that heaven is a place?"

Tim pondered for a moment, and took a swig off his beer.

"Well, yeah. Maybe the streets aren't lined with gold and all that, but heaven's definitely a place."

James didn't need any time to prepare his own response to the question.

"Heaven is a place where the righteous who have lived up to God's plan and who have asked for forgiveness, will go to experience everlasting life."

"Then what about hell?"

"Eternal damnation for those who failed, and yes, it's

a place."

"Well brother James, my son asked me the other day if he was going to hell. Can you believe that? I thought to myself, something must be really wrong. He said he had lost sight of heaven, and he was actually considering whether he deserved to go to hell? That made me sick, and makes me question my religion."

James tried to speak, but Thomas wouldn't let him.

"I know what you're going to say before you say it. Hell can be avoided by a fervent belief in our Lord Jesus Christ and a sincere confession of sin. As long as we are forgiven for our sins, even at the hour of our death, we can still go to heaven, as long as we believe! Blah, blah, blah, blah. But you see, that's not helping John right now. It's too abstract for him."

Rufus was concerned that he was witnessing a brother/brother breakdown. At first, he wasn't sure how to address the heightening frustration. Holding some very strong opinions of his own about heaven, hell, and conceptions of life after death, he was usually quite willing to voice them, and accept his plight as theological lightning rod. But this was not one of those times. Rufus simply felt compelled to do whatever he could to lessen the metaphysical shock the brothers were experiencing in that moment.

"Thomas and I have mused about life everlasting. Everyone does. We all know that sometimes life events cause us to question. But it's been a long day, and I am concerned that this discussion is cutting into much needed rest time for all of us. I know you have to work in the morning, and Thomas has been up since three. I propose that we postpone these deliberations about heaven and hell. In fact, I insist. This isn't the time or place for such a heavy discussion."

Rufus sensed that Thomas was feeling regret about bringing John into the discussion.

Uncharacteristically proactive, James responded by getting up, going over to his brother, and placing his hand on his shoulder.

"I promise we'll talk about it soon, OK, Thomas."

Thomas was fighting back tears, so he merely nodded agreement.

Tim, a welcome catalyst for a return to normalcy, rushed to lighten the load.

"Aw, Rufus, they said you didn't have any sense. But tonight, you're actually doing pretty good."

He reached out to shake Thomas' hand and wished him luck in the morning. Then, turning toward Larry, who had gotten stuck with Ginny and Katie, he yelled.

"C'mon Larry. I need my beauty sleep!"

In the middle of the men's exit, Robert and Matthew returned from the valley. They were wet and filthy, but obviously happy. Their cell phone videos of beavers slapping their tails on the water at dusk served to seal the fate of any seriousness that had pervaded the west side porch.

Everyone seemed to have gotten something out of the day. Thomas went to bed more secure in his friendship with Rufus, and felt a bit closer to his brother James. Katie was proud of the way Rufus had handled things, and was gratified that her sister agreed. Matthew finally got to meet Rufus face to face, and Ginny enjoyed the opportunity to publicly praise her son. James felt proud that he had stood up for his religious beliefs.

The pre-dinner discussion about forces offered an excellent springboard for Matthew to dive into the astrology pool with Robert. The two friends were to have yet another thing in common. Robert began teaching his friend the basics that very night. It was a good thing Matthew planned to spend the night at Robert's because his mother might not have let him in the house, as dirty as he was from the adventure at the beaver pond.

Chapter 14. Country Reality

Robert found out at dinner Monday evening that Thomas had in fact gotten a turkey. It was hard for James to hide his immense pride as he presided over the evening meal. In spite of the sensitive discussions of the evening before, everyone, even Angela, reported having had a good time at Rufus and Katie's.

The road project was just about completed. The result for Robert's family was actually to gain some ground in the front of their house. Taking the sharp turn out of the road had essentially moved the road farther away from their house and added almost a half an acre to their property in the front.

It was beginning to appear that the most important road, the one to higher education, was leading right back to the City. The Jesuit University was offering the best deal, and Robert couldn't help but wonder what part Mr. Dempsey had played.

For the current school year however, it was about experiences that would change him in a way that had nothing at all to do with academics, college plans, or career. During the coming winter, Matthew was to introduce Robert to aspects of life that were totally new to him.

It all started one day after school when they were to meet at his car. There was Matthew, skipping along toward him, arm in arm with two girls. The one on his left arm was Mindy. Robert had met her a few times because she sometimes hung out with Matthew in the lunchroom. Skipping a very tenuous skip, she looked like a scared rabbit. He wasn't sure if he had seen the other girl before.

"Robert, I know you remember Mindy."

She smiled, projecting a kindness and a sincerity that one could easily accept, like the surprise offer of a beautiful, fresh picked flower, spontaneous and natural. When she stopped smiling, having greeted Robert without any words, just a curtsy, she reverted to scared rabbit, shy, and unwilling to initiate even a glance.

The other girl was very calm, and spoke softly but confidently.

"Hi, I'm Jane. Matthew has told me a lot about you."

Robert mustered a respectful 'nice to meet you' that was intended to apply to both girls at once. Flattered at the attention, he quickly reverted to responsible Robert. Knowing that the girls had already let the school bus go, he took Matthew aside and warned.

"You know I can't have anyone in the car but you! What's going on?"

"I know Robert. Just get us as far as my house and then I'll drive my truck. It'll be a little crowded in the truck, but that's the best plan. We've got to babysit!"

Robert was a bit confused, but texted his mom that he was going to be at Matthew's for a while after school to work on their computer science project. The girls had waited patiently during the negotiations and were ready to get going. They got into the back seat.

Robert knew the way to Matthew's house like the back of his hand, and was very careful with his driving, but he was definitely distracted by the gorgeous face in his rear view mirror. He kept stealing glances at Jane as he drove. It was the way her wholesome greenish blue eyes glanced back at him that provoked his distraction. Her cheeks were like that soft yellow orangish-pink part of the peach that just screamed luscious. She was on the short side, a bit pudgy, but oh, that face. He drove on, wondering what the afternoon was really about.

After switching vehicles, the foursome headed south of town for a few miles and turned onto a county gravel road. Within a half mile, and a lot of playful moaning and groaning from Mindy and Jane, they stopped in front of a broken down old mobile home. As they got out, the girls squawked about how rough it had been riding down the gravel road, with Jane complaining the loudest because she was the one on the bottom. But it was all in good fun. Even though they were country girls, neither had wanted to sit on Robert's lap, for fear of giving the wrong impression.

A woman that was apparently Jane's mother came flying out of the trailer. Matthew was still in the truck and the truck was still running. She yelled at the three barking dogs to shut up, went straight up to Jane, gave her a big hug, and jumped in the truck. Noticing Robert as they were pulling away, she leaned out of the passenger window.

"Oh, Hi honey. I'm sorry. . . . . I have to go."

Within a span of two minutes, Robert was marooned with two girls, three dogs, and as he would soon discover, three little kids. Jane shooed the dogs away from Robert's trembling legs and settled his fears in that consistently calm voice.

"Don't worry. Matthew will be right back. He just had to take mama to work 'cause her car wouldn't start. Mama's name is Sarah. I'm sorry you didn't get a proper introduction."

The girls invited him into the trailer where he met Jane's three younger siblings, a girl twelve, and boys four and six. They were bright eyed and well-behaved, and didn't pay much attention to Robert. They were fresh off the bus and transitioning to their after school life. As Robert and Jane headed back outside, she couldn't help but ask.

"So Matthew says you're from the City. You act like you've never been any place like this before. You haven't, have you?"

"No, I guess I haven't."

Over the next little while, sitting at an old picnic table on the side of the trailer, looking out on the neighbor's horse pasture, the three of them talked while they waited for Matthew to return. Jane disclosed the facts about her father's incarceration, for conspiracy to cultivate and distribute marijuana, being careful to stress that he was a really good man who had just gotten in with the wrong crowd. Jane then went on to re-introduce Robert to her girlfriend, disclosing that Mindy was the mother of a one year old boy, and lived with her grandparents up the road. The girls identified themselves as juniors, and admitted being fascinated with hearing about Robert at school because they had met so few people that had grown up in the City.

In the midst of a dog trodden landscape in which the driveway and the yard were as one, Robert felt refreshed by the honesty and integrity in Jane's smooth voice. Matthew had dropped him into a cultural swamp with no warning, perhaps to see if he could survive on his own. Robert felt that he was not only surviving, but thriving, because of the forthrightness in the character of this girl Jane. But it was all happening too quickly for him to realize that she was to be the medium for his transformation.

Matthew returned and pulled right up by the picnic table, beckoning Robert to approach. He gave him the choice of coming along while he dropped Mindy off at her house, or staying with Jane until he returned. Robert had good reason not to leave this girl that he obviously liked, but he opted to ride along. He really felt he needed to get home, and feared that allowing Matthew too much freedom would be risky. Leaving Jane was the price he had to pay for some control over the situation.

Goodbyes said, Jane watched the truck ramble down the dusty road, before heading inside for an evening of babysitting and homework.

Within about a mile, the truck approached what looked like the end of the county-maintained road, and a gate that accessed Mindy's grandparent's property. Other than the faded white wood-sided house with the rusty tin hip roof, the most prominent feature of the landscape was the saw mill. Mindy's grandfather was one of the last of the small time saw mill operators in the area, making his living timbering small tracts with mules, sawing out and selling tie logs, pallet lumber, and custom lumber.

Mindy's grandmother greeted them with the baby in her arms, insisting of course that the boys come in, so she could check out the new friend. Mindy took the baby from her grandmother, offered a simple but sincere thanks to Matthew for the ride home, and disappeared upstairs, leaving the two boys at the mercy of grandma. It was clear that the elderly woman felt very comfortable with Matthew.

"So who do we have here?"

"This is my new friend Robert. I felt like he needed a taste of the country ways, at least the poor people country ways, so I brought him. He stayed with Jane and Mindy while I took Sarah to work."

"Oh, that's good. Jane is such a sweet girl, and her mama Sarah is a real gem. I'm glad to know 'em. Nice to meet you Robert."

Robert responded with all the politeness in his being while he tried to hide his fascination with everything he

115

could see around him inside the home. It was like a step back in time, like a museum. Rufus talked and walked a nature lover kind of country existence, but Mindy's grandparents were the real article. The kitchen was adorned with all the devices and furniture of a bygone era, much of it apparently not just for show, but for everyday use. Butter churn, cream separator, egg boxes, slaw cutter, wash board, and ice box, each a fitting complement to the sturdy antique furniture, homemade cabinets, and wooden kitchen countertops. Shelves full of a vast variety of canned meats, vegetables, and fruits dominated one of the walls in the kitchen. The smell of fresh baked bread made it hard for the boys to turn down the offer of a country ham sandwich.

"We promise we'll come back soon, but we have to get home and get started on our homework. Say goodbye to Mindy for me. Tell her I'll see her tomorrow at lunch."

Matthew was used to escaping grandma's offers. In a whisper, he bragged about it, as the two of them headed for the truck.

Grandma yelled after them.

"I'll be sure to send a piece of pie with Mindy tomorrow. Thank you Matthew."

Robert was glad to be headed back to his car. He didn't ask Matthew to explain the events of the afternoon because he didn't want to reveal how shook up he really was.

Matthew didn't wait for an invitation.

"So you probably haven't been around too many poor people. You don't really notice at school, but about a third of the students you see everyday live in conditions similar to Jane's. Sometimes it's just a way of life that is as natural as life itself. Sometimes it's a family tradition of ignorance. Sometimes it's drugs, or alcohol. Sometimes it's inescapable health problems that force disability or reliance on welfare. Sometimes it's just a family tradition of dependency, with no clear cause. Sometimes, as in Jane's case, it's just really bad luck."

"I'm glad you brought me out here. I've definitely never been anywhere like Mindy's place, or Jane's place. I don't mind saying, and you probably already know, that I really like Jane. So her Dad is a pretty good guy?"

"Oh yeah, he's alright. He's a good guy, and a great mechanic. He was working hard, doing what fathers are supposed to do, I guess. He was trying to make enough money for his family to have a better life. But with three kids, it was difficult. So he got involved in the marijuana trade. He participated in growing local weed to bring in a little extra cash. Unfortunately, one of his partners screwed up big time. The partner, and supposed friend, started messing around with the wrong guy's wife and the whole marijuana bust thing was payback. Everything would have been cool if his partner would have just realized how bad he was screwing up. No pun intended."

He continued when Robert didn't say anything.

"Mindy's story is just the opposite. Her Dad was quite the piece of work. Not only did he totally reject the hard work road to prosperity offered by his father, the saw mill guy, but he always seemed to end up with the most messed up women. Mindy really paid the price. With an asshole for a Dad and never a stable mom, she got in with the wrong crowd starting way back in junior high. By early high school, she was getting used by guys not so different from her Dad, and she didn't see the light until she got knocked up. Thank God for her grandparents. She's got a lot to work through, but she's going to be OK."

"Wow. So much for the cozy little middle class family I grew up in."

Strangely, the whole experience made Robert think of Andrew, and gave him an idea.

"Matthew, I think I'd like to turn the tables on you. What do you say we figure out how to go to the City over

Christmas break?"

"I'm not sure how we're going to do that, but OK."

Robert didn't stay long at Matthew's. They would have to work on their computer technology project some other time. Robert drove home to an evening of thinking about Jane. He now had yet another compelling reason to look forward to going to school.

CHAPTER 15. COUNTRY COMFORT

As November slid toward Thanksgiving break, Robert had established his own relationship with Jane, apart from the afterschool ramblings of the original foursome. Matthew had to work most days after school. So the most common occurrence was Robert driving Mindy straight home and then spending time with Jane at her place if she had to babysit, or at the local creek getaway spot if she didn't have to come home right after school.

Robert had never had a girlfriend, or a girl who was a close friend. All he knew was that he felt comfortable around Jane. He spoke freely about how he felt, like he hadn't with any girl before. It wasn't lust, and it wasn't needy, and it wasn't romantic. It was just honest and easy relations, direct and to the point, unconfused. How refreshing for Robert to be truly operating outside of his intellectual self for once. It was equally satisfying for Jane. Her natural shyness seemed to fade away when she was with Robert, almost as much as it did when she was with her siblings.

Jane declined the invitation to Robert's house for Thanksgiving dinner, but accepted the offer to accompany Robert, Matthew, and Mindy out to Uncle Rufus's place the day after. The first snow of the season came over night, so the foursome didn't actually make it out to the farm until almost lunch time.

Rufus was ready for them. After a lunch of Texas chili and sandwiches, they went sledding. The starting line was in the backyard up by the pool. After a gentle run around the west side of the house, blind to their destination, the sleds would cross the driveway, and then accelerate down the long steep hill. The boys showed the girls how to steer, to avoid crashing into the trees, and how to slow down at the end, to avoid screeching to a halt on the gravel road. The excitement of it all even got Mindy to open up a bit. She laughed and talked much more than usual. Nothing like a fast run down a snowy slope to uncork a quiet person.

Once in the house, after a brief stint by the wood stove in the basement to warm up, Katie served them hot chocolate in the kitchen upstairs. The conversation was mostly 'getting to know you' small talk, but the girls seemed very comfortable, considering it was the first time they were meeting Katie and Rufus. Jane had heard a lot about Rufus, including his fascination with astrology, and other equally eccentric topics, so she didn't see him as a total stranger. Rufus made it easy for her and Mindy to relate, having had much experience with similar young people as a small town teacher.

Robert was elated when Rufus invited him and Matthew along to feed hay. The sheep's reaction to the provision of the nutritious fodder was nothing short of remarkable. The snowy landscape had sealed them off from the grass. So the appearance of men with sustenance induced a hearty demonstration of animal gratitude. Relieved of the prospect of surviving on stored fat reserves, the sheep chomped on the fibrous feast with unbelievable enthusiasm. It was something to behold. Robert was happy that Matthew was there to share the experience.

Having heard from Robert that Matthew's interest in astrology was genuine, Rufus talked freely. Presuming that Matthew was aware of his ideas about improving data collection, he poked around about how adept the boys were at computers. The boys didn't really understand what he was getting at. They thought he was asking their opinion about the astrology apps that were out there on the net, not realizing that his true motivation for evaluating their cyber aptitudes.

Rufus was glad to know that Robert had facilitated the generation of Matthew's natal chart, and was growing comfortable with Matthew's astrological integrity as he listened to the young man's comments and plans for future study. Careful to avoid sounding like he was worried, Rufus did make a point of asking the boys to keep their astrology enthusiasm to themselves, implying the dangers of divulging too much of such a thing in a small town school. The boys assured him that it was all on the QT, and that Jane and Mindy were cool.

The foursome thanked Rufus and Katie for the fun time and hit the road. Robert was feeling good because he knew he had succeeded. He had made his friends happy by getting them away from the hum drum of the small town scene. On the way back, everyone chattered about how much fun it was to go sledding, and how much they appreciated the warm welcome and good refreshments.

As they approached town, Jane reminded Robert of the promise they had made to Jane's mother, to stop at the grocery store on the way home. They pulled into the parking lot. As the four of them got out of Robert's car and walked toward the store, they were confronted by a group of boys, the sight of whom wiped the smiles off their faces in an instant. It was Mindy's baby daddy and his low life friends, a total of four young, stinky cowboy boot wearin', unkempt losers.

One of the boys stepped out in front of his little group and seemed intent on manufacturing some kind of confrontation.

"So, how's my kid I never get to see, Mindy, and who's your new boyfriend here?"

Mindy didn't answer him in words. She bit her lip, gave him a brief hateful stare, and stepped to the rear. Matthew was not a fighter, and neither was Robert, but they had learned how to posture to face down an obvious threat. These four young men, who appeared high or drunk or both, were representatives of that pitiful local element that had fallen prey to the monster meth. Even though they probably weren't using at the time, they couldn't hide the telltale signs.

The baby daddy's name was Jason. Matthew had known him all his life, so he was the obvious choice to engage him. Jason had been expelled from school for fighting long before Mindy had given birth to their child. With no education, no support system, no gumption, and no job, he had been convinced to give up his parental rights. It was apparent that he approached the world with many chips on his shoulder.

"Jason, you know we don't want any trouble. Mindy isn't my girlfriend. You know that. We were just out goofin' around 'cause it snowed, and it's a holiday. How you guys doin'?"

Jason's friends were just dying for him to show out. One of them started in on Jane, mouthin' about how sweet she looked and maybe she'd want to go with them for a good time. Robert was frozen with fear on the outside, but on the inside his superior brain was processing a way out. When he spoke, the ruffians didn't really know what to think.

"Jane, just give me your list. You and Mindy and Matthew go back to the car. I'll just run in and get the stuff so we can go."

Robert had assessed the risk and made a calculation. He was the person with whom they had the least problem, if for no other reason than he was an unknown quantity. He was gambling that making an unexpected move, on his own, as if it were no big deal, would confuse the opposition. As Jane handed him the list, he nonchalantly tossed the keys to Matthew, who escorted the girls back to the car.

Robert was betting that, without the familiar buttons to push, the miscreants would have trouble processing. They would not be able to figure out fast enough how and why they should hassle someone they had never met.

Robert turned and calmly walked by Jason, who appeared confused as to whether he should confront him, or re-engage Mindy and Matthew. Robert took a deep breath, held it, and trying desperately to control his nerves, proceeded into the store.

The maneuver gave Matthew and the girls time to lock themselves in the car. Jason ended up looking like an idiot. His friends quickly lost interest in the game. As Robert safely entered the store, he considered asking for assistance from the store manager, but it wasn't necessary. The trouble makers had tired of the game and were leaving the scene. He waited a few minutes and then went back out to the car to rejoin his friends. Jane got out of the car and gave him a big hug.

"Robert, you did good, but don't ever do anything like that again. I don't think you realize what these guys are capable of."

"All I did was come up with a plan to defuse the situation. That guy is obviously hurting. By not confronting his pain directly, I gave him a chance to reconsider."

Matthew apologized to Robert for never having explained Mindy's unfortunate relationship with her baby daddy. Mindy started crying, mostly out of relief that the experience was over. She and Matthew got into the back seat of the car, while Jane and Robert went into the store to get the groceries. Matthew knew how to get Mindy settled down. He had been like a big brother to her for a long time.

It was a struggle for Jane to obtain all the items on the list with the amount of money that her mother had given her. She didn't want to disappoint her mother. But even with the food stamps, decisions had to be made about quantities and sizes so that they could get everything on the list. Robert's mathematical brain was a big asset in accomplishing the task. Jane wouldn't let him throw in any money to make it all work, but she did let him buy the younger kids some candy.

They got Mindy back to her baby. As she said her goodbyes, she asked everyone to please resist telling her grandfather about the confrontation with Jason. She was more afraid of what her grandfather might do than she was of what Jason might do.

Sarah invited Matthew and Robert to stick around for a while as they brought the groceries in. Knowing how little fun her eldest daughter usually had, she wouldn't let them stop talking about the joy of sledding. She was ho hum about the Jason episode. She was a tough lady who had handled many of his kind, and she was confident that she had taught Jane how to take care of herself and her friends. Sarah wasn't the shot gun totin' type that Mindy's grandfather was, but she had solid friends who could come to the defense of her and her family. Most importantly, she knew that Jason was well aware of that.

Robert dropped Matthew off and went home with a real sense of accomplishment. His family was gathered in the big living room trying to figure out how to make a fire in that wonderful big stone fireplace.

CHAPTER 16. WINTER JOY

Robert's eighteenth birthday fell on a Saturday and coincided with his acceptance letter from the University. He had been awarded a full academic scholarship. For once in his life, Robert felt he was in control. His relationship with Jane was steady and fulfilling. Family life in the new home was warm and supportive.

When he came in from the mailbox, he knew right away that something was up. He had not seen his mother Ginny so happy for a long time. She was absolutely beaming as she hurried toward him. He stuck the letter in his pocket.

"Gary's coming home!"

"For Christmas?"

"Yes, he'll be home on Christmas Eve and will be home for two weeks!"

"That's great news Mom. I can't wait to see Gary. I worry about him all the time."

"I'm planning a big party for the weekend after Christmas. I've already talked to your father."

"I was going to ask if I could invite Jane for Christmas dinner, but maybe I should just invite her to the party. Maybe Matthew can come too, and bring Mindy. Does that sound OK Mom?"

"That sounds perfect Robert. I'll invite some of Gary's old school buddies, and your Uncle Thomas and. . . . . "

Ginny had to pause to catch her breath.

"I think, just maybe, that John may be able to come too. That would be wonderful, wouldn't it Robert?"

"That would be wonderful Mom. I haven't seen my cousin John for a long time, since before, you know . . . . "

"We're going to make it work. Gary's going to be so happy to see everyone."

Robert hustled upstairs to call Jane. He was so excited to tell her the news about college, and about the Christmas party. Initially, when he offered the invitation, she was flattered and excited. But the more he talked about his brother Gary, and how thrilled his Mom was, the less she said. He wondered if it had something to do with the fact that her father would not be coming home for Christmas, not for several more years.

Rufus was next on Robert's list. He couldn't wait to share the news about his college acceptance letter, so he telephoned. Katie answered. Rufus was at work, but would be off on the following day. He told her the great news about Gary and about the scholarship.

Robert wasn't able to escape the Sunday family scene until late afternoon. He made a bee-line for the farm. When Katie was finished congratulating her nephew, Rufus rushed him down the basement steps and invited him to take a seat on the couch in front of the wood stove.

"Well, first of all, congratulations! It's a big deal to get a full scholarship. I remember when it happened for me and I have never lost my sense of gratitude. Corporate America didn't exactly get a very good return on their investment, but I sure have appreciated all the knowledge!"

"But Rufus, they think I want to be an engineer. That's what I need to talk to you about."

"You mean all the grade point averages, aptitude tests, and interest inventories don't lead to the same conclusion as your gut? What a big surprise!"

"Something like that, yeah."

"I don't think you should be too worried. You won an academic scholarship because you have proven yourself an excellent student. I'm pretty sure, if you choose a different major, you can still have your scholarship. What are you thinking about studying?"

"Well, I've been researching their psychology and sociology degree offerings. I think I want to be some kind of counselor. The last three months of working with kids at school has made me forget about building dams and bridges. I just don't know."

Robert was teetering. Insecurity was creeping in. It was a hard habit to break. Rufus remained silent, giving him time to shake it off.

"Obviously, I will need to talk to them directly about acceptance into a specific counseling program, but I'm feeling pretty good about my decision. I think I want to help people build bridges for themselves. I think I want to go in to counseling."

"You'd be good at it. You impress me as one of those rare people who would be good at anything you would choose, but you have to admit, this is a big change. What happened?"

"I've always loved to analyze people's individual differences. But now with the astrology, I'm even more curious about what makes people tick. I can't think about anything else."

"Robert, you do know there are no college offerings in astrology."

"Very funny, Rufus! I know I'll have to follow a conventional course of study. I'm just saying that astrology has made me think about people in a more structured way. Isn't that what psychology's supposed to do?"

Rufus couldn't contain his curiosity.

"Did meeting Jane have anything to do with it?"

"I guess so. In a very short time, she has made me, well. . . . . . . , more confident maybe?"

Rufus had never felt so connected with a young person. He had taught and counseled thousands of young people, and was all too familiar with the strange feelings that can come with having no children of one's own. But this time was special. He wanted to help Robert any way he could, and secretly hoped that Robert could one day help him in return. Rufus had not purposely steered Robert in the direction he was heading, but he also wasn't surprised by it, or unhappy about it.

Without warning, Rufus stood up and began to preach in a loud gospel tempo.

"Confidence, oh yeah! Sweet Jesus, confidence! Bless me with some confidence!"

Rufus slowed it down, softened it up, and added melody.

"Robert, my friend, I'm so tired. . . . . , so tired of being sad. . . . . . . , so tired of being mad. . . . . , so tired of being confused. . . . . , so tired of being worried. . . . . . . , so tired of being fearful. . . . . , so tired, ... so tired, ... , so tired. Sweet Jesus, bless me with some confidence!"

Without asking his spellbound nephew, Rufus hollered up the stairs to Katie that Robert would be staying for dinner. Then he grabbed the phone and called Ginny. He told her that there was some work he needed help with and he didn't want Robert to have to hurry home for dinner.

When he got off the phone, he checked Robert's reaction to the idea and asked him if he wanted a beer. Robert was a bit confused, but happily accepted the beer. After all, why shouldn't he celebrate the good news?

"Robert, I think you are making a good decision. But most importantly, remember that choosing a direction in life does not always have to be high drama. You can always change course. Never say never, and nothing is forever. Your choices should be based on what you know and what you feel at any given time. Your choices can turn out to be forever. But even if they're not, it's OK. If new circumstances, new learning, or new experiences cause you to change your direction later on, that's OK too. Right now, if counseling is what you're feeling, then go with it."

Robert sipped on the beer, nestling into that provocative sense of manliness that went along with forays into the forbidden. It was just a beer, but for Robert, it felt like his confirmation. Rufus proceeded to reinforce.

"Robert, at the risk of sounding overly profound, let me tell you something. The fulcrum on which we balance our approach to life is the choice between financial security and personal fulfillment. If your see saw is weighted toward personal fulfillment as a counselor as opposed of the hefty salary of an engineer, then good for you. It's your life."

This was one of Rufus's favorite subjects, and he had a feeling that Robert was more than willing to listen.

"In addition to making a personal decision about what kind of life work will bring you fulfillment, you are actually setting a course consistent with the needs of a modern economy. It's inevitable that humanity choose a less materialistic, more spiritual path. The Earth can only support so many people. Man's original economy, which is based on the exploitation of natural resources, will inevitably be replaced by the service economy, and then the information economy, and then what I call the efficiency economy, where people will achieve personal fulfillment without using so much energy and so many material resources. It'll be like. . . . . .where new age spiritualism meets 21st century robotics. More leisure time will mean a greater need for people to know their true selves. Psychologists, and hopefully astrologers, will be more in demand than ever."

Robert was enjoying Rufus's show of support. Empowered by his half a beer buzz, he asked if they could go for a walk. The ultimate outdoor person, Rufus couldn't get his boots on fast enough. He threw Robert a stocking cap to protect from the chill of the evening wind, and then led the way out the basement door.

They walked down to the county road where they could gaze out over the south-sloping fields. There was barely enough light to see, as the stars were beginning to dimly glimmer on the milky sky that was December dusk. Some ewes were grazing on the snow melt pasture, while most were either eating hay or preparing to bed down. It was a refreshing site. Rufus confirmed that sheep farming during December was a peaceful affair, as all the lambs had long since gone to market.

"Robert. I totally support your decision. You have grown in your appreciation of the idea of helping other people. It could be that the people you were around in your old school did not challenge your sense of who you really are. They were too focused on following their college prep mandate, preparing young men to join the corporate economy and make their fortune. I'm not saying they would have discouraged your current decision. You just may never have had the experiences that caused you to consider it. By a simple twist of fate, your mother's decision to be close to your grandfather, you may have been given a chance to wake up to who you really are. I'm happy for you."

"I am feeling pretty good about things right now, Rufus. You have helped me see that there may actually be some kind of order to the universe, and that I have everything I need to discover how that order affects me. On top of that, Jane has helped me with my communication. I'm not afraid to say what I mean."

"Well, for my part, I want you to know, I'm continuing with my efforts to enable people to get more out of astrology. I'm refining my ideas about how to make it a stronger science. Not only that, but I'm actually making good progress on my book."

"Your book?! Let me guess. It's either about astrology or it's about heaven."

Robert knew that Rufus was fascinated with afterlife theories. When he wasn't talking astrology, he was exploring how different religions address what happens to a person when he or she passes from this life. He enjoyed astrology, but he was obsessed with concepts of heaven.

"Heaven it is."

The younger man was feeling a bit tipsy from the beer. Feeling playful, he let out a loud holler of joy, knowing that the valley below was a pretty fair echo chamber. Impressed with himself, he walked closer to Rufus and reached out to shake his hand. Rufus was so endeared by the gesture that he deflected the young man's hand and gave him a big old manly hug instead. The moment would be forever imprinted on their collective memory. It would serve as Robert's initiation to the club, the new apprentice, on his way to becoming philosopher king and astrology aficionado.

Robert was in a trusting mood. He took the opportunity, however unplanned, to share the gist of his encounter with Kristin that night in the guest room at Andrew's. He was hoping that the older man could help him understand why his relationship with Jane was so confusing when it came to sex.

When he realized the extremely personal nature of Robert's confession, Rufus cleverly diverted the discussion to something more akin to an 'astrology of sex' lesson.

Rather than comment on Robert's actual relationship with Jane or Kristin, he instructed Robert on the differences between relationships based on Sun, Moon, Venus, Mars, Uranus, and Neptune. He also emphasized the overwhelming importance of how house placements affected the type of relationship one might have with another person. Robert was doing his best to comprehend all that was coming at him. When Rufus focused on the meaning and importance of seventh house relationships, Robert began to understand. With a September 12th birthday, Jane's Sun was right on his Descendant, which helped to explain why the relationship was so direct and powerful, but not necessarily sexual.

"Jane's prominence on your seventh house cusp may have set the stage for the lighting of a flame. But it is not the fuel. That comes from inside each of you. You are discovering how each of your whole selves can intertwine, and that's a beautiful thing. Just try to enjoy it."

This didn't really help Robert with his original question, which was about sex, but it made him feel that someone cared. He had always wanted to talk to someone about the magical encounter with Kristin, but he couldn't possibly know who or how. Having now met Jane, sex had become even more confusing. How could he get his hands on that magic? Kristin had allowed him a sexual fantasy, but with Jane, the emotions were so raw and powerful, they seemed to overpower the sensual aspect. He realized that Rufus was simply telling him that he would arrive at the answer on his own, in due time.

Then, like a falling star enabling the fulfillment of a wish, Rufus decided to take a chance and help the kid out.

"As a young man, if you're lucky, you'll find yourself in situations with girls, you know, like you did on that night. It's inevitable. Being an impulsive, virile male is part of who you are. When those kinds of experiences come your way, and your conscience approves them as free and mutual, then, by all means, enjoy the experience to the fullest. It's OK. It's part of growing up. You will know when you are using someone, or when someone is using you."

Robert didn't say a word, as if he were asking for more.

"You will learn that you are a sensitive, loving human being who will owe your ultimate survival mostly to platonic relationships, often inexplicable in their psychological and emotional complexity. Jane may be your first one of those. If your sexual urges need to be suppressed right now in order to avoid complicating your friendship, then by all means, suppress them. But when your heart allows you to be impulsive, be impulsive, and feel good about it. When your heart tells you to be patient, be patient, and feel good about that. There's no 'one size fits all' with relationships, or with sex. Does that help?"

Robert was relieved, but it wasn't just about Jane. His entire adolescence had been a struggle, having to hear about his friend's sexual escapades and feeling like the proverbial late bloomer. He felt self-conscious about his relative sexual inexperience, and he hated the sense of inferiority that came with it. Jane meant a lot to him. He just had to accept that the confusion he felt when he was physically close to her was a natural part of growing up.

Sensing Robert's thoughtful appreciation, Rufus decided to risk making it even more personal.

"When the time is right, you will talk to Jane about these feelings. Ultimately, that's the only thing that will help. But right now, just follow your heart. Sometimes, when we're young, because of what we see other people doing, we think we need to grow up faster than we really do."

Robert finally spoke. All he said was, "thanks, Rufus". Then, raising his arms up above his head as if he were praising God, he let out another holler. He propelled his burden down into the valley, and let it bounce around over the waters of the beaver pond. As the two of them listened intently, Rufus hoped that the fading echoes were signaling a sense of relief for his young friend.

The solemnity of their union on the county road was interrupted by the voice of Katie crying out that it was time for supper. With a new sense of mutual fascination and bravado, they headed for the house. Rufus knew that open and honest discussions about astrology, counseling, sexuality, and personal growth represented strong underpinnings of what he hoped would become a collaborative relationship. He didn't share all the details of his plans with Robert, but he knew that it wouldn't be much longer before he would have to.

After a dinner of Katie's famous store bought frozen pizza topped with an extra pound of cheese and pepperoni, Robert was ready to head home, probably more confident and self-assured than he had ever been in his life. He decided it was time to stop asking so many questions, and just appreciate the sensations.

Chapter 17. Gary's Party

Christmas with Gary was absolutely, without a doubt, the best thing that had happened to James and Ginny since they moved to the country. Without him, they had been feeling that the move was incomplete. Now that he was finally home, the peace and happiness they were experiencing was beyond anything proclaimed in the most sacred of Christmas messages.

Gary didn't really know what to do with himself in civilian land. He had been fighting terrorists in the Middle East so exclusively that he could only tentatively appreciate the softness of the bed linens and the sophistication of the cuisine. Had he been able to return to the home he had known all his life, he may have had less difficulty. War has the power to force an unnatural change of personality, often leading to an urgent need for new masks, to protect what is left of one's fragile self-image. Arriving at this new place, so different from where he grew up, Gary was clearly struggling to adapt.

Midnight mass all together as a family, breakfast in the middle of the night, and the opening of presents on Christmas Day all seemed quite magical. But it took a lot of awareness on everyone's part to create a supportive environment for Gary. The combination of his reluctance to talk about his military life and his general lack of recent experience with civilian life sometimes made conversation awkward.

Thank God for Grandpa Samuel. It was obvious, beginning on Christmas Day, that Gary felt the most comfortable around him, so he gladly accepted the invitation to spend as much time as he wanted out at the farm. Gary had a lot of good memories of his grandparent's country lifestyle. Because of his age, he had a better recollection of the happy years when Grandma was still alive and Samuel was starting up his cattle operation. By contrast, Robert and Angela remembered mostly the sad years, when Grandma's decline took such a toll on their mother Ginny.

Gary spent most of his time with Samuel during the days between Christmas and the weekend party. They rabbit hunted. They played cattle farmer. They talked. It was quite alright with everyone that Gary and Samuel shared something unique, especially considering how therapeutic it seemed to be for Gary's post-traumatic mindset.

The invitations to the party called for people to show up as early as two o'clock, and they did. "Let's get this party started" was the attitude of many. The invasion included Thomas and his family, Rufus and Katie, high school and army buddies of Gary's, as well as a multitude of country relatives. Gary hardly recognized some of the country cousins.

Robert and Jane had been elected to pick up Grandpa Samuel. They brought Matthew along for good measure. Even though Matthew assured Mindy it would be OK to bring her baby, or even her grandparents for that matter, Mindy declined, staying in character as the shy, scared rabbit that she truly was.

Angela managed to entertain her school girlfriends and her church girlfriends, each of whom had their own cute way of suppressing a squeal when they encountered Gary, the totally handsome soldier.

Limited by the weather to an indoor affair, Ginny opened up the greenhouse off their bedroom to provide a place to congregate besides the living room and the kitchen. As the afternoon progressed, it became the preferred gathering place for some of the closest family, as it was accessible only through James and Ginny's bedroom.

Gary eventually escaped the guest of honor congratulatory madness by making his way to the greenhouse with Thomas and Rufus. This enabled the long overdue reunion of Gary and his cousin John. They had not seen one another since before Gary entered the service. Gary was only vaguely aware of John's difficulties, and greeted him with the kind of unconditional acceptance one might only expect from a long lost cousin.

The four men had just a few moments to bond before they were mobbed by Angela showing off the greenhouse to her young friends. Luckily, Matthew, Robert, and Jane were right on their tails, and summarily shooed them away.

It wasn't long before the call came from Ginny for everyone to gather in the kitchen and make a plate. Fried chicken, fried catfish, and all the fixings, with beer and wine for those so inclined.

After everyone had their fill, most of the guests squeezed into the fire-warmed living room, while James invited Thomas, John, Gary, and Rufus for a little after dinner stroll, the lake being the obvious destination. Gary not only felt good about escaping the crowd, but he needed to smoke. Pleasantly inebriated and full of food, Gary was in a really good mood. But little did this guest of honor know, he was about to go under his Uncle Rufus's theological microscope.

When Rufus opened with a question to Gary about Islam and suicide bombers, James immediately protested. His fatherly instinct was to protect his son and keep the mood on the lighter side. But when it was obvious that Gary had no problem with the subject, James backed off. Gary seemed to appreciate the directness of the question, and responded in a way that demonstrated that he had given the subject a lot of thought.

"It really is about the concept of a martyr's death, as far as we could gather from the Muslims who would actually talk to us. Don't forget. The martyr's death comes complete with virgins, paradise, and skipping to the front of the line. Even though it seems like an extreme view, that's really what they believe."

There was not a word from anyone in the group, just silent attention, so Gary went on.

"Even for the regular Muslim, the non-jihadist, it's about Paradise or Hell, you know, Heaven or Hell. Same thing to them, but they prefer the term Paradise. They believe that when someone dies, they are kind of dormant in their grave until the Last Day, when they are judged as deserving one or the other. According to Islam, on Judgment Day, their physical bodies are restored, and the pleasures of heaven are spiritual and physical!"

Gary emphasized: "physical". He repeated it emphatically several times. This was by far the most he said at one time all day.

Rufus thanked him for his perspective, and explained that he was really interested to know what Gary had been told by actual Muslims in the Middle East. All Rufus knew was what he had researched in the literature.

"What exactly did you mean when you said something about going to the front of the line? Muslims, like Christians believe in the Final Judgment, but we all have to wait, in a sense, for the end of time."

"According to some interpretations of Islam, when

the jihadist dies, it's different.   I can almost quote the passage from the Koran. Most of us GIs know this one. It's good to know what you're up against when someone is trying to blow you up. Let's see. . . . . 'Warriors who die fighting in the cause of God are ushered immediately to God's presence'. That really gets 'em goin', because they don't even have to wait for judgment day! Is that messed up or what?"

Rufus was like an attorney who was excited about such graphic testimony, as if there were a case to be won. He decided to lead the willing witness.

"But even an average devout Muslim believes that their physical body is restored or re-created and will reside in an actual physical place called Paradise?   Am I right?   We're talking mansions, streets lined with gold, that kind of thing, eerily similar to what many Christians believe."

"That's right."

"But there's nothing in Christian teaching that compares to the shortcut reward option that Islam reserves for its holy warriors. At least I'm not aware of it."

"You're the expert, Rufus. I just know what I know, but I think you nailed it."

Gary lit another cigarette and asked if anyone had brought any beers with them. Thomas retrieved a beer from his coat pocket and handed it to Gary, who thanked him with an explosion of sarcasm.

"But don't forget the virgins, lots of virgins, you know! How bizarre is that?"

As if he was thinking a million thoughts at once and needed to reset, he stopped and kicked a stray rock into the water. The other men watched and waited, collectively well aware that Gary was showing all the signs of needing to vent.

"The most revolting thing is this belief that Paradise is only available to true believers in Islam.   But, hell is big enough for all the bad Muslims and all of us too! Hell must be really big. Good Muslims go to heaven. Bad Muslims go to hell. But a lot of us regular schmucks who have tried so hard to live a good life automatically go to hell, just because we're non-believers!"

Gary began to laugh hysterically. When he settled down, he was more circumspect.

"But maybe all religions automatically exclude the other guys."

Extremely impressed with Gary's observation, Rufus wanted to respond but wasn't quick enough.

"Rufus, apparently you know a lot about this kind of thing. I never gave it much thought growing up. I mean why would I think about what happens to people of other religions when they die? But, hey, figure it out. These guys come right out and say that all non-believers go to hell. Boom. Done. So let me ask you. Are all six billion people on this planet making reservations for the right heaven? Is there more than one heaven? 'Cause if there is only one, a lot of people are gonna to be really disappointed. What the hell is going on?"

When he heard himself say 'hell', Gary started laughing again. This time he could barely stop. James came over to him and put his arm around him and told him how extremely proud he was. They looked into each other's eyes and smiled. Gary was gratified that people cared, and James was happy to find out that his son was not as much a closed book as he thought.

As if he wanted to preserve the important father/son moment in its current state, Thomas interjected for the first time since they had arrived at the lake.

"Who wants another beer?"

Rufus knew his response would have to wait, and he was fine with that. There was implicit agreement that it was time to return to the house, as if their mission was completed and there was nothing else to be done. They headed up the hill in a flurry of small talk.

Gary probably wasn't sure exactly why Rufus had pursued the subject. But Thomas was beginning to figure out what made Rufus tick, and he wanted to know more. Like his father, John didn't say a word throughout the entire episode, just listened intently. Thomas was convinced that being exposed to different ideas about religious interpretations of the afterlife was excellent therapy for his son.

Back at the house, Gary was very much in demand. He was the catalyst that seemed to enable everyone's reaction to all things political, especially things having to do with terrorism and homeland security. He graciously suffered through the bravado and flag waving, as he gradually shifted his focus to his old friends from the City.

Most of the country relatives departed early. The drinkers were concerned about the alcohol affecting their driving, while the temperance-minded were tired of being around the drinkers. Either way, for the locals, the party mood was fading.

Grandpa Samuel was the key to Gary spending quality time with his old buddies. Samuel had invited them to spend the night at his farm. Although he was less than enthusiastic about their propensity for hard partying, he understood that Gary needed to make the most of his time with them, and in his own way. Robert, Matthew, and Jane were elected to take Samuel home, with Gary and his friends to soon follow.

Angela's local girlfriends were spending the night with her, and would rejoin their families before or after Mass the next day. To make room for some of James and Ginny's old friends from the City, Thomas and his family planned to head westward to Rufus and Katie's. Rufus would catch a ride with Thomas and John, leaving Ellen and her daughter to ride with Katie.

CHAPTER 18. TWENTY-FIVE MILES

As they drove westward, Thomas conversed with John about his reactions to the party. Thomas had pre-arranged with Rufus for him to join the conversation from the back seat whenever he saw an opening. Thomas hoped that Rufus could help John re-establish his path forward after an adolescence characterized by disillusionment and frequent scrapes with authority. John needed a new beginning. Thomas wasn't satisfied with how he was responding to traditional counseling, whether it was from a secular source or from the Catholic Church.

John was first to bring up the discussion at the lake, making it way too easy for Rufus.

"Robert says you used to be a Catholic, and now you're an astrologer. So why do you care so much about heaven and hell? Gary seemed like he was talking mostly to you."

Taken aback by such a poignant question, Rufus carefully considered his response.

"Well, I believe in God, and I consider myself a Christian. I have an inquiring mind, I'm a critical thinker, and I like to check out what people believe happens when they die. Astrology doesn't have that much to do with it. Astrology doesn't replace religious beliefs. It's just a system of thought that some people use to help understand themselves and others. It can help refine religious beliefs, but it's not a substitute for them. Does that make sense?"

John responded to the frank response with a little candor of his own.

"Whether I'm going to go to heaven or hell when I die has always really messed with my mind. They'd have you believe they know some kind of secret and they're going to let you in on it. But then they also kind of try to scare you, you know, into being good. Like scare you straight. It doesn't really work for me. I have done some bad things, but it's supposed to be OK as long as I'm sorry?"

Rufus felt John's confusion and decided on a path.

"I have some problems with the traditional views of heaven and hell, John. That's why I spend so much energy and time trying to understand it. Where can I begin? Oh, I know. One day I was down at my lambing barn and this powerful feeling came over me. I was right where I was supposed to be, you know, at that very moment. All my thoughts and feelings, and what I was doing, all combined into an incredible sense of certainty. I was in sync with the energies of the universe. It just happened, like a revelation. It was not the kind of thing that you could try to do. You couldn't just decide you wanted to feel that way. It was my little glimpse of heaven. Since that day, I have considered that heaven might be nothing more than a feeling, a profound feeling of satisfaction, a spiritual contentment, a momentary affirmation that what you had done with your life up to that moment was exactly what you were supposed to have done. A kind of perfect fit."

Relying on what Rufus had told him about the powerful oppositions in John's horoscope, Thomas joined the conversation. Rufus had helped him understand how

John tended to think dualistically, black or white, good or evil, right or wrong, heaven or hell. He thought it was a good time to intervene.

"What Rufus is saying is that maybe there isn't any such thing as hell. Maybe hell is nothing more than a sense of frustration about the lack of heaven. During our lives, we have momentary glimpses of what heaven must be like. Each and every time we get a glimpse, it's because we have done all we can do to follow the teachings of our Lord Jesus Christ. We are blessed with a sensation of peace. The trouble is, life goes on. We don't get to stay in that moment. We don't get to stay in any moment for that matter. The forces of life propel us forward in time, and we have to go on."

John was intrigued by what his father was saying. He had never heard him put it quite that way. He wondered about what effect Rufus might be having on his father. He liked what he was hearing.

"So heaven is that feeling Rufus is talking about, like you're right where you're supposed to be, only, it's forever, and it's forever because you're dead."

John was really throwing Rufus a bone.

"That's exactly what really got me, that forever part. You see, I was fascinated with being in that sweet spot in that moment. No regrets, no expectations, just pure contentment. But how could you have that forever? You live your whole life, full of trillions of moments of being lost and being found, sinning and succeeding, and then, somehow, when you die, you enter a state of happiness for eternity? You lead a marginal life, you ask for forgiveness for your sins, you die, and you somehow continue to exist for eternity. Do you actually experience the sensation of yourself as an individual, as Thomas, or John, or Rufus, reaping a reward for eternity?"

Rufus was really getting wound up. Thomas was getting worried that they were going to give up some of their gains if Rufus got too philosophical too fast. But there was no holding Rufus back.

"I have a hard time with all that for three reasons. Number one, it's too easy. Follow the yellow brick road. Line starts around the corner. Sign here. Get our deal. Tickets please."

"Number two, it places the emphasis on a reward after death, instead of a maximum effort to do God's will while we are here on earth. Lead a marginal life, apologize sincerely, and presto, maximum absolute payoff. We are supposed to emulate the life of Jesus while we are here on Earth because it's the right thing to do, not because we are expecting a reward."

"Number three, it's narcissistic. To think that you retain your individuality after death, physical body restored or not, seems kind of arrogant. Jesus told us that when we died, we would join our Father in heaven. He did not say what heaven was exactly, just that we would be with Our Father."

The old man with a pony tail was really preaching, but John just wanted the answer to one question.

"So what do you think really happens when you die?"

Thomas didn't let Rufus answer.

"Rufus, you are confusing me and John. You seem to be saying more about what you DON'T believe than what you DO believe."

"You're right. I am. So let me give it a try. To put what I've been working on for over ten years into a short summation while we cruise down the road in the dark after a long day is not so easy to do. I should just stop right now, and make you both wait until I've finished my book."

John seemed to accept that response better than Thomas, but was compelled to re-visit the astrology angle.

"But what does all this have to do with astrology?"

"Astrology has offered me a framework for understanding what God wants me to do with my life. When I was born, I was given gifts, attributes, qualities, talents. That can mean strengths, and depending on how I handle it, can mean weaknesses. So how do I use that knowledge to help me praise God? By realizing that my share of the gifts is only a very limited part of the total gifts that God bestows, I embrace humility. You and your father also have your own limited parts of the total gifts. Each person's obligation to God is to do his best with the gifts he has."

"Now, to clearly profess why astrology plays such an important role for me, I must bare my soul. I have concluded, and truly believe, that the sum total of all human effort to glorify God, is God. All the gifts manifested in all the horoscopes of men, is God. Each person, each sinner, doing their best with what they have been given, is what God is. God is nothing more than the sum total of the goodness of men."

He paused as if he had actually overwhelmed himself. He realized that his penchant for reductionism may have caught up with him. Were his statements sounding simplistic? Did they appear to belittle people's personal concepts of God? Thomas and John did not seem offended in any way. They were simply blown away by Rufus's theological and philosophical stamina.

"Forgive me for returning to what I don't believe instead of what I do believe, but I do not believe in God the Father as a distinct deity, or entity, that will sit in judgment of us as individuals. In order to maintain a successful relationship with their maker, most humans down through history have depended on such an image of God. I understand the need to describe God as God the Father, an actual being. But, I personally prefer to believe that God is primarily the Holy Spirit, and that we are all part of the Holy Spirit. While we are alive, we are to do our best to love our neighbor as ourselves, just as Jesus taught. We are asked to rely on individual strengths and overcome individual weaknesses, but there is no individual God the Father, and there is no individual Rufus after Rufus dies. My soul will rejoin the universal Holy Spirit, which is God. Over time, the efforts of all the souls praising God leads to the perfection of God. Moving closer and closer to perfecting the love of God throughout eternity, both on earth and in 'heaven', is the idea."

". . . . 'Thy will be done, on Earth, as it is in Heaven'. These are the most important, but some of the least emphasized, words in The Lord's Prayer. Heaven is already perfect. Our sacred obligation is to bring that perfection to man's existence on Earth. That is our task. That is our call to action."

"Time is infinity. There is no end. Final Judgment and Eternity don't jive. I say 'World without end, Amen'. Eternity's already here. It's continuous. Infinity doesn't start after some finite event. This is it."

"Well Rufus, I think you did it. Now I don't have to buy your book."

John was slightly dumbfounded, never having met anyone like Rufus. Thomas sought clarification on one point.

"So Rufus, I know a little bit about world religions. What you're saying sounds like eastern spirituality. Pretty soon you're going to start talking about how energy is recycled, or how souls are reincarnated. That being said, allow me to expand on that aspect."

Rufus interrupted only to make sure Thomas didn't miss the gravel road that led to his farm.

"The Christian and Muslim concepts of afterlife rely on a deity that is some kind of active being, planning on making some kind of final judgment about each individual's relative success in achieving compliance with behavioral expectations implied in a set of teachings.

Right?"

"Right, Thomas. I like how you said that. Can I use that?"

Rufus laughed, but Thomas could tell he was serious. Rufus offered a clarification.

"I'm saying that Jesus Christ Is OK, and that the Holy Spirit is OK. But I'm also saying that God the Father doesn't quite compute. Everything Jesus taught was about being selfless. When he died on the Cross for us, Jesus was as selfless as one can get. The Holy Spirit is obviously selfless. How could a Spirit be anything but selfless? But, our working models for God the Father seem to provoke a certain kind of selfishness. What does He think of me? What happens to me? What do I get out of it?"

Thomas broke in as he pulled up the driveway.

"So what I hear you saying is that the God the Father part allows for the judgment of an individual by an individual God, which has the appearance of being selfish?"

"Right, and I think we're better than that. I say 'duty first'."

As they prepared to go into the house, with John looking totally exhausted, Rufus summed up his belief.

"I am of the opinion that there is only the Holy Spirit. We are supposed to live our individual lives in a way that contributes to the achievement of perfection of the Holy Spirit. When we die, our soul, as a representation of all we have accomplished, will return, and add or subtract from the truth inherent in the Holy Spirit. This goes on for eternity until perfect love is achieved. But remember, you can either have eternity, like 'world without end, amen', or a finale. You can't have both. Eternity, by definition, leaves the door open for higher and higher states of enlightenment."

After they entered the house and obtained the beverage of their choice, Rufus steered them to the basement so that he could feed the wood stove. After a few minutes, he brought the discussion to a solemn end. He knew that his guests were tired, and he could hear the ladies arriving upstairs.

"Thanks so much for engaging in such a provocative discussion. I apologize if I talked too much, and John, I apologize to you for not answering your questions in a straightforward manner. My ideas are no better than anyone else's. Perhaps I have spent more time pondering these subjects than most people would consider reasonable. I don't know. But I sincerely believe that we should offer our lives for the greater honor and glory of God, and that we do not retain our individuality after we die, except in the memories of the people who survive us. We simply transform from an active, working part of the Body of Christ, to a passive, spiritual part within the Soul of Christ, which is the Holy Spirit, which is God."

Thomas capped it off just as Katie and Ellen were descending the basement stairs from the kitchen.

"I'm just happy to be here. Thank you, Lord, for allowing me to participate in the wonders of this day."

John seemed pretty happy to be a part of his father's relationship with Rufus.

"So I just have to do my part to contribute? No more threats of hell? No more anxiety about whether I'm good enough to go to heaven? I'm down with that."

Rufus knew Thomas and John were not quite ready for the rest of it, given their lack of astrological knowledge. He was just glad that the three of them could share ideas. For the time being, he would keep his ultimate goal to himself. Rufus wanted to bring all the heaven concepts of all the world religions into one unified theory.

The next morning, over a breakfast of Rufus's famous bacon and hot pepper cheese omelets, Thomas suddenly resurrected the subject of the afterlife.

"Rufus, I laid awake for a while last night thinking

about what we discussed. Setting aside the question of whether we maintain our identity as individuals after we go to heaven, and admitting that any concept of forever is surely unfathomable for a human mind, I'm fascinated with how you seem to be begging the old argument between belief and works. I think I'm hearing you say that a lifetime of faith in God and a sincere effort at repentance before death is just part of the equation. I think I'm hearing you argue for the importance of a person's responsibility to grow in their ability to do good works, and that I guess you might also believe that we are supposed to be actively engaged in interpreting astrological forces as a way of helping in that effort."

Rufus was totally impressed with Thomas's inference, but was tentative about responding in front of Katie and Ellen, who probably had no earthly idea what Thomas was talking about. So he tried to keep it simple.

"Thomas, I'm flattered that you have given my ideas so much thought. In a way, it's hard for me to simply agree. I'd rather take your statement as an invitation to expound on my beliefs at a later date. But I will tell you this. You are exactly right to pick up on my bias for Christian 'acts' as opposed to just Christian 'faith'. We have been afforded countless gifts, and we are obliged to recognize them, polish them, perfect them, and offer them up to others."

Katie and Ellen clearly didn't want to get involved. It was time for them to leave anyway. The two women, along with John and his sister, would be travelling to pick up Gary and Samuel, so that the six of them could attend Samuel's church. Ellen wanted John to see Gary one more time before they left for home, and Katie had promised Ginny and Samuel many weeks before that she would facilitate Gary going to Church with his grandfather.

Rufus, Thomas, and the dogs, went for a long walk in the winter woods.

Chapter 19. Old Friends/New Friends

Robert's idea of taking Matthew to meet his suburban friends got a boost when Gary asked his mother to borrow her vehicle for a trip to the City. He wanted more time with his high school buddies before he had to report back to base. Robert and Matthew were on Christmas break with old vehicles and no money. How could their parents say no to them riding along with the super responsible soldier boy?

Andrew was all for the visit, but warned that they would not be able to spend the night at his house because his parents were entertaining guests from abroad. So Robert turned to Petey. The timing couldn't have been better, because Petey's parents were about to head out of town.

The conversation on the way up to the City was pretty much about girls. Touting his age and experience, Gary told tales of sexual conquest, while Matthew hinted that his sexual experience was more extensive than they might expect. Although he found it stimulating, Robert thought it was kind of silly that he was being subjected to advice from these two supposed relationship experts, when neither of them had a girlfriend, and he did. Go figure.

After a while, Robert was only pretending to listen. He was thinking about Jane. Their relationship was tight and light at the same time. Each had their own reasons for playing it cool even though the attraction was undeniable. Jane accurately perceived herself as the overly dutiful daughter of a mother with extremely limited opportunities for pleasure, in other words, a hard life. Her mother Sarah had four children, no husband to depend on, and made very little money. Jane was happy to help out, but was deathly afraid of following in her mother's footsteps. Robert fascinated Jane, but he stirred not even the slightest trace of true emotional commitment in the young lady at this point in her life.

Robert's own self-examination revealed that there was absolutely nothing that was going to keep him anywhere near that Podunk town. He would always appreciate the country hiatus, but was determined to pursue higher education, and hopefully a professional career as a counselor, or even a psychiatrist. In the meantime, hopelessly smitten with his first real girlfriend, it probably wouldn't be long before he and Jane would have that talk about sex.

Daydreams hit the skids as they approached their destination. Gary needed directions. When they finally arrived at Petey's, Robert was relieved because he could finally talk to Matthew again. His friend had been so intent on playing up to Gary that Robert was beginning to wonder.

In spite of glaring physical and cultural differences, Petey and Mathew seemed to hit it off. Petey grabbed Matthew's attention with demonstrations of his latest cyber schemes. Computer savvy Matthew was genuinely interested. Quite familiar with Matthew's talent for social adaptation, Robert was not at all surprised how quickly they achieved a comfort level.

When Petey finally tired of impressing Matthew with his latest programming project, the three of them smoked a joint and headed over to Andrew's. Millie let them in through the kitchen without much fanfare, and they spent the early part of the evening playing games in the recreation room. Given the extravagant feast of snacks prepared by Millie, the munchies were relieved in style.

Andrew was cognizant of their intoxication, but tried not to judge. At the right moment, he shared his bittersweet news. He had not been selected for the baseball scholarship. Instead of attending the state university, he would be staying in town. Robert struggled valiantly to emphasize his empathy for Andrew, but it was hard to hide his ecstatic satisfaction that he and his friend would be school chums again. Andrew was OK. He knew he could still play baseball, just not at the level he had hoped.

So far, Andrew's relationship with Cindy was immune to some of the potential problems that can occur with long distances. The west coast was a long way off, but Cindy was able to travel home more often than the average college freshman, as her parents' wealth rivaled even that of Andrew's parents.

When Andrew took off for Cindy's house, the three young men headed back to Petey's place. Fueled by marijuana and wine, they stayed up late. Petey went right back to showing off his latest computer conquests. He had actually figured out how to hack the high school's system. He was not only able to access personal information on all the students and faculty, but he could re-program the security files to cover up each intrusion. Robert didn't approve. His moral compass was spinning just about as wildly as his head was, from all the spirits and the smoke.

Matthew had attempted to do the same at his own school in the country, but he lacked Petey's skills. The idea was to access the student data base to correlate student birthdays with their responses on the survey project they were doing for their computer technology class.

Before he could express his concerns about Petey and Mathew's cavalier attitude toward hacking personal information, Robert was shocked by another revelation. There was a decent chance that Petey would be enrolling in the computer security program at the same state college that Matthew planned to attend in the fall. Petey explained that he was trying to avoid college altogether, but if he was going to have to go, he wanted to go to an "easy school". As someone who was just glad to have the opportunity to go to college at all, Matthew didn't appear to be insulted by Petey's attitude.

For two young men who had never before met, Petey and Matthew's lives appeared destined to intertwine. Matthew would commute the 30 minute drive from home, and Petey would live in the dorm.

Petey's parents were very successful computer scientists who had been lured away from academia by the opportunity to create cutting edge software in the lucrative, brave new world of smart phones. They were not the idea people. But as technical people, they were gaining an excellent reputation for building easy-to-use apps that people liked.

Petey wanted to join his parent's firm directly out of high school, but his father was against it. He would not have his son working in the family business without a college degree. Dad was playing hard ball. Petey could either venture out on his own, with a trust fund inaccessible until age twenty-five, or he could enjoy virtually unlimited financial support while he pursued a bachelor's degree. Tempted by the initial down payment, a brand new car, Petey was leaning toward taking his father's deal.

Robert was awakened early the next morning by a

call from Gary. Successful with one of his high school doll babies, he told Robert and Matthew that they would either have to stay in the City for a few more days, or find another way home. With Matthew having to work the next day, sticking around was not an option. The boys would have to find a ride, or get Gary in trouble with Ginny.

The idea for that day was to take Matthew to visit Robert's old high school, after which they would meet Andrew, Cindy, and a few of her friends for lunch near the University, which just happened to be close to one of Andrew's father's corporate offices. Cindy was applying for a summer internship in marketing and had an interview that morning.

It didn't take long for Matthew to recognize the incredible differences between Robert's private school and the small town public school he knew. Even with no students walking the halls, he could sense that the physical plant was built for intense education. The three boys walked the entire facility, exchanging stories about their high school experiences. Robert assured them, as the only one who had seen both sides of the private/public school divide, that the most important thing was what each individual student brings to the game, and that it was not about the physical plant. Matthew, envious of the private school facilities, appeared skeptical, but he didn't argue.

Soon after they arrived at the restaurant, a text from Andrew directed Robert to go ahead and get a table for seven. Andrew, Cindy, and her friends would be their momentarily. They hadn't been waiting long when Robert heard a voice behind him.

"This wouldn't be that shy boy I had to invite to the prom, would it?"

Samantha hugged him around the neck from behind and pecked him on the cheek.

As Robert got up to return the embrace, he couldn't help but look past Samantha for just a second to admire the incredible heat he knew as Cindy's friend Tina. It felt like nine years, not nine months, since he had been sitting on the bleachers with these same three girls watching Andrew run the bases. He remembered how intimidated he used to feel around Tina, and how he used to fantasize about being with her. He had to struggle to maintain his composure with Samantha. Surely, he thought, no one noticed his lustful reminiscence.

Robert directed his attention to Samantha, and then to Cindy. He was relieved when Andrew took over the introductions. What he had hoped were improved social skills seemed to vanish. In his new life in the country, he was something of a big fish in a small pond, but at that moment, he felt more like a tiny minnow in a large lake.

"Robert, it's so good to see you, and to meet your friend."

Cindy had a wonderful presence about her, as always, and from the head of the table, she charmed everyone into a comfortable place.

"One of these days, Andrew and I are going to make it down to the country to see you. He probably doesn't admit to you how much he misses you, but I know the truth."

Robert's confidence slowly recovered. Intent on avoiding the temptation to compose a perfect response, he replied quickly.

"There's not a whole lot to do down in the country. But my Uncle Rufus did introduce me to canoeing, and it's wonderful."

Andrew raised his glass of iced tea into the air, as if it were champagne, and made a toast.

"Next summer, we're goin' floatin'! Is that how you say it?"

"Here here" was the refrain, from a bunch of people

who really had no idea what a float trip was. Andrew and Cindy had each been on whitewater raft trips with their parents. When Robert explained the basic idea of a float trip, Andrew and Cindy shared longing glances, as if they were imagining the erotic seclusion of a lonely gravel bar.

After lunch, the group attempted a walk around the University campus. But the cold, windy day quickly convinced them it was time to go their separate ways. Andrew vowed to call more often, and suggested a possible spring break happening at this parent's house.

By the time they got back to Petey's, they had a solid plan to get home that evening. Petey would drive them to the halfway point, where they would meet up with Rufus. Robert had called his uncle right after they received the news from Gary.

When rush hour subsided, the boys headed southward. As if to preface Petey meeting Rufus for the first time, Robert and Matthew really opened up about their burgeoning interest in astrology. Petey may have been way ahead of them when it came to computers, but they fancied their astrology talk fitting compensation. Petey was intrigued, and gave them kudos for putting their energies into something unique and unconventional.

At one point, he made a remark that really tickled Robert.

"Sounds interesting, but I don't have enough data."

Rufus was always using the data word when he talked astrology, and here was Petey doing the same.

When they arrived at the rendezvous point, Rufus struggled to conceal his excitement. From the little bit Robert had described, Petey was someone he definitely wanted to meet. Inside, he was overtaken with wild speculation about the day he would ask for Petey's help. Any way you sliced it, a successful data collection effort would require a lot of computer expertise of the clandestine variety. To accomplish the task at the scale

Rufus dreamed of, there would probably have to be a lot of Peteys.

But what was he thinking? At that point, Rufus had little more than abstract plans. His few allies in the astrological world didn't seem ready to help. On top of that, he hadn't even shared anything specific with his young protégé Robert.

As Petey came forward to greet him, Rufus collared his exuberance and simply focused on making a good first impression. The introduction was a pleasant, but awkward stalemate. Rufus couldn't move on the computer front, and Petey didn't dare make anything more than a casual reference to astrology. Neither Rufus nor Matthew had time for a sit down dinner, so the four of them lingered for only a few minutes on the restaurant parking lot before it was time to go.

It was weird, but strangely comforting, to transfer from the Lexus Petey had commandeered from his parent's garage to the old pickup truck of the sheep farmer. As they rode three abreast, Matthew truly enjoyed the opportunity to ask astrology questions of the master, having spent way too many hours with Robert's second-hand answers. Rufus was impressed, particularly by Matthews's recognition of how much the astrologer must struggle to synthesize an interpretation from the many individual components in the chart. Matthew demonstrated an instinctive reluctance to get hung up on one planet, or one house placement. When the young man actually used the word synthesis several times, Rufus realized that Matthew was well worth the mentoring.

Robert, the social scientist wannabe, promoted astrology's potential as a counseling tool. In an attempt to "one up" his friend Matthew, he paraphrased things he had read, and heard from Rufus, about how the horoscope could be a kind of platform, useful for facilitating discussion of personal attributes and life goals.

The boys didn't realize how much they appeared to be competing for Rufus's attention. Matthew said the priority should be chart interpretation methodology. Robert defended the importance of applicability to psychological issues. It had never been Rufus's conscious intention to get these two young men irrevocably hooked on astrology, but the depth and quality of the discussion convinced him that it was probably too late.

Rufus bid the boys goodnight as he dropped them off at Robert's. In the spirit of gratitude for his providing them a ride, they offered their services out at his farm, which nudged him to explain that he would be going out of state for the second half of January. He did not divulge his destination or his specific purpose, and the boys were gracious enough not to ask.

He wished them a Happy New Year, and promised that he would contact them on his return. He made a point of asking Robert to check with Katie, starting on about the 15th of the month, to see if she needed any help on the farm. The two young men, satisfied with the promise of a full report later on, thanked Rufus for the ride home, and bid him a warm, respectful good night.

Chapter 20. New York

Katie loved Rufus very much, and was fully aware of his eccentricities and interests when she had married him some 23 years before. So she wasn't surprised or upset that he was leaving her in the middle of winter. The ewes weren't due to lamb until mid-February. Rufus had stockpiled plenty of firewood in the basement and arranged hay in the barns for the sheep. The heaviest work for Katie would be feeding grain and providing water. She had neighbors and relatives she could call on if need be.

The only thing Katie dreaded were those first few minutes when she arrived home at night after a long twelve hour shift at the hospital. She felt so horribly alone. Once she'd accounted for the dogs, and was re-connected with her home, she was fine with being by herself.

When Rufus arrived in New York, he was greeted at the airport by a woman who had become a very important part of his life over the previous couple of years, even though he had not actually seen her in thirty years. Her name was Elizabeth, but she went by Liz. Rufus had met her at a peace rally on the lower east side when he was trying to forge a life in New York City as a young man. As a literary agent all those years since, Liz was the person Rufus contacted when he became serious about his book. He was in New York City to meet with Liz and her staff for several days to iron out any changes necessary to get the book to press. He would finally be signing a contract.

"Evan, darling, it's so good to see you".

She accepted a kiss on the cheek and a brief embrace from Rufus, who kind of enjoyed hearing his given name used by someone besides Grandpa Samuel. Liz knew very little of Rufus's life, and he saw no reason to complicate things with tales of Rufus T. Schicklgruber.

"You look fantastic. Liz, I must say that those photographs of you on the web don't do you justice. You look beautiful."

"You can stop right there Evan. I know I'm looking quite the old woman these days, but I'm happy, and I feel good. But thank you for your kind words."

Liz was twenty years Rufus's senior. Their relationship had always been strictly about literature with a healthy dash of good old fashioned liberal philosophy thrown in. Thirty years earlier, Rufus had impressed her with his poetry. Their friendship, though brief, was totally genuine, and devoid of expectations.

When the airport limousine dropped him at the hotel, Rufus confirmed his appointment with Liz for the next morning. She warned him that after a brief meeting with the executive publisher, the day would be about Rufus working intensely with a couple of her assistants. Rufus was not to make any other plans.

He was so grateful that Liz was willing to help him. The old adage "it's not what you know, it's who you know" was in play. Liz was the first person who had ever read his manuscript, and that included Katie. So when she told him that she thought it was "excellent", he felt like a winner for the first time as an author. He had worked on the book for almost seven years. It was his lifelong dream to write a book. He had always assumed it would be fiction, in the mold of the great American novel. Now here he was, wanting to publish a non-fiction work on theories of heaven, hell, and the afterlife, in spite of having no theological, philosophical, or academic credentials whatsoever.

The book was entitled: Heaven: The Unified Field Theory. Rufus's insistence on the title, one that provoked an analogous reference to Einstein's proposition of a unified field theory in physics, initially sparked resistance from Liz and the publisher. They thought it sounded kind of cold. They were afraid that the vast majority of people would be unfamiliar with Einstein's attempt to unify the general theory of relativity with electromagnetism. They wanted a simpler, catchier, more straightforward title, but they eventually relented.

The premise of the book was that there could be only one heaven. Whatever one's concept of God, as the Almighty, or the Creator of the Universe, or the Father, or the Spirit, Rufus contended that heaven could not be proprietary. Heaven could not be a brand. Heaven could not be exclusive.

Rufus was arguing that Jews, Catholics, non-Catholic Christians, Muslims, Hindus, Buddhists, and every other believer in redemption, had only one common denominator, a soul. People embracing different beliefs about what happens to a soul in the afterlife was imminently reasonable, and to be expected. But that did not mean that there were actually different afterlife realities. There could be only one. This was Rufus's challenge, and based on considerable research, he nobly presented his case.

He was not just a man on a soapbox. Rufus documented and expertly referenced everything he found in the literature. He very carefully and skillfully presented the beliefs of all religions, according to the highest standards of non-fiction, scholarly work.

But Rufus's solution to the problem did put him on a slippery slope, religiously, and fundamentally. He hinted in the final chapter that the only way to unify all the afterlife theories under one banner was if the banner read "Astrology". Only hinting at a justification for such a contention, Rufus seemed to be foolishly setting himself up for a barrage of criticism. But he convinced the publisher to allow it, in the name of a possible sequel. The idea was to sell books, after all.

Liz was supportive of the venture because she saw what Rufus was trying to do. He was writing a book for the masses, with the goal of selling a million copies. At the same time, he was pre-empting the inevitable attack from the academic theologians. They would be entitled to criticize his theory but they wouldn't be able to fault his research. From the publisher's standpoint, it was still a gamble. They were afraid that Rufus's desire for scholarly credibility would mean that his book wouldn't be sexy enough of the masses.

The fact that Rufus was willing to gamble was clear in the contract. The publisher would pursue both hardback and e-book, with Rufus getting essentially nothing until 10,000 of each were sold.

The foreword began with a quote from Revelations 2 :7.

"He that hath an ear, let him hear what the Spirit saith unto the churches: To him that over-cometh, will I give to eat of the tree of life, which is in the midst of the paradise of God".

Rufus embraced the reality that there was more than one church and more than one path. He believed that the astrological forces of the universe were intended to help us navigate our existence from birth to death. If we listened, we could overcome, but everyone's starting point was different. Everyone's strengths and weaknesses were different. The only unifying factor was that all our souls combined after death to complete the perfection that we call God, however many eons it takes.

Chapter 21. The Desert

Rufus did not call Katie until he arrived in the desert. He could have called her before he stepped onto the plane in New York, but he made a conscious decision to wait. He desperately wanted to avoid hearing something from Katie that would make him consider cancelling his trip to the Southwest. If he were already physically present at the conference, the chances were much less that he would stress over some minor crisis at the farm.

He got the full report about all the 'goings on' at the farm, the ones that seemed so important when you're there, but sound kind of funny when you're on the phone with someone who's there. He even got the skinny on Gary and his new/old flame. As Rufus ended the call, he had that familiar thought, that Katie had no earthly idea what he was trying to accomplish with all this philosophical gyrations, but thankfully, she supported him anyway. She was indeed the sweetest pea he knew.

The astrology conference was held every year during the third week of January. The fascination was with the planet Saturn, the Ruler of Capricorn. Saturn was widely believed to be the planet with the most recognizable influences. Its thirty-year revolution cycle seemed to correlate well with lessons learned during a human lifetime. The aspects it formed in an individual's horoscope were of the highest significance. At sixty, Rufus was completing his second Saturn cycle, and was excited about his third.

Participants were there to pursue their favorite past time, while taking advantage of a beautiful, warm winter environment. Perennial attendees like Rufus only spent a few nights at the conference hotel before moving to someone's private home for the balance of their stay. The area was something of a Mecca for astrologers, and Rufus was relatively well known to the Capricorn crowd.

Unlike their brothers, the astronomers, astrologers' forays into star gazing were more about using the luminous magic of the desert night to stimulate conversations about the effects of the planets than they were about capturing telescopic images. There were many interesting testimonials offered over a delicious cocktail or two.

The only focus group that Rufus really cared about was to meet the third day of the conference at the home where he was staying. Charging themselves with monitoring and assessing the impact of astrology products currently available in the media, from cheap shot smart phone apps to astrological websites, this rather large committee started the day by the pool and ended the day by the pool. Members heaped praise on those that adhered to the strictest of standards, and expressed disdain for practitioners resorting to obvious commercial trickery.

The group was the best Rufus had found for making new contacts. He was always on the lookout for serious astrologers who expressed an interest in finding a way to collect more astrological data. He was anxious to meet people who believed as he did, that astrology was ready to be put to the test. Rufus wanted to apply modern technological tools to the task of collecting astrological data on individuals. One or two charts at a time, with the anecdotal interpretations that accompanied them, would never really prove anything to anyone. Not only was there no formal committee with such a mandate, even at the Saturn Conference, but much to Rufus's chagrin, like-minded people were few and far between.

When he felt people out, Rufus was careful to avoid over-using the term "data collection" in public. It tended to immediately evoke an image of a surveillance crazy world, obsessed with intrusions into people's privacy, and that was not at all what Rufus meant by data collection, or was it?

His luck was about to change. Accompanied by a woman whose plain appearance was in stark contrast to her own flashy vibrancy, a young brunette approached Rufus and his two male friends as they enjoyed morning refreshments in the shade. Introducing herself as Monique, her French accented English was as flawless as her body. Easily any of these three men's top shelf fantasy, she was obviously most interested in Rufus. After some pleasantries and a little playful homage to Saturn, the young woman asked Rufus if he liked to swim. That was like asking an eagle if he liked to fly.

Rufus rose up and removed his shirt. He acted like a man who would swim through boiling oil to find out more about what this woman wanted with him. Monique's acquaintance, introduced as Jo Ann, was not too happy when the couple suddenly dove into the pool, leaving her stranded with two older gentlemen. Apparently she had a thing for Monique.

When they surfaced on the deep end, Rufus and the young lady hugged the poolside. She explained that she was a friend of the owner of the house, and that she was visiting from Switzerland. Then she got right to the point.

"I am an operative. It was decided that I meet you here, in this way. There are people from previous conferences who have recommended you. I am here to convince you to accept an invitation."

Captivated by her beauty, Rufus had to remind himself to listen. The swim had been exhilarating, but not as exhilarating as the woman. He had never before been intimidated by a female at an astrology conference, and he resolved that this would not be the first time.

"The only invitation on my mind is the one I'm offering to you. Have dinner with me this evening."

"Merci, Monsieur. J'amerais"

Rufus did not expect such a reply, especially not immediately. Did she really say, "I would love to"? It was clear that Monique was testing his French, and indirectly, his worldliness.

"Magnifique, madam."

"Je suis mademoiselle, mon pere."

She clarified her marital status and swam away. In one continuous motion, she left the pool and disappeared into the house.

With a multitude of seductive memories of young women, Rufus found it almost impossible to act his age when it came to romantic encounters. He knew he had no chance with this goddess and knew he would never cheat on Katie anyway. But his actions and feelings were those of a man who just could not turn away from the excitement of the pursuit of exotic beauty. In spite of having a few miles on him, Rufus was in great shape, and most women considered him charming, if not brutally handsome. For Rufus, it was like riding a bicycle. He had a way of engendering trust. But most importantly, Rufus was judicious, careful to reserve his talents for that one special woman he simply could not resist. He was not an "any port in the storm" kind of guy.

However activated his highly discriminating woman sense was, he was still at a loss. With no idea how to contact Monique, Rufus didn't want to consider that the whole thing might have been some kind of strange game or practical joke. However enticing the prospect of dinner with beautiful Monique, he reminded himself that he had been with her for barely five minutes.

As he dressed for dinner, he was feeling quite unapologetic about his lack of self-control. He was in the mood for a manly fantasy. He really was hoping that his wish would come true, to once again experience the joy of chasing another erotic rabbit down another hole.

Just as doubts were starting to creep back into his brain, there was a knock on the door of his room. It was the owner of the house. He entered and asked Rufus if he was having a good stay and if there was anything he needed. Sincerely appreciative of the accommodations, Rufus indicated that there was nothing more he could possibly want. The man smiled and then delivered a twisted message.

"We have a wonderful dinner planned for this evening. Too bad you're going to miss it."

"I'm afraid I don't understand. I met your friend Monique out by the pool and was hoping to see her at dinner."

"Rufus, let me be quite candid with you."

When he paused, Rufus thought for sure he was about to get shot down for even thinking about pursuing Monique. But the man just wanted to choose his words carefully.

"You have gained a reputation in the astrological community as a progressive. You want to, in your own words, 'take astrology to the next level'. Am I correct about this?"

Rufus was extremely flattered by the reputation part. Whenever he considered how his persona might be impacting the world of astrology, he presumed himself a minor player. Eccentric by his own admission, at least he tried. Now here was a man before him, uttering one of his

173

favorite phrases, "take astrology to the next level".

"Yes, I think you have me pegged."

"Good. You have a decision to make and a promise to keep. I'll just lay it right out there. Monique wants to take you to meet some people. The purpose of the meeting is to brief you on some of their activities, and to ask you to join them. Once briefed, you are sworn to secrecy, and there will be no turning back. Your decision is, go down to the garage right now, where Monique is waiting for you, or decline the invitation and disavow any knowledge that it was ever extended. The promise is, that whether you decide to go with Monique or not, you will say nothing of this meeting right now, or any future meeting, to anyone, ever, for any reason."

Rufus started to ask a question. The man stopped him.

"You're in or out, right now. All you get to know is that these people share your passion for improving data collection. I cannot say anymore, or answer any questions. When I walk out this door to go to dinner, I will consider that this conversation never happened. I must stay apart from the activities of this group. My only purpose is to lend credibility to the offer, and to be a witness to your promise of secrecy. Monique is involved as an extra layer of cover for you. If people think you are just chasing a skirt, they won't ask as many questions."

Rufus had no doubts about the decision, or the promise. Wanting to show unfettered respect and gratitude, he replied without delay.

"I'm in. Thank you. I understand totally."

After shaking Rufus's hand, the man departed without speaking another word.

As Rufus entered the parking garage in the rear of the house, he noticed car lights flash on/off, on/off. He heard an engine start, and soon found himself in the passenger seat of a blue Mustang. Monique said nothing as she opened the garage door by remote and sped away down the driveway towards the desert sunset. Only when they were well underway did she speak.

"I'm so happy that you have accepted our invitation. This may not be the dinner with me that you wanted, but we are together now, and I will not be leaving you alone."

Rufus was charmed. He didn't know if the thrill he was feeling came from this gorgeous woman, the invigorating ride, or the prospect of the meeting. He was infatuated with the woman and intrigued by the idea of the meeting, all at the same time.

"I am enchanted, to say the least. But I do have one question. Are you just an operative, or will you be participating in the substance of the meeting that I presume we are on our way to attend?"

Quickly and succinctly, in that sweet French accent, she offered her dodge.

"I know that you're thinking. Jupiter on your tenth house Venus is just beginning to bring you good tidings as it transits onward toward your natal Jupiter at 29 degrees of Gemini."

"OK, OK, you've done your homework, but you haven't answered my question. Will you be part of what I assume will be an ongoing effort, or will you fly away after tonight? After all, you are an 'operative'."

"We will discuss that later, monsieur. You have enough to think about this evening. Just know that I will not be leaving you alone tonight."

They arrived at an exclusive hotel, parked, and headed for the front desk. Monique was flirting with Rufus and pretended to be drunk as she asked if there were any messages for her. She made the hotelier promise to hold all her calls and practically dragged Rufus toward the elevator. She was quite the actress, skillfully selling the idea of a romantic tryst to anyone witnessing their arrival. Once in her hotel room, the young beauty dropped the act and offered him a drink.

"Sorry about that, monsieur. I had to make them believe that we are, as you say, an item."

Rufus said nothing as he made quick work of the beer she had provided. It made his lack of control so much easier to tolerate.

It wasn't long before she received a text, and they were off down the rear stairs and out the exit where a car was waiting. This time it was a non-descript SUV. They got into the back seat and were on their way again.

What little the driver said was steeped in a heavy Mexican accent. Although he insisted he was just the driver, he did provide beer and tacos. Monique explained that the refreshments were to hold them over until they arrived at their destination.

The half hour ride gave them a chance to get better acquainted. Everything had been happening so fast. Rufus told her about his farm, and a select few of his life choices. Eventually he brought up the book. Monique expressed admiration for Rufus's determination.

Monique disclosed that she was the granddaughter of one of the most renowned astrologers in Europe, and made her living as a model. She did favors for friends of the family with regard to astrology, and in spite of having learned from some of the best astrologers in the world, she was not a practitioner or an activist. She had grown up taking astrology for granted.

After a rough ride up a canyon, they arrived at what was no more than a desert encampment. A half a dozen small campers and winnebagos formed a circle around a central fire and chuck wagon. People were sitting in lawn chairs around the fire. Laughter was the primary sound heard by Rufus and Monique as they got out of the SUV. The driver handed them each a serape to protect them from the cold desert air and then, as if he were following instructions, drove the SUV back up the road about one hundred yards, parked on the side of the road, and turned out the lights.

Monique was obviously well known to the ten or so people at the fire. Rufus, as a country boy, was happy to find such an informal outdoor gathering. It was ironic that the only thing that made him feel awkward was the way he was dressed. For a formal dinner party!

Monique introduced him all around, one person at a time, to a varied group of men and women, only one of which Rufus recalled meeting before that night.

What he thought was going to be an intellectual affair focusing on the subject of how to improve data collection turned out to be more like an overnight float trip from his hard partying past. There was a lot of alcohol, a fantastic assortment of campfire food, primo marijuana, and even peyote for those inclined to be so brave. It was a bonding experience, an initiation, a leap of trust that would profoundly affect Rufus for the rest of his life.

The group's mission was to find innovative ways to bolster the astrological data base. The days of relying on observations handed down from ancient times, or sifting through catalogues of horoscopes of famous people were numbered. His new friends wanted to mine birth data, generate millions of horoscopes, and investigate whether there were credible correlations with people's life choices. Just like Rufus, they wanted astrology to finally, once and for all, prove its worth, or, God forbid, its weakness.

The principal organizer of the desert camp was a man named Simon.

When Rufus was about as high as a man could get, Simon took him out under the stars and explained the reason for all the secrecy.

"Rufus, since we started this effort, we are feeling a persistent threat from what we call the 'prediction people'. Instead of making improvements to methodology for the sole purpose of helping people lead better lives, the

'prediction people' are unapologetic about their desire to
use astrology for their own purposes, some of which we
fear are both political and economic. We embrace
astrology with honor, as you do, as altruists, whereas
there are many scoundrels ready to steal our potential
discoveries in a heartbeat, to make an extra political point,
or an extra million dollars in the stock market."

Rufus assured him that he understood, and went on
to make his own point about the importance of secrecy.

"I believe you correctly anticipate the threat. But I
suggest that there is yet another force, perhaps embedded
in the far right, conservative, religious movement that
could be a problem, for a different reason. There are
people that would try to disrupt our efforts simply to
discredit us and denigrate the science. In my part of the
world, and in many of the other 'red states', there are well-
meaning people who feel that astrology threatens their
beliefs."

"Point well taken my friend. They told me you were
a thinker, Rufus. Indeed, after that statement, I'd say they
were right. In any case, we are glad to have you on
board. Now, let's join the party. Tonight, enjoy yourself,
and just get to know some of the other players. There will
be plenty of work to do down the road. My message to
you is simple: welcome to our merry band of data
collectors."

Simon gave Rufus a long powerful hug, and the two
to them headed for the fire.

About 3 AM, at the behest of Monique, the two of
them headed for the hotel. At 9 AM, Rufus woke up on the
couch to the sound of room service at the door. There was
a note from Monique, indicating that she would soon
return. As he got up to shower, he found a note in his
pocket, with an email address. He remembered the man
that had given him the note, but not his name. On the
back of the note it said:

"Welcome to the DCG. Be patient."

Even in his hung-over state, Rufus smiled ever so widely in the shower. It was an unimaginable breakthrough, one that came just when he was feeling there was nothing that could top getting his book published.

Rufus didn't see Monique again after that morning, but he felt certain that he would see her again. He spent most of his last two days in the desert by the pool, helping some of the younger members of the focus group with their projects, and peacefully catching rays. He was intentionally a bit selfish for the rest of his stay. Before he knew it, he'd be back to "playin' in the blood and poop" at the hospital and spending late nights at the lambing barn.

Rufus could not have been happier. He resolved to wait patiently back on the farm, not only for the first news about book sales, but for how he might contribute to the efforts of the data collection group. The incredible sense of good fortune he felt from being asked to join the DCG became more real as each day passed. He had attended a conference that honored Saturn the task master, and ended up supremely grateful to Jupiter the beneficent.

Chapter 22. Robert's Flock

When spring break rolled around, Robert decided to bring Jane and her siblings out to the farm. Robert hadn't seen his uncle much at all. When Rufus returned from his dual purpose NY/desert trip, he was either working long hours at the hospital, giving Katie some much deserved attention, or being a good shepherd, in the literal sense.

Jane's mother Sarah was about to make the long trip to the state prison to visit her husband. She would have liked to take the kids to see their father, but Robert and Jane encouraged her to go by herself. They knew she was badly in need of a break.

Robert arranged for the kids to visit Rufus's farm for the two days and one night that she would be away. That way, she wouldn't have to worry about Jane being alone with the three young ones, or Jane being alone with Robert. Jane was only seventeen. Katie made the idea more credible and comfortable for Sarah when she made a point of visiting the restaurant one day and offering her assurance that she wanted to help. Sarah didn't know Katie very well, only that she was a really good person.

Robert had been busy with school. Having made a good impression on the high school counselor, as well as the Division of Family Services people, he couldn't find enough room in his schedule for all the tutoring opportunities available. He was getting valuable experience. For many of the "special needs" kids, who were often the "extreme poverty" kids, tutoring was essentially a euphemism for counseling. Not only did these kids need someone to empathize, but it was very clear that their emotional and socio-economic circumstances were much more of an issue than the correct answer on a worksheet. Mostly, they just needed someone to model appropriate behavior. Unlike some of their parents, that's where Robert excelled.

When the kids piled out of Robert's old car on Holy Thursday, you'd have thought Katie was welcoming her grandchildren for Christmas. She was so excited.

"Well, who do we have here?

The littlest one, Todd, didn't know what to think.

"I see you even wore your boots. You look like you're ready to help Rufus with the lambs. Welcome to our farm!"

The little boy looked around in bewildered amazement. No amount of preparation from Jane could have gotten him ready. He didn't cry, but almost. Not only didn't he see a farm, or know what a farm was supposed to look like, but he was seeing a back yard that was way more stimulating than the one he was familiar with. He said nothing, and shyly walked over to stand behind Jane. Luckily, he was familiar with Robert, who was throwing him little cues the whole time.

Jane stepped up and introduced her siblings from oldest to youngest. Susan, who genuinely liked and trusted her sister, was twelve, soon to be thirteen. Jeremy had just turned seven, and took every opportunity to let Jane know that she was not his mama. Todd, at four, didn't care whether Jane was his mama or not. He was hanging onto her for dear life, no matter what.

"I can't even tell you how much we appreciate you

letting us come out here. My mother will have a much better trip knowin' that we're stayin' here. When the boys get adjusted, you'll see, they won't be no bother."

Katie finally started to relax. Rufus said nothing. He wanted the reception to have Katie's face on it.

"Don't think a thing about it, Jane. We are honored you could all visit. Why don't you come on into the house?"

After a simple lunch, Rufus asked Jane if she thought the kids would enjoy going to see the lambs. Rufus had hooked a wagon behind the tractor and filled it with straw, for a kind of springtime hay ride. He suggested that Jane go on ahead, with the two littlest ones, to gauge their acceptance of the idea. Rufus was concerned that the combination of the sound of the tractor and the newness of riding in a wagon would scare them if it were sprung on them too suddenly.

After just a few minutes in the wagon, the answer was clear. They loved it. Rufus and the others had been watching from the kitchen, and after some last minute wardrobe adjustments, they joined Jane and the kids. Robert marveled at their adaptability as he and Susan climbed into the wagon. With no room for Katie in the wagon, she stood on the hitch, and held on tight to the back of the tractor seat for the ride down to the lambing barn.

It was a good time of the year for the kids to view the lambs. The youngest lambs were in the smaller lots near the barn, making it easy for Rufus to catch one, for the obligatory "holding of the lamb". Little kids looked so silly and sweet the first time they held a lamb in their arms. The lambs let out high pitched "maaas" and tried to get away, while the kid's wild-eyed expression screamed "could somebody please help me with this thing?" Susan seemed rather enchanted by the sheep experience, asking a million questions, and following Rufus very closely.

With the one exception of astrology, there was nothing that made Rufus happier than a person being interested in sheep.

Rufus asked the whole group to follow him a short distance to another nearby pasture where there was a group of ewes with slightly older lambs. Knowing what was coming, Robert encouraged the little kids to keep up. He knew that when Rufus distributed the bucket of grain in the long feeder for the ewes, the lambs' reaction would make for a delightful scene.

Their mamas getting fed a generous portion of nutritious grain was a clear signal to the lambs that they would soon be getting their allotment of milk. Having learned the hard way that trying to move in too soon on mama's teat could be counterproductive, if not dangerous, they passed the time with a bizarre kind of play. As if on cue, several pairs of lambs would face off, and playfully challenge one another, as the rest of the lambs watched. They would stomp their feet, posturing as if ready to duel to the death, and then pretend to butt heads. For a split second, they would all freeze in place, and stare each other down. Without warning, a self-appointed leader would take off, running up the field as fast as his little legs would move him. All the other lambs would follow. When the leader stopped, they all stopped. Then, another virtual freeze frame, before a new self-appointed leader would initiate a return run right back to the point of beginning. Rufus called it the "lamb races".

The part that Robert dearly loved, the part he especially didn't want the young people to miss, was when some of the lambs would get so excited that they would do the "pogo stick". Stiffening all four of their legs, they would wildly hop as if they were on a pogo stick, somehow running and hopping all at the same time, right in the middle of the lamb race. It was spontaneous, unpredictable, and incredibly funny to watch. Little Todd giggled at the lambs as he exhorted them, over and over, to "do it again".

When the mamas finished their repast and called their progeny, the lambs gave up racing for some voracious suckling. Surprisingly quickly, depending on their age and whether they were twins or triplets, the mamas cut them off by raising and then lowering their rear leg and turning their body. The lambs then heard a different kind of baaa', one that roughly translated to "you may now follow me out to pasture".

As the four-legged entertainment rambled westward toward lush grass, the humans had to decide on their next move. Noting her interest in animal husbandry, and wanting to offer her a much needed break from the little boys, Rufus invited Susan to stay behind with him at the lambing barn while he performed the more serious, less exciting chores. When Katie took over as tractor operator, the little ones didn't notice. They were hooked on wagon riding.

Back at the house, Robert and Jane asked Katie if she would mind watching Jane's brothers. Katie was quite confident that ice cream and a few good animated films would make her a well-qualified baby sitter. She not only relished the child care role, but she was really happy that Robert and Jane were finally going to have some time alone.

Robert showed Jane the trail that accessed the logging road to the north of the house beyond the swimming pool. It led eastward, through the neighbor's farm, all the way to the low water bridge at the main creek. They worked their way upstream about a quarter mile to a private gravel bar that faced southwest toward the afternoon sun. It was a gorgeous spring day. They lay back on the fine, sun heated gravel, closed their eyes, and listened to the sound of the water.

"Thanks for bringing me here, Robert. This is just

what I needed."

He rolled over in her direction, and put his arm around her just below her breasts, gently snuggling his face into her shoulder.

"It's just what I needed too."

They lay like that for a long time, the sound of the water massaging their thoughts, with no need to speak, or even move.

After a while, inevitably, Robert's hand started to roam. Ever so slowly, ever so gently, his hand slid up toward her breast and then down toward her ass, trying so hard to be nonchalant. Jane wasn't normally touchy about his boyish advances, but the gravel bar wasn't quite private enough for her, so she deftly rolled right out of his embrace, and stood up. She obviously wanted to talk. She picked up a big rock, and threw it into the water with great force, trying to make the biggest splash she could.

"Robert, you're the best boy I've ever known. When you start to touch me like that, it makes me feel one thing. I want to do it with you."

She picked up another big rock and made another big splash.

"But I just can't. I can't do it because of what it makes me think about. It makes me think about babies. My whole life has been about nothin' but babies, and if I was to do it with you, I wouldn't be able to stop thinkin' about babies."

Robert got up, and joined her at the water's edge. He picked up a big rock and handed it to her.

"Here, try this one."

She made another big splash. Robert grabbed her by the arm, brought her toward him and kissed her hard and fast on the lips.

"I understand. You really didn't even have to tell me."

"There you go again, being sweet. But Robert, I know

you think about it. You've figured out by now that over
half the boys in your senior class have done it. You know
Matthew has."

"Jane. Stop. We've known each other for six months
and they have been the best six months of my life. Of
course I think about it. When the urge wells up, it feels
wonderful. It's overwhelming. But my brain tells me that
I might not know what the hell I'm doing. For me it isn't
babies, but I know what you mean, I do, and I admire you
for telling me how you feel."

She hugged him around the waist, and would not let
go. After a long time, when she finally loosened her grip,
he took her by the arms, and gently laid her down on the
gravel in almost the same spot as before. He lay down
beside her. This time he beckoned her to roll toward him
so that she could rest her head on his shoulder. They
stayed like that for the longest time without saying a
word.

When the sun dipped low enough to be blocked by
the trees on the west bank of the creek, it quickly became
too cool for good snuggling. They picked themselves up
and began to retrace their path, back up the creek, across
the field, and up the hill into the forest. They walked in
silence.

As they walked, Robert's thoughts turned to the
encounter with Kristin the previous summer. As much as
he had grown accustomed to kissing and caressing Jane,
he suddenly realized how different it felt, compared to the
erotic encounter with Kristin. In that instant, he found
himself able to embrace each form of desire
simultaneously. He was able to admit that he craved a
lascivious sexual encounter, and yet thoroughly enjoyed
his deep platonic connection to Jane. The weirdest part
was that it didn't feel confusing at all. It felt natural. He
considered that maybe even young people have
epiphanies.

Nearing the house, Jane shocked Robert back to reality when she asked what they would be doing the following day. She was concerned that she and her siblings might be a burden, and offered to go back to the trailer in the morning to await the return of her mother Sarah. Robert assured her that Katie was expecting them to stay at least part of the day.

At dinner, Rufus announced that he had to work at the hospital the following day, and that everyone would be turning in early. Rufus was just that way. He told it like it was, and no one dared protest.

Katie not only had the sleeping arrangements figured out, but she had the entire next morning planned. She confirmed with Rufus that it was OK to take the tractor and wagon down to the beaver pond. The only stipulation was that no one take the boat out onto the pond. He wasn't comfortable with even Robert and Jane taking the boat on the water without him being present.

With Jane and her siblings bedded down for the night, Rufus asked Robert to accompany him outside. They each donned a jacket and stocking cap and walked up to the pool bar. Rufus turned on the light, proudly exposing his new creation. His friend had finished the porcelain tile bar top, featuring a one of a kind, in laid horoscope. The beautiful, perfect, twelve-section circle, about sixteen inches in diameter, was ready to assist the portrayal of any astrological happening. Rufus thought it was really cool, even though he knew that most people would think it a little odd. To him, it was an evocative symbol of the progress he had made in his life, artistically conveying his willingness to share his astrological knowledge with those he deemed worthy.

Then he explained that the real reason for their excursion to the pool bar was not the porcelain horoscope.

"Robert, I wanted to get you alone so I could give you something. I want you to keep it to yourself for now, but I want you to have it."

He reached up and retrieved a book from the high pool bar shelf. He opened the front cover, and taking a pen from his pocket, he wrote:

"To my good friend Robert, a Master of World Religions".

He signed his name Rufus T. Schicklgruber. It was a first edition copy of his book, Heaven: A Unified Field Theory. Robert was lost for words.

"Jesus. That was pretty quick. You just made your deal in January."

"Only when you have read it in its entirety, and we have discussed it, do I want you to talk about it with other people, OK? I want to keep a low profile in this part of the world. The bible beaters around here would have my head if they were to read some of the stuff I've written. After I make my first hundred thousand, I won't care so much about what they say."

"I understand. Congratulations."

Under the circumstances, Robert decided against telling Rufus about the experience with Jane. Instead, he asked a favor.

"Can I ask you an astrology question?"

"Well, of course."

"The books you gave me don't really explain aspects very well. I get the elements, and the signs, and the planets, and I'm starting to get the houses. But the aspects really have got me going. I'm not sure what to think, especially when I look at my chart, where the moon seems to be opposing just about everything else."

Rufus nodded acknowledgement, motioned to Robert to stay put, and ran to the house. He returned with a small paperback, and an apology.

"Things have been so crazy. I haven't kept up with you like I promised I would. I believe this book will help. This guy does a good job with chart interpretation, aspects in particular. In the preface, he actually discusses how he got feedback from people after his first two books. It was the aspects that were causing the most difficulty. So he wrote this book with that in mind."

He looked Robert right in the eye.

"A word of caution. Read this book from start to finish. Don't just use it as a reference to look up a particular aspect. This is your chance to get oriented to proper chart interpretation. The author stresses the importance of the whole chart, the whole person. Too many teachers and too many students of astrology fall into the trap of cookbook astrology. They look up an aspect like their looking up a recipe, but they never develop an overall ethic, or interpretive approach, that will transform them from cook to chef, from simple-minded astrologer, to master. This guy can help you with that. You'll know what I mean before you are even finished with the introduction. Do you want to be a chef, or someone who can just follow a recipe?"

"Thanks, Rufus. I'll read the whole book."

"Robert, I know you haven't had the opportunity to see a lot of charts, so you're not sure what to think about all those planets in your tenth and eleventh houses. So, here's a little tip. Remember to balance all those planet and house influences with the opposing force of your Moon in Cancer. Your fifth house Moon sits opposite all those planets in your tenth and eleventh houses. Remember when we talked about the fulcrum, the see saw? In your horoscope, your Moon will always be the counterbalance to all the more worldly influences, as represented by those other planets. You will be tempted to disregard your Cancer Moon tendency, which is to help all those less fortunate. As long as you are aware of the need for balance, you'll be fine. We are all constantly in the process of finding balance."

He used the inlay chart in the countertop to illustrate

what he was saying.

"Throughout your life, everything that happens in the more public domains of the tenth and eleventh houses, as pre-disposed by those natal planets and triggered by transiting planets, may seem to conflict with how you feel deep down. Everything you do will have to be reconciled with your most intimate feelings, as represented by that very sensitive, very dominant Cancer Moon. Sometimes it will not be easy to do so."

Robert was grateful for the attention, and for the lesson. Not only did he understand what Rufus was getting at, but he realized it didn't make him feel uncomfortable. Maybe he was learning the basics better than he thought.

Grateful for the astrology discussion, the impulse to talk about Jane crept back into Robert's mind. He remembered how good he felt that winter night when he had talked to Rufus about his dilemma. The memory gave him courage.

"Speaking of feelings, I finally had that talk with Jane. We know we can't have it both ways, so we're going to keep things cool. Thanks for talking to me about that before."

The older, wiser man didn't press Robert for details because he knew exactly what Robert was implying. Robert was poised to race down a very fast track in the coming year. Prom, graduation, and a summer transition to an independent life in college may very well relegate Jane to nothing more than a lucky penny. As Robert sought his fortune, Jane could be his wonderful treasure, his eminently safe place, willfully and wisely reserved by innocent love, unencumbered by mortal, physical commitment.

"I'm glad to hear that things are more clear. Often times, it doesn't matter what the answer is, so much as there is an answer. I hope that makes sense."

"It does actually. In a way, it makes me wonder why I even brought it up. I guess I just wanted you to know that I feel better about it, since you were nice enough to talk to me about it before."

At that moment, Robert had a strange vision of his future. It was not about Jane, but it still included Jane. The distinction was important. He was reminded of his thoughts on the trail, as he and Jane walked back from the creek that evening.

Rufus ran his finger around the porcelain circle and started humming. . . .

"And the seasons, they go round and round, and the painted ponies go up and down. . . . . "

It was a little too hypnotic for Robert after a long day. He was glad when Rufus stopped.

"Robert, there is one more thing. I may miss your graduation. Now that the book is published, I'm ready to pursue another project that will take me away from the farm."

Rufus could tell Robert was disappointed, but not surprised.

"I promise you I'll make it up to you. I really, really want to take you, and whoever you want to invite, on a float trip adventure in June. I think you'll enjoy that much more than having me at your graduation. Trust me. I would just be a big distraction."

"That sounds fantastic. It's about time we got those city slickers on the river. I've never let them forget about it. But, hey, what's the project?"

"Astrology related, as you might have guessed. But I cannot tell you any details until the time is right. It's kind of funny. I will definitely need to tell you all about my project at some point, because I think I may need your help to pull it off."

Robert was used to the ever cryptic Rufus, and affirmed his willingness to help any way he could. For very different reasons, each of them was excited about the future as they walked to the house to go to bed.

Chapter 23. Back to New York

Rufus had fond memories of the intriguing encounter with Monique and the wild night at the desert camp, but was left to wonder for months what the data collection people were really about. He sent the email as instructed, purposely making it as innocuous as possible. The message was:

"I really enjoyed our visit. Hope to see you again soon".

It drove him crazy that there was no reply for so long.

When the reply finally came, in early May, it read:

"You're welcome. See you at the book signing." Whoever his contact was, they were very clever. How many people could have known about the book signing coming up at the end of the May? Rufus had just confirmed the invitation.

The initial success of the book gave Rufus the confidence to make two important decisions. He converted to PRN status at the hospital, and he purchased a brand new 'luxury' crossover. He was gambling that proceeds from the book would pay for it.

His enthusiasm for a little extravagance was only accentuated by having an actual invitation to a book signing in Manhattan. It was quite enabling for a man who was already prepared to throw caution to the wind. Rufus had worked hard all of his life, and though he was not a wealthy man, he was pretty sure it was time to gamble.

His only regret was missing Robert's graduation. When he had warned Robert of the possibility, he had no idea it would be because of a book signing. He assumed, or rather hoped, it would have something to do with the data collection group, as it was named that night in the desert. Rufus missing the graduation didn't make Katie very happy at all. Although she was more than fine with Rufus leaving, and extremely proud of both him and Robert, she just wasn't looking forward to driving herself to the ceremony.

On the other hand, Rufus was looking forward to driving himself to the book signing. He couldn't let go of a hunch that events might occur that would make him glad he opted for the flexibility of driving instead of flying. Besides, he had not owned a new vehicle for many years, so the journey would be quite liberating for a man who was more accustomed to driving a truck to a small town for feed and groceries than he was taking a road trip to Manhattan.

Just before he left the farm, Rufus received a parcel. It contained a twenty-five page, untitled document that outlined ideas for how and where to obtain mass data to support an astrology validation effort. Someone was trying to bring him up to speed, but no names were on the document.

It was as if Rufus had been mailed the suggestion box. Reading like a collection of cut and pasted ideas from numerous sources, as evidenced by the varied syntax, the document provided a welcome diversion from the monotony of interstate travel. Rufus was intrigued by some the ideas, and was largely familiar with most, having heard them at astrology conferences over the years. But he had never met anyone, until the desert, who was interested in actually doing something.

As he drove the thousand miles to New York, Rufus had a million big ideas rambling around in his brain. Synapses fired up limitless possibilities ahead, powered up by one monstrous shot of energy from the night in the desert. His ego as unrestrained as his imagination, Rufus had no apologies for fancying himself one of the more valuable members of the DCG. He felt that his education, his science background, his vast astrological knowledge, and his track record of finding innovative solutions, added up to perfect preparation for playing a major role.

At the same time, Rufus had to admit that accomplishing data collection on the scale the group was envisioning would require significant computer skills and an enormous amount of processing capacity, neither of which he was in a position to provide. Not only was he not a hacker, or a programmer, but a couple of PC's and a tablet were the only computer hardware currently at his disposal.

In New York, he was booked at the same four-star Manhattan hotel as in January. Normally, luxury accommodations were only offered to the writer as persuasion to sign the book deal, but Liz had convinced the publisher that Rufus deserved to remain on a diet of extravagance.

The day of the signing, Rufus was delivered by cab to a book store in Greenwich Village, where he was ushered around a long line of admirers to a table. That was his first time seeing Liz since his arrival. Rufus considered her more than just an agent. The two of them were only able to visit for a few minutes, but it was enough to wash away all of Rufus's apprehension about the new experience at hand. After many hugs, handshakes, and photos, Liz said she had a meeting and left him to the task.

The fans of Rufus's Heaven came in all shapes and

sizes, and from all persuasions. In addition to the admirers of all new books with an air of controversy, there were literary types, academics, theologians, and even a few print media critics. At first it was exciting for Rufus. He enjoyed the flattery and talked just a bit too long with each admirer. But after a while he mastered the art of working the line with a quicker style.

When nothing could seem to slow him down, Rufus was suddenly stopped dead in his tracks. An older gentleman approached him, and opening the front cover of the book, revealed a note card that read "Monsieur Rufus, Comment ca va?" As Rufus went to sign the page, he froze for just a moment when he realized that the note may very well be from Monique. He signed the book and retained the note with the excitement of a school boy who had received one from his girlfriend all the way across the classroom. But "how's it going?" was all it said.

When the scheduled lunch break came, Liz's assistant made a point of asking Rufus whether he preferred to go to lunch on his own, or with her and her friend. Given even a small glimmer of hope of seeing Monique, he politely declined their invitation, made his excuses to the lingering patrons, and nervously ventured out the front door of the bookstore.

He had no idea Monique was following him when he started down the sidewalk. He wasn't even sure where he was going. She soon caught up with him and whisked him down an alley before he could react. They had their reunion behind a dumpster.

"Rufus, it is so good to see you again. Come on, hurry. I know a little place on the next block where we can talk. I know you don't have much time."

She took him by the hand and pulled him energetically and relentlessly down the alley, then around the corner to a small deli. Once inside, and seated in a booth, she let him speak.

"Monique. Your flair for the dramatic leaves me a little out of breath. It's good to see you too. But isn't this too public for you? Doesn't everything have to be a secret?"

"Monsieur Rufus, I understand why you would feel that way. How shall I say? If people think we have found romance, this is OK. It is only when we are around the astrology types that we need to be careful. Comprend?"

"Comprend."

Settling into a simple lunch, they did their best to catch up. Monique had been in Europe most of the time since the Saturn conference in the desert. Rufus spoke mostly of his joy over the success of his book.

"I want you to know that I have read your book. It is quite fascinating, and a very unique perspective. I predict much success for you."

"Thank you. I'm happy about it, but I have so little experience with this kind of success. I have no interest in fame. It's a strange feeling."

At that point she began to whisper.

"Monsieur, you know that the committee plans to use your travels to promote your book as your cover, you know, to be involved with the DCG. It could not be better. Tonight is the first official meeting, if you would like to go with me."

Rufus could not have been more excited. His mind was racing over the craziness of this fascinating woman, travel, freedom, his book, and finally, a real opportunity to pursue his number one life dream. The farm seemed light years away.

"All I can say is, of course I will go with you. I received the package. I have a lot of ideas. When do we start?"

"I will pick you up in front of your hotel at six o'clock."

When they left the deli, she kissed him on the cheek,

pointed him back the way they had come, and
disappeared down the sidewalk in the opposite direction.

Chapter 24. The Veranda

It was difficult for Rufus to relax at the hotel. Even though he was tired, after a day that reminded him way too much of his teaching days, he could not rest. Afraid of over-indulging at the hotel lounge, but in need of something to calm his nerves, he ordered a couple of exotic brews from room service and got lost in a long hot bath.

He was so glad that he had taken a rain check on the invitation to dinner with Liz. Cancelling on short notice would have made her way too curious about his reasons.

In her typical fashion, Monique did not divulge much about the plans for the evening. She encouraged him to relax, to lower his expectations, and simply enjoy an evening out with her. But he'd been there before. This time, his gut was telling him that there was more to it. He was anticipating, or at least hoping for, something much more serious and substantive.

At precisely six o'clock, he was hailed to a private car in front of the hotel. He recognized the two men in the front seat from the desert camp, and was very happy to see Monique in the back. They talked about a lot of things as they drove eastward. Rufus quickly realized he wasn't the only one excited about the evening. The two men were bubbly with anticipation. They shared Rufus's hope that the DCG was about to move beyond the concept stage, and acknowledged receiving a package identical to the one Rufus had received.

The hilltop residence didn't quite exude opulence, but it was in a great neighborhood, on a lot that was much larger than those in the immediate area. A half a dozen cars were parked along the circle drive. Music could be heard, along with laughter and conversation, coming from a second floor veranda that provided horizontal relief from the large white columns that graced the front of the home. Monique was clearly familiar with the vast majority of the attendees, greeting them by name as she walked Rufus and the other two men up the massive internal staircase and through the study, to the doors that opened onto the veranda. The atmosphere was one of a cocktail party.

When he arrived on the veranda, Rufus was singled out by a cigar smoking man of robust stature. Rufus did not recognize him from the desert. The man was intense, with a warm, but stern stare, like a CEO getting ready to address the Board. He had a beer in his hand, something that endeared him to Rufus immediately, and confirmed with his handshake that he was very much used to being in charge.

"There's that rugged mid-westerner that I've been so anxious to meet. How are you? Monique and some of the others have told me a lot about you. Now a published author, I hear. Good for you. My name's Walter."

After all that, he finally let go of Rufus's hand.

"I'm just glad to be here Walter. Is this your place?"

"Yeah, isn't it great? I know it seems out of place up north here, but I'm from Atlanta, so I had to have a veranda. You know what I mean?"

Walter was appearing a little inebriated, which made Rufus feel even more comfortable with him. Rufus could appreciate a man who communicated better with a few beers in his belly. Predictably, Walter continued.

"After dinner we'll talk. Make yourself at home."

He patted Rufus on the back, hollered for someone named Erica, and wandered off through the study.

Monique was waiting to rescue him. She could tell that Rufus was rocking on the edge of serious. She knew he was perfectly capable of having a good time drinking and meeting new people, but at the same time, was suffering under a load of pent up curiosity about how this DCG thing was going to work.

"Monsieur Rufus, you look so handsome this evening. I'm so glad you have met Walter. You'll get used to his ways. Don't worry. Without him and Erica, the DCG would not be very far along at all. So you'll have to take him with a grain of salt. Is that how you Americans say it? Let me introduce you to another big player. OK?"

They stepped to the far right corner of the veranda. From there, Rufus noticed something quite fascinating. The veranda continued around the side of the house, where it provided a magnificent view of the distant night lights of New York. It was a satisfyingly subtle sight, enabled at such a great distance by the relatively dark, down-sloping foreground of Walter's back yard and neighborhood.

"Stephan, mon cheri, I would like you to meet Monsieur Rufus."

Stephan was seated in a high-back whicker chair. He was about the same age as Monique, perhaps mid-thirties, of medium solid build, with brown curly hair, and dark heavy-framed glasses. He appeared quite healthy, and eminently comfortable in his own skin. He did not get up to greet Rufus. Instead, the man seated near him, as if on cue, got up and offered his chair. Monique leaned over and whispered something in Stephan's ear. He laughed quietly at whatever she told him. As he kissed her on the cheek, she turned her gaze toward Rufus. Not taking her eyes off him while Stephan continued whispering in her ear, she smiled warmly. Then she quietly departed with Stephan's companion.

Rufus sat down. Although he might have felt uncomfortable with the less than warm reception from Stephan, he did not. He sensed a style more European, like that of Monique. This was confirmed when Stephan proceeded, without any hesitation or small talk, to explain his relationship with the DCG. His accent may have been German-Austrian, but his English was superb.

"I have no idea what Monique or Walter have told you, and I'm not sure it will matter. What I know about you is that you are a devotee of astrology and you have the ability and the desire to help us. So let me explain."

He pulled his chair closer to Rufus, took a sip of his wine, and began.

"I am, shall we say, a representative, of one of the largest, most successful, most legitimate, horoscope services that exist today. Our online horoscope product and the associated services have stood the test of time. We are well respected. But some of us are feeling a bit stagnant. We think that more is possible. Are you familiar with how our algorithms were developed in the first place, Monsieur Rufus? I know that you are familiar with our little business."

Rufus, however comfortable he was with this virtue called patience, was indeed glad to finally be allowed to speak. Although he wasn't actually upset about the way things were going so far that evening, he was unaccustomed to being so submissive.

"Yes I am familiar. I have often wondered whether revisions are made, how often, and on what basis. Your program accurately and quickly prepares a chart for the user, and I admit to using it myself, if only for the chart preparation. None of us miss the tedium of constructing a natal chart the old-fashioned way. But I have always assumed that the chart interpretation, even though it is offered by way of a website, is based on the same books, the same rules, shall we say, as if it were done 'by hand' by any capable astrologer. The automation aspect of your interpretation program saves a lot of time, but does not necessarily produce a better product. In fact, it may not be as good. Don't you agree?"

"I would say that you have offered a fair analysis of what we do. Our chart interpretation product lacks the interactive aspect that many consider important to a good reading. It is 'one size fits all', and could certainly be criticized as superficial. Also, as you suspect, there have been revisions to the program since it was developed, but only minor ones."

Rufus felt he had successfully established his credibility, and was now more comfortable with just listening.

"Your hostess here tonight, Erica, believes as you do, that with actual, real life data, we can improve on the current computerized chart interpretation algorithms. But you see, we can hardly ask our subscribers to submit their lives to intense scrutiny, just to help us improve our product. It would be like admitting that we are not quite sure whether we have it right. I know you understand. You see, such a move has been suggested, and fortunately, in my view, has been vetoed. But I fear that the resistance to change may be for the wrong reasons. Some of the people in charge simply prefer the status quo. Our website generates quite a lot of revenue in its current form, and they have no desire to take a chance, or rock the boat, as you say."

Stephan took another sip of wine.

"Monique and I have approached the people with the ultimate control over these valuable algorithms, and after much negotiation, they have finally agreed, with certain stipulations, to allow Erica to use them. This is a very significant development, and in part, explains the incredible secrecy that you have noticed surrounding the DCG's activities. These people are simpatico, but they do not want to be identified as part of the effort, for many reasons."

Rufus had processed multiple rationales for the secrecy, but had never considered this one. He presumed that keeping the group's activities secret was a logical hedge against people who may want to impede such an effort for political or religious reasons. Not only that, but advanced astrological interpretation capabilities could be dangerous in the wrong hands, as Simon had pointed out during their starlit break from the bonfire at the desert camp. Mostly, Rufus was mindful of the fact that many of the methods under consideration for collecting the vast amounts of data were not exactly legal. Pushing his thoughts aside for a moment, he responded with appreciation.

"In other words, your people are going to save us the trouble of re-inventing the wheel? They're going to give us something to start with."

Stephan's facial expression signaled his growing acceptance. The succinct nature of Rufus's comment had made an impression.

"Yes, with two main conditions. First, if your efforts are discovered and such a discovery could potentially harm our organization, we will reserve the right to disavow any involvement in your cause. Second, if your efforts result in any real improvements to astrological interpretation, we will have certain rights to that new intellectual property. This second point is what has made the negotiations difficult. Even now, it is unclear exactly what this means. It will have to be negotiated on its merits, if and when the DCG is successful. There are those in your group who want absolutely no commercial use of your work, for any reason, never, ever. On our side, there are people who believe that you will be able to share your success without compromising your principles."

"Stephan, will you be involved in our effort?"

"I will monitor progress on behalf of my people. Monique will remain your primary contact. Erica is really the one in charge because she is footing the bill. The DCG will receive the most actual assistance from a man named Lukas, who you will meet tonight. He will work closely with Walter. Lukas is the software guy. He will install your copy of our program, and prepare it for acceptance of the new data as it is collected. If the effort is as successful as we hope, he will be the one to write the code for the new chart interpretation software. The project will take years, not months."

Not knowing Walter's actual role, Rufus could not help but ask.

"I just met Walter, but only for a minute. What is his role?"

Stephan appeared surprised that Rufus did not know.

"Walter, my friend, is the hardware guy. He will be the man to whom all the data is funneled. He may not look like it, but Walter is a computer genius. He doesn't write software, but he has a great deal of experience building servers to handle huge amounts of data. On top of that, he was one of the pioneers of the cloud. As if that weren't enough, Walter knows so many people in the data storage business that he may be one our biggest assets when the front-line hackers are trying to gain access to this or that."

Their conversation was interrupted by a dinner bell. Monique brought Rufus another beer, and offered to show him the way to the dining room. Stephan declined the invitation to join them, indicating that he would await the return of his friend.

Rufus was a bit overwhelmed at all he had learned from Stephan. Monique took advantage of this, leading him around the corner to the side of the house where the veranda offered the view of the City. Physically facing him in the direction of the lights, she put her arm around him and pressed her small frame into his side, hugging him, as if with appreciation, or celebration.

"Monsieur Rufus, I know you are feeling good. You now know that you are not alone. Your dreams can come true."

For Rufus, in that moment, Monique felt like an angel. She was this mysterious, beautiful spirit, offering him guidance and support on his journey. But it wasn't just about this woman Monique. Rufus could not even feel her physical body embracing his own. Instead, he felt that incredible feeling, of being exactly where he was supposed to be in that moment. It was capturing that fleeting sensation, experiencing it more often, and making it more accessible to people, that was his motivation. If a person's actual life path coincided with his astrological path, even for an instant, the sensation was ecstatic and indescribable.

Chapter 25. Money Talks

After a sumptuous four course dinner in the large formal dining room, the fourteen guests were alerted to Erica's remarks by the ceremonial tapping of silver on crystal. During dinner, Rufus remembered that Erica was one of the people he had met in the desert. Instead of jeans and flannel, this elegant heiress, dressed to the nines, was ready to address her dinner guests from the head of the table.

"Thank you so much for coming tonight. I have had such a good time, and it appears to me that you have had a good time as well. If I have neglected to visit with each and every one of you, please forgive me. I will get to you."

She looked right at Rufus when she said that, which made Monique giggle just a bit.

"The basket of benefits I have reaped from my association with some of you eminent astrologers is over-flowing. Even before I started my foundation, I consulted astrologers. But so many of the principles inherent in my philanthropy were only truly refined through the insights I have gained from you. Thank you."

She raised her glass, looked at Walter for approval, or perhaps guidance, and then continued.

"As some of you know, we are moving the headquarters of our foundation to the mountains. We are very excited about this. We are constructing a wonderful facility, one that will rival the features of a small college campus, while having the appearance and amenities of a resort. We are calling it the Institute for Humanistic Innovation, or IHI."

Monique began to politely applaud, inducing the other guests to follow suit.

"We will be providing an environment where deserving people, with noble ideas, can come and work on their particular campaigns. Religious, sociological, cultural, scientific, environmental, whatever we deem worthy. I am dedicating all of my time, and great resources, to the pursuit of whatever will make this planet a better place. I do not presume to have the answers, or even know the questions, but I can offer support to those who propose innovative ways to help mankind. It is my opinion that many charitable and philanthropic endeavors are at risk of becoming stagnant and ineffectual. In some cases, the efforts are too bureaucratic, and in others, too authoritarian. We are dedicated to finding creative ways to approach humanity's limitations. We want to support the people with the most innovative ideas, thus the name for our new Institute. My dear people, I know I am rambling, so I will now turn things over to my dear Walter."

Walter stood up and held her chair while she sat down.

"Thank you my dear. I am honored to be your right hand man on this project."

Turning to the guests, Walter made his pitch.

"You know why you're here. You all want to make astrology more accountable. You want to make it a more useful tool. Although I am not personally well versed in astrology, I do know systems."

He paused, going for his wine glass.

"We've decided that one of the best ways to help some of these well-meaning people that Erica refers to is to get them some computing power. So, one of the major distinguishing features of the Institute will be the supercomputer that I'm going to build. Your astrology project will be just one of many tasks for my supercomputer."

Walter, looking so proud and 'chairman of the boardish', impulsively grabbed his cigar, but Erica quietly shook her head "no" as she reached over to remove his hand from his lighter.

'We're going to be upfront about its existence. Besides, making the kind of hardware purchases necessary, in a surreptitious manner, would be impossible. But we don't necessarily have to be upfront about everything we're using it for, if you know what I mean. After dinner, Monique will visit with each of you. She will be the one who will let you know what happens next. In the meantime, enjoy yourselves, and thanks for coming."

As it turned out, Monique's role was nothing more than telling each guest when it was their turn to meet with Lukas. He had set up shop in the wine cellar. Relying on dossiers prepared by Monique, Lukas planned to interview each of the DCG operatives individually, before any final decisions would be made about assignments. There were nine of them, including Rufus. They would report only to Walter, or his appointed representative, and only as specifically instructed. They were not to meet without Walter's approval, communicate with one another, or collaborate in any way, without specific permission.

Rufus's reputation as one of the most avid supporters of advanced data collection, along with Monique's talent for persuasion, earned him the honor of being interviewed first. Monique escorted him to the wine cellar and left him alone with Lukas.

Slightly taller and more muscular than Rufus, yet eerily similar in terms of certain Germanic features, Lukas appeared more the alpine athlete than the computer nerd. A little older than Stephan and Monique, he spoke with a thick accent, explaining that he was actually an Austrian citizen. Unlike Stephan, Lukas approached Rufus in a very sensitive, inquisitive manner. He wanted to hear Rufus's thoughts first.

The alcohol and large meal served to soften the delivery. Considering Rufus's pent up desire to seriously communicate his ideas, this was a very fortunate thing for Lukas. After politely gauging Lukas's knowledge of astrology, Rufus shared his thoughts about data collection. The traditional approach, erecting a natal chart and searching for correlations with the actual events of people's lives, during some kind of personal interview, he believed, did offer some justification of astrology's worth. But Rufus contended that these bodies of work, these portfolios of chart interpretations compiled by the greatest astrologers, didn't really prove anything. According to Rufus, what traditionally served as "data collection" was limited to the subjective examination of the lives of far too few people, and was more anecdotal than empirically scientific.

To skilled astrologers and their followers, these pseudo-objective chart interpretations appeared to support the possibility that the motion of celestial bodies had some kind of influence. But they don't evoke any meaningful sense of credibility in the mind of the average person. This wishful veil of objectivity the astrologer draped over the chart was indeed a thin one, easily pulled back at the first hint of suspicion. Rufus was the first one to admit, like it or not, that most people considered astrology to be a totally subjective art form, an intriguing first cousin of tarot cards, séances, and ouija boards.

Rufus confessed that he was not surprised that astrology had remained nothing more than an interesting activity, a curiosity, a pastime. But he wanted so desperately to raise its stature to something more significant and enduring than cult or superstition.

When he finally finished his diatribe, Rufus seemed relieved, and then strangely embarrassed, when it struck him that he was preaching to the choir. Lukas was already well aware of the limitations of modern astrology's idea of data collection, or he wouldn't have been there.

"I believe you have presented an excellent rationale for the endeavor we are undertaking. Considering your background as a scientist, I'm sure you know that we will never really be able to 'prove' anything. We will merely lend support to the theory, yes?"

"Yes."

"Rufus, other than your enthusiasm, and your vast knowledge, what data sources can you personally help us access?"

Rufus arrived back on earth with a thud. Lukas's question instantly let all the air out of his eloquent philosophical justifications. It was time to put up, or shut up.

"Well, I may have a way into the census bureau, and I'm working on access to internet marketing data, browsing history, credit card use, that kind of thing. I realize I need to make the transition from concept to actual data gathering. My biggest concern is birth times. How will we get to all those birth certificates?"

He felt self-conscious for the first time since he arrived at Walter and Erica's home. Lukas's challenging question had brought him right back to reality. How was he going to contribute to the actual acquisition of data? The DCG didn't need leadership. It needed operatives with computer skills and people who could make inroads into the world of big data. Lukas seemed neither

impressed nor disappointed, but Rufus, at the risk of
appearing defensive, offered more.

"I do know some young computer geniuses who may
be able to help."

Rufus knew he was being presumptuous to think
Petey or Matthew would actually agree to help him, but he
felt it was time to pull out all the stops. Besides, he had
given their involvement a great deal of thought. He just
didn't have all the answers yet.

"That is excellent. I mean, that you have people you
can trust, and perhaps control. You will need people who
can help you with the chain of deniability. Now, let me
lay out for you how I think we should proceed. Feel free
to interrupt or ask questions at any time."

Rufus listened intently, distracted only by the
sensation of certainty that Lukas was definitely someone
he could work with.

"Reflecting on what you have so eloquently implied,
the data set has to be large, and it has to be random.
Stephan has probably told you what some of our
colleagues prefer, to acquire data on the people who
currently make up our customer base. But even if every
person who requested a horoscope agreed to offer the
actual details of their life for examination, and astrological
correlation, the sample would still be way too small.
Also, if the results were only based on people who sought
out astrology, the study could be criticized on the basis of
confirmation bias, or pre-conceived notion theory. How
would we determine whether particular tendencies had
been suggested to these people, or whether they were
actually indicated in the natal horoscope?

"I agree completely, Lukas."

"We can start with census data, assuming that your
contact will help us. By itself, it will be only so useful, but
it offers a foundation. Next, we will pursue birth time
data. This will be more difficult to obtain, as you have

mentioned. If we can obtain birth time data for a large portion of the individuals in the census sample, that would be great. As we go forward, there will be many things that will limit the eventual sample size. But, in the long run, we need to have a sample size in the tens of millions."

Rufus wasn't shocked by Lukas's goal for a sample size. His goal was more like one hundred million, but it was no time to quibble.

"I agree that we have to start with the census data, or something like it."

"What do you mean, 'something like it'?"

"I'm hoping that we can discover a link from census to some higher level, a data base that has already reconciled census data, name, address, all that, maybe even social security number, IP address, and phone number."

"Yes, we may stumble across a pot of gold, Rufus, but I am not at all certain that the DCG has that much of an appetite for risk, especially at this point in the campaign. The chances of getting caught stealing census data or birth time data will be relatively low. But dangling your noodle into government data bases, or data bases controlled by certain powerful, information age people, could easily land you in jail, or even somewhere more permanent, if you know what I mean."

"I know, you're right, but I just can't help but think about the amount of data that is being accumulating by the government, internet search companies, and social media companies. If we could figure out how to access it without getting caught, that would be the berries. We're not trying to steal peoples' identities or peddle their credit card numbers. We just want to profile people."

As Rufus spoke these words, both men started to laugh. However convinced the two men were about the worth of their project, they had to admit that Rufus's profiling statement sounded pretty ridiculous.

Feeling satisfied that they had accomplished great things, Rufus was the one to suggest an end to the meeting. It had been a long day, and he just wanted to rejoin Monique. With his desire for the serious finally fulfilled, all he really wanted was more of her.

"Lukas, this experience has been better than I could have ever imagined. We are of like mind. We know what kinds of information we need to collect, and over time, we will. But right now, we're beginning to sound like a mutual admiration society, and you have many more people to interview."

Appreciative of Lukas's laugh of agreement, Rufus rose from his seat and stretched his long arms above his head, and then out to the side, several times. He was feeling physically tight, right when his spirit was loose and soaring. He offered his allegiance to Lukas.

"You know my resolve. I find you a very capable warrior, and I cannot adequately express how happy I am to meet you. I look forward to our next meeting."

"Likewise. But there is only one more thing. You must agree with the idea of zero communication between you and I, unless it is in person, of course."

"I understand. At every turn, we will learn another reason for absolute secrecy. I assume you will contact me through Monique?"

"That is the most likely way. You may occasionally receive instructions or information by regular mail, or delivery service, which you will know to trust when it includes the word 'extropian'."

Rufus smiled, wondering if Lukas realized that he was actually familiar with this very obscure term.

"Not too many people know that word, Lukas. I am only a meliorist, but I do understand that extropians exist. Can I now say I have met one?"

"Do you mean me, or do you mean Walter?"

The two men shared yet another laugh. Rufus couldn't help but wonder how long it would be before he would see Lukas again. He really liked him, and felt an overwhelming sense of certainty that he would be spending time with him in the future.

Lukas shook his hand and showed him to the door. He had apparently texted Monique to bring the next DCG operative, because Rufus met them coming down the stairs to the wine cellar.

Chapter 26. Leaning Home

An early breakfast meeting with Liz was exactly what Rufus didn't need. Only the bounty of choice hot tea offered hope that he would get through it. Besides, it was his only commitment until afternoon. He couldn't wait to spend the late morning in the hotel Jacuzzi.

"Rufus, I want you to know you were right. I have gotten so many comments from academics that say they cannot fault your research. So, no attack from that corner, as I feared, praise the Lord. That's one less thing to worry about. Who knows, if the John Q. Smith sales keep picking up, we might be onto something. There are a lot of people out there who may be reshuffling their views on religion."

She took off her glasses and reached over to touch the hand of this sleepy man.

"How are you Rufus? Sorry to talk shop before breakfast."

"Not to worry, Liz. I don't know how I could have done it without you. You have been fantastic. I'm really happy. I had a late night, as you can probably tell. I may look pretty on the outside, but on the inside, I'm struggling."

"I understand, honey. I just hope it was worth it."

"It was, Liz, and that's all I'm saying."

Liz assumed that Rufus had gotten caught up in the New York City night life, and politely let him off the hook. Liz had never met Katie, but she had no reason to assume that Rufus was anything other than happily married.

"I wasn't sure how long you would be in the City, so I brought the updated tour schedule with me. I'll email you any changes, OK?"

She placed his copy on the table so he could read it.

"Other than here in the northeast, sales are best out west and up north. You can just about imagine how the book is being received down south. Let's just say, not at all."

She laughed and playfully feigned righteous indignation, as if to say, "what do they know, anyway?"

"I don't know how you really feel about these events, but let me tell you, they sell books. Especially for a book like yours that may have a limited audience on the front end, we need some buzz, and frankly Rufus, you are a compelling character in person."

Although Rufus was not crazy about personal appearances, he was ready to do what he had to. He was already beginning to savor the freedom that the book money could bring.

"I've arranged for Minneapolis and Seattle in July, and saved California for November. After a book fair in West Hollywood, we'll drive up to San Francisco for the Symposium. By then, you will have had enough practice to handle those ecumenical types."

"We?"

"Yes Evan. You're not the only author I have, and you're not the only reason I have to go to California. But you are one of the more interesting people I know. Besides, we need to talk about your next book."

"Boy, you really know how to take advantage of a man with a hangover."

"If you ever want to take Katie with you, the northern trip would be the one she would probably enjoy the most, you know. I'll see that everything is paid for. Think about it."

"Whatever you say, my dear Liz. I owe you. But keep in mind that my wife is not crazy about flying on airplanes."

"Well. OK. Let's see. I'm working on something in Chicago for December. Weather permitting, maybe you two could drive up there."

"I promise I will give the Minneapolis/Seattle trip my best shot. I'll let you know. I do think Katie would like Seattle. It's one of the places we have talked about going."

After breakfast, Rufus returned to the hotel. There was a message for him at the desk, to be in his room at 2 PM. It was from Monique.

After breakfast, he called Katie. Everything was OK back home. Liz's suggestion that his wife accompany him on one of his excursions gave him something more exciting to talk about, since he wasn't ready to share anything about the DCG, and obviously couldn't talk about Monique. He was smart enough to leave it to Katie's imagination how he was occupying himself when he was not signing books.

Rejuvenated by his time in the hot tub and pool, Rufus alternatively napped and pondered the discussions of the previous evening. Given Monique's penchant for intrigue, he had no way of predicting what was going to happen at 2 PM. He was ready for anything when he answered the knock on the door.

It was Walter.

"I can't stay long partner. Lukas and I decided to split the follow up duties. All nine of you had to be contacted with your final instruction, and one of these."

He removed an envelope from his suit pocket and laid it on the table.

"We'll get to that in a minute. Here's our near term strategy. Each of these nine illustrious members of this DCG thing have at least some chance of helping us access the kind of data we need. Your contact in the census department sounds pretty good, for example. For now, just find out if the person is really willing to help us. We can help mitigate risk. You won't have to operate on your own."

Walter walked over and stared out the window.

"The main reason I'm here this afternoon is to assure you that whoever does the hacking will be supported, financially and legally. Very few of the nine of you are proficient hackers. But at least some of you can arrange for someone who is, and provide the necessary guidance. In many cases, the hackers are young people who feel they have nothing to lose, and everything to gain. I'm sure you remember the 'devil may care' attitude of youth."

With that, he turned to make eye contact with Rufus.

"But they also need cash. You probably remember that about your younger days too."

Rufus was feeling a little anxious. He couldn't guarantee being able to deliver Petey or Matthew.

"Walter, I'm not absolutely certain these two young men I have in mind will be agreeable, but I will try."

"Oh, don't worry about it. I'm sure it'll work out. If not them, then some other young upstarts. They're out there. It would just be better if you have some guys you can trust. Just remember to tell 'em we can fix it so the hacks will be hardly noticeable, or seem innocuous, or just cannot be traced. We have lots of tools at our disposal. The most important thing is to proceed in a workman-like manner. We never want to get desperate. We'll always stop and look at the big picture before we push any buttons. We'll never proceed with a hack unless we are absolutely sure that we can pull it off without being detected."

"Walter. Thank you for that. It makes it easier to consider involving these young people. I keep reminding myself, we're not trying to steal credit card numbers or tap bank accounts. We're collecting jigsaw puzzle pieces, billions of puzzle pieces, from millions of different jigsaw puzzles. When we have enough pieces, we'll try to construct a scene that makes sense. The whole process will take some time."

Walter shook his hand in a gesture of admiration, the way he did at their first meeting.

"I've got a couple of things that will help."

Walter walked over to the table where he had left the envelope, picked it up, and began thumbing through its contents.

"First, here's twenty-thousand dollars. Each of the nine of you gets your allowance today. Keep it in reserve for paying your hackers or greasing the palms of people who can help you access the data. I can get instructions to you after today, but this way, I won't have to worry about getting you untraceable money. Some things have to be done in person."

"Second, I'm giving you a phone number of a technical support guy. Commit it to memory. Later on, when your little hacker boys need help, this will be the number to call. You must personally make the call, and it must be from a throw away phone. The person on the line will have ways of verifying that it is you. Once he knows it's you, he will talk to your boys. Rufus, don't even think about letting one of them call the number. You understand?"

"Yes, Walter. I understand."

"Good. I know you do. I hate to be so abrupt. It's kind of ironic, me being in a hurry, because this whole thing is actually going to move at a snail's pace. The actual construction of the Institute is moving along nicely, and I've ordered most of the hardware I need for my supercomputer. I'm feeling quite confident, actually. Besides, it will make my wife very happy. She's working so hard to give away her inheritance. She says she's especially excited about the Institute, because it's a more permanent legacy. I think she likes the idea because she'll be able to spend the money faster. It's fine with me either way. Not only do I get to spend more time in the mountains, but I have a great project to work on in my retirement."

As Walter exited the hotel room, he turned to Rufus and winked.

"Monique said she'd pick you up downstairs at six, and that you should dress casual."

Walter out the door, Rufus just stood there for a moment, as if he were trapped in a time warp and needed to reboot reality. He was overtaken with the sensation of being an actor in a film, uncertain if he were really Rufus, or some character being subsumed by forces of a plot over which he had little control. In an attempt to calm himself, he lay down on the bed, on his back, and closed his eyes.

The next scene in the movie came when Monique found him in the lobby of the hotel. Always eager to have fun with the ruse of romance, she greeted Rufus like a long lost lover. Thankfully, Rufus was accustomed to her seductive ways, and knew better than to take her 'over the top' performance too seriously. But he did enjoy it.

"The third time is the charm, Monsieur Rufus. This evening is strictly about you and me. Whenever I invite you to dinner, it turns out to be something more, something different. Tonight we just have fun."

Rufus was excited, but strangely calm, as he headed out into the street with Monique. His readiness for a good time was tempered, though only a little bit, by thoughts of returning home with so many secrets. He would be departing in the morning.

Monique apparently knew just what Rufus wanted to

do. She took him to the after work hot spots that featured pretty girls, handsome young men, and copious amounts of friendly chatter. Travelling on foot or by taxi, they visited many such watering holes before settling into a quiet dinner at a French restaurant.

Monique shared stories of her thirty years on the planet, opening up to Rufus in a way that she had not done before. Her accounts of young love gained and lost stirred memories for Rufus, whose twenties were a tumultuous time of obsession and romance. On this night, Rufus couldn't help but fantasize that Monique was the living breathing composite of the two women he had fallen so deeply in love with when he was young. His first was a vivacious temptress, who possessed a pouty power over his youthful penchant for lustful experience. His second was a naturally mysterious woman, a Neptunian goddess, spiritually evocative to the core, who introduced him to a vast ethereal landscape that he may never have discovered, if not for her. Each had broken his heart. Each had made him the tragic character that he would always be. Each had given him the strength to explore and embrace what made him unique.

Monique allowed him to revisit all those dormant feelings, without eliciting actual sensual desires. She was the excitement of untying the bow, tearing off the paper, and opening the present, knowing all along what was in the box.

Eventually, the conversation turned to the love affairs of the present. Rufus offered Monique a polite peak into his relationship with Katie. She made it easy for him to become so vulnerable by confiding that she was involved with Stephan and considering marriage. She claimed she loved him, but was reticent to marry him, because of her ambivalence about having children. This gave Rufus yet another chance to feel close to Monique. Knowing the reality of a childless marriage, he was able to empathize, but knew better than to offer advice.

After dinner, it was north to Harlem for jazz and blues. Rufus was a man who knew his music, and Monique was a woman who was familiar with New York. The two of them settled into a multi-layered, wholesome, genuine friendship, as they finally stopped questioning what their relationship was about. "Tonight we just have fun" was a prediction that was coming true.

Before Monique said goodbye to Rufus outside the door of his hotel room, she signaled to him that she wanted just once to feel his embrace, not as her friend, not as her contact, and not as her partner in a ruse of romance. She felt compelled to offer him one chance to steal a taste of forbidden fruit. She didn't know why, and she knew it was crazy, but she wanted him to know he could actually have her, if that was his final choice.

The kiss was long, and sweet. For a moment, only their spirits existed. When the physical body was about to overrule the spirit, Rufus let her go. He locked his eyes with hers and thanked her. As she slowly backed down the hallway to the elevator, she never stopped grinning. The look on her face was like "I know a secret and I'm not going to tell".

Rufus worshipped her essence. He knew how much he wanted to bask in the warm glow of her soul. But strangely, even in the midst of what was undeniable ecstasy, there was nothing overwhelmingly erotic. He could value her. He could idealize her. But he could not possess her. Monique was a rare, beautiful bird who proudly shared her courtship dance, but had to fly away, to preserve herself.

CHAPTER 27. BACK TO KATIE

Katie was ready for Rufus to be home. The sheep were no problem, but the dogs really missed him. The coyotes seemed to know when Rufus was away. Katie knew there was no real danger, but she worried anyway, not about the sheep, but about the dogs. They could sense that the shepherd was not there to back them up.

Despite the backlog of farm chores, it was an excellent time of year to be coming home. Katie had the swimming pool sparkling, and Mother Nature had provided supportive weather for early garden crops, filling dinner plates with organic spinach, peas, and asparagus.

For Rufus, the most important item on the agenda for June was fulfilling his promise to take Robert and his friends on the river. He and Robert had discussed some tentative dates before the New York trip, but he couldn't wait to find out the latest. He was hoping that the boys would select a three day period that would work for Thomas and his son John.

Rufus called Robert very early on the morning of his trip to town to buy feed for the sheep. They agreed to meet at Grandpa Samuel's farm around lunch time. It was only a few miles from the feed store. Rufus had this thing about talking to someone in person, if at all possible, rather than on the phone.

Knowing that Samuel and Robert would be working in the hay all morning, Rufus decided to show up with BBQ carry out. He had no doubt that Samuel would work Robert hard and then offer him little more than bologna sandwiches for lunch. Besides, Rufus welcomed any chance to make points with Samuel.

After a wonderful lunch, with entertainment provided by Rufus's skillful deflections of Samuel's inquiries as to why he was leaving his daughter alone all the time, and "running around God knows where", Samuel went out to service the baler. This afforded Rufus and his nephew a chance to talk before Robert had to remount the tractor to rake hay.

"Rufus, it couldn't be any better. Andrew and Petey are definitely on board. Matthew is pretty sure he can get off work. He's just worried about money. I told him the float trip wouldn't cost him anything. The neat thing is that he seemed more committed when he found out Petey was coming. He really likes Petey."

"Good. But did you make sure to invite your father?"

"Yes, but let me tell you. There is no way. Not only is he kind of afraid of getting out on the water, but he's always talking about how he can't possibly take off from work. His new job really keeps him busy. They have a lot of new projects."

"That's fine. Not only do I want him to feel included because he is your father, and it's your graduation present, but I've taken the liberty of inviting Thomas and John. Too bad Gary isn't stateside. I know he would enjoy it."

"Yeah, I miss Gary. That would be so cool. By the way, Dad knows you invited Thomas. He seemed to be very glad that you did."

"You haven't mentioned the girls. Was it Cindy? Isn't that Andrew's girlfriend?

Oh my goodness. Robert, what about Jane?"

Forever egalitarian, he wanted Robert to know that he would be glad to have girls on the float trip, if that were the consensus. But Rufus was secretly hoping that there were would be no girls, and he was pretty sure Robert knew his true feelings. Wanting the float trip to be more "outward bound" than summer camp, Rufus was relieved when Robert said the girls would not be coming along.

Rufus laid out the plan.

"I will take care of everything, almost. Each person will be responsible for their own sleep gear, including sleeping bags and tents, if they want to bring tents. All the way up until bedtime, I will be responsible. But how comfortably everyone sleeps will be up to them. The gravel bars are hard and the night air can be chilly, even in summer."

Robert was captivated. He looked like an "A" student sitting in the front seat of his favorite class, intent on capturing each and every detail in his notebook.

"Each person will have their own canoe. I've chosen a stretch of the river that will allow for the first day to be about learning how to steer. I will provide all breakfast and dinner each day we are on the river. Lunch and snacks will be up to each individual. I will take care of camp fires and cooking fires, but recommend each man bring multiple light sources. Remind the boys to pack their gear in something waterproof, even if it's just trash bags. Five gallon buckets work great. Everyone will have a life jacket. Any questions so far?"

"Yeah, I can't seem to shake the image of you standing waste deep in the river trying to catch a fish. Is it OK to bring fishing gear?"

"Of course, just make sure to go online and get a license. Now where was I? Oh yes, the schedule. I want everyone to meet at my place on Monday evening. That way, when we get up Tuesday morning, we'll be ready to hit the road. We'll be on the river from Tuesday noon until Thursday late morning. We won't leave a lot of miles to paddle on the last day, so the guys coming from far away will have plenty of time on Thursday to get back home."

"Rufus, it sounds fantastic."

"Now all we need is some good weather. Traditionally, the last week of June in this part of the world is a pretty good bet."

Samuel returned to the house to wash off the grease and announce to young Robert that it was time to get back to raking the hay into 'windrows'. All the alfalfa he had mowed that morning needed to be baled because there was a chance of thunderstorms that evening.

"Samuel, you'll be happy to know that I'll be bringing Katie to church this Sunday."

"Well, I'll be. Maybe there's hope for you yet."

Samuel gave Robert one more gentle nudge and headed for the tractors.

"Robert, call me if you have questions, or have the boys call me direct. I don't mind."

As he finished cleaning up the lunch mess, Rufus made a suggestion, that he was afraid even Robert would consider a little strange.

"Maybe you could collect everyone's birth info before the trip. We can print out everyone's horoscope and have a little fun around the campfire."

"I'm so glad you brought it up. I was thinking about asking them, but I was afraid it would seem a little creepy. If I say it's coming from you, and they can get a free reading. . . . ."

"We'll have them if someone wants to ask a question. No pressure. No planned activity. We'll just have them if we need them."

"I like the way you're thinking."

As he prepared to leave the kitchen, Robert gathered

up his gloves and hat. Suddenly, he turned back to Rufus.

"You didn't tell me anything about your trip. I feel bad for not asking."

"We'll pull our canoes together on some slow stretch of the river, and I'll give you a full report."

Rufus returned home with the sheep feed to find that Katie had decided to take the afternoon off. She was lounging at the pool. With a birthday in just a few days, she was happier than Rufus had seen her in a while. After leaving a voice mail for Thomas, he joined her.

They swam, and drank beer, and talked, in the hot June sun. One thing they had in common, for sure, was a love of coconut oiled bodies soaking up solar radiation. They often joked about absorbing enough to last them through the dingy, cold winters.

"Rufus, I saw your note. I can't believe you're going to church with me on Sunday. Dad must have had a fit."

"I told him I could use some good preachin', after my trip to that heathen haven they call New York City."

She gave him a look that wasn't too different from the look he had gotten from Grandpa Samuel. He swallowed hard and changed the subject.

"Katie, I know I've been leaving you alone too much, but you do understand how important this is to me?"

He approached her chair with a little smooching on his mind, but she wasn't having it.

"When are you going to take me on a float trip? Ginny told me about Robert's graduation present. What about my present?"

She knew Rufus would do just about anything for her, but she couldn't resist screwing with his head a little bit. She didn't really want to go canoeing.

"Katie, you know I'll take you floating whenever you say. But what I really want is for you to go with me to Minneapolis and Seattle in July. Have you decided? I can get Robert to stay here. He's not working this summer, except for your father, and all the hay will be in soon. C'mon, girl. We haven't been anywhere together for a long time. I know you'll love Seattle."

"If you get Robert to stay here, I'll go. Someone I trust has to be here to take care of the dogs. I won't leave them alone. You know that. And I mean stay here, not just come by and feed."

Rufus was so happy. He tried again to get all kissy face, and started to meet with some success.

That evening, Thomas called back with the good news. He and John would be able to come. After discussing the schedule and who was bringing what, the two men pursued a rather intimate conversation about Rufus's book. Thomas was almost too impressed. Rufus was beginning to realize that Thomas was transforming from friend to disciple, which caused him some concern. It was important that Thomas agree to help the DCG, but Rufus wanted it to be of his own free will. After their conversation, Rufus descended into a solemn, private place for a long time, and came up resolved to put their friendship first, regardless of whether Thomas offered to help the DCG.

Chapter 28. Canoe Club

When he watched the reunion of the boys on the pool deck that Monday night before the great float, Rufus could not help but reminisce about his younger days. He had enjoyed so many great friendships and experiences. He was sensitive to the fact that America had become so conservative, and worried about present day young people having enough room to move.

Other than an occasional reminder to Robert that John was the odd man out, he left the young men to their own devices. They had a lot of catching up to do. Rufus fed them, answered questions about their gear, but didn't try to direct their activities. Rufus knew the boys would get plenty of exposure to him on the river.

Thomas expressed great joy at being away from the city life. Freely acknowledging that it had been far too long since he had done anything fun, he was quite animated. Sharing a bottle of homemade wine, he and Rufus prepared the food and beverage coolers for the trip. Tuesday lunch through Thursday breakfast meant preparing two lunches, two breakfasts, and two dinners, for seven men. Tuesday breakfast on the way to the river would be the boys' last taste of "fast food", while Thursday lunch would be at Rufus's favorite country café near the takeout.

In the morning, John opted to ride with Rufus and Thomas. He thanked the other boys for the invitation to ride with them, but said he preferred to stretch out in the backseat of Rufus's vehicle. Only Robert knew the truth, that John was hooked on listening to the older men.

John's decision was problematic for Rufus, who was ready to ask Thomas to consider helping the DCG access the census bureau data base. But the forever philosophical Rufus rationalized that spending quality time strengthening his friendship with Thomas might prove just as valuable.

Thomas was proud to report that John was not only gainfully employed as an apprentice at a cabinet shop, but he had been accepted to pursue woodworking at the local vocational school. After considerable work on John's chart, and hours of consultation with Thomas, Rufus had come to the conclusion that John's way forward depended on his ability to work with his hands. It was something worth trying. Previous attempts to divert John from a path that was strewn with destructive relationships had failed because they only suggested what not to do. John needed something to do. His only sin growing up was being too impressionable. He was often victimized by friends with crazy ideas and easy access to alcohol. John's current push down the path toward genuine self-esteem, the only true defense against temptations dangled in front of an idle mind, was now literally in his own hands.

They arrived at the "put in" to find seven canoes poised to head down the river. The canoe outfitter had provided drivers to deliver Petey and Rufus's vehicles to the "take out", some twenty-six miles downriver. As the drivers departed the gravel bar, the boys started to grasp the reality of the situation. Their transportation was now a canoe, and their communication capability was as basic as a caveman's. Rufus had required that they leave their smart phones behind in the vehicles.

Robert's friends on the river were a sight to behold. Given the boys' widely varied athletic abilities and water related experience, the first couple of miles were quite bizarre. In spite of a lot of minor crashes and zigzagging, the need for expert advice was not as great as Rufus had expected. But the boys did have lots of advice for each other. Unfortunately, it was the kind where everyone was talking and nobody was listening.

For the most part, Rufus's initial canoeing lesson appeared to be sufficient. In the first few miles, no one crashed or capsized. The truth be known, Rufus wasn't even worried about the boys. They were young and durable. He was concerned about the coolers each one was asked to carry in the front of their canoe. Lots of good food and drink was at risk.

When they stopped for lunch, Rufus took care of a little business. He reminded the boys of the legalities associated with fishing. Also, having been told by Robert that both Petey and Matthew liked to partake of the weed, he told a true story about an old friend whose float trip was ruined by the actions of an overzealous conservation agent. But mostly, he wanted them to understand his dilemma as the person responsible for the float.

"As the most experienced river man, I have to bring up the rear, in case one of you has trouble and needs assistance. But I'm also the one who knows how to recognize the best gravel bars for camping. So here's what we're going to do."

He pulled a river map from his bucket and beckoned Robert to come and look.

"Never venture more than a hundred feet ahead of Robert. He will be the one to spot the trail to the old mill spring. When you get there, stop, go on up the trail to the spring, and wait there for me and Thomas. Hopefully, the gravel bar just below the spring will be open for us to

camp on   I want you to have fun this afternoon. Stop and
swim, fish, whatever you want, just have fun. But don't
overshoot the spring, because that would mean
overshooting the camp site."

All the boys chimed in, guaranteeing Rufus that they
understood. Robert remembered his float with Rufus the
previous summer and assured him that he would spot the
trail to the spring. He was confident even though this was
a completely different river. Robert was notably nervous,
but apparently not about his assignment

"Rufus, can I talk with you alone?"

"Of course, Robert. C'mon, I have to pee."

No one paid much attention as they traversed the
gravel bar in the direction of the woods.

"Petey wanted me to ask you if it was really OK if we
get high, since you brought it up. I know Matthew's on
board. The thing is, Andrew heard them talking about it,
and he's interested, which I'm a little surprised about. But
I thought I better ask you about John."

"You can't very well keep it from John. So be upfront
about it with him and let him make his own choice.
Thomas is prepared. We talked about it. Don't worry.
Thomas knows it's a risk, but he also knows that John has
to make his own decisions. I'm all for smoking some herb.
The only reason I mentioned it was that I didn't want
people to get careless. Being on the river can elicit a
wonderful feeling of being totally free, and make you
forget that someone could be watching from a cliff top.
It's one in a million, but that's what happened to my
friend."

"Thanks, Rufus. I'll make sure everyone is cool."

As expected, Robert did successfully identify the trail
head. As Rufus and Thomas completed the short walk up
the trail, and observed the boys enjoying the mind
numbing dives into the cold clear water of the mill spring,
it was obvious that the boys had settled the marijuana

issue. The sun was hot, and the first day of the journey was exceeding everyone's expectations. Petey felt good about his coronation as king pot head and proudly designated Matthew as his loyal prince. Robert and John pledged their allegiance, and helped Andrew with how to smoke just enough to fit in and have fun, without getting totally fried.

After the spring, they stayed together so they wouldn't miss the gravel bar that Rufus had in mind for their first night's camp. Providing the perfect river experience was a lot of work, but Rufus had only himself to blame. He insisted on providing gourmet meals and as many of the amenities of home as he could. He put the stoners to work collecting firewood and preparing their beds for the night.

Feeling their age, and having had too many beers in the hot sun, Rufus and Thomas turned in early, leaving the boys to share starlit stories around the campfire. As he prepared for sleep, Rufus enjoyed the thought that the hard part was over. He looked forward to more relaxation on day number two. Many times, he had experienced the transition day phenomenon, and he never failed to appreciate its power.

Each of the boys would wake up the next morning, dew soaked by the moist night air of the river, and emotionally captivated by its relentless gentle flow. Having allowed the river to transport them to a place where they could dream pure dreams, they would wake up transformed by the constancy of its spirit. Feeling like they had grown taller over night, they would rise, and effortlessly settle into a day of self-discovery that they would remember for the rest of their lives. As Rufus drifted off to sleep, he surely looked forward to the next day, when he would bare his soul, confide his plan, and beg recruits.

Chapter 29. No Guts, No Glory

The group would encounter the most challenging water on the second day. There were two runs that would test their nerves and athleticism, the first one in the morning, and the second one later in the day.

They hadn't gone very far down the river before Rufus ordered them to pull over. They had arrived at one of his favorite spots. It had something for everyone: fishing, swimming, bathing, depending on your persuasion. Being careful to promote a sense of excitement rather than a sense of danger, Rufus assembled the group and apprised them of the day's first canoeing challenge.

The first interesting run they would encounter couldn't really be called a "rapids". It wasn't all that fast, but it was long, and strangely alluring. Essentially straight, it required nothing more than a good approach, a watchful eye, and timely changes of direction. Many large boulders lurked just beneath the surface. The only clues to safe passage were portrayed in the subtle shimmers and swirls of the water flowing over the top of them. There were no sharp turns, so it wasn't about being an expert paddler. But if you didn't identify your path far enough ahead of time, you risked scraping the top of the boulder just enough to be helplessly twisted around and dumped into the drink. It was about lead time. Complacency or indecision could spell disaster.

An hour later, when they arrived at the head of this long captivating run, Robert signaled them all to pull over. Rufus had told him what to look for. Everyone assumed that it was time for last minute instructions, but Rufus actually just wanted to share a story.

"One time, after I had been canoeing for over thirty years, I was invited by some friends to float a fast river in the spring. Toward the end of the first day, there was a rapids that demanded respect. The five canoes stopped at its head, just like we're doing today. Each person shared their experience with that particular run, at that water level. When the conversation turned its focus away from the river, to a completely unrelated topic, I became impatient. Slightly inebriated, and feeling way too proud, I suddenly proclaimed that I would go first, and prepared to depart. No one said a word. Aware my vast canoeing experience, they just let me go."

"I chose the left side of the run. It took less than thirty seconds, with the help of some indecision, to expose my poor judgment. My canoe struck a large boulder, capsized, and ended up completely underwater, hopelessly wedged against some submerged rocks, crossways. I was not seriously hurt and managed to stay with the canoe. After their own successful runs down the middle and the right, my comrades had to come back upstream on foot, along a shear granite bluff, to help me. I was cold and humiliated."

Intrigued by the story, but notably anxious to get going, Matthew bravely interjected.

"I think we get it. I will be glad to follow you, Rufus. We will all be glad to follow you. I just want to get to that swimmin' hole you been talkin' about."

"Enough talk then. Let's go. I'll go first. Start twenty

seconds behind me. One at a time, every twenty seconds, first Robert, then Petey, then Thomas, then John, then Matthew, then Andrew. I've got Andrew last because he is the strongest amongst us, and may also be the best swimmer. Same reason that Matthew is second to last."

Just about to step into his boat, Rufus turned toward them once more for that all important comprehension check.

"I hope you know the moral of the story."

The boys offered their various takes. When they were finished, Rufus helped them out.

"Don't screw up, because we don't want to have to save you."

That got a cautious laugh all around, each boy wondering whether or not he was joking.

"OK, now let's do as Matthew suggests. On to the swimming hole!"

Just as the second man was about to set off, Rufus stood up in his canoe, held his paddle high over his head with both hands and screamed.

"C'mon, you sodie suckin' cake eaters! You pixie stick lickers."

This time he was the only one laughing.

Caught off guard by Rufus's playful insult, their newfound motivation had them falling all over themselves to ready their boats and get in position to take off. Rufus was still laughing.

On the way down, Petey actually did encounter one of those boulders. Although he did make a few scary noises, and some awkward, unplanned rotations, he never lost his cool. In other words, he kept his side-to-side balance. He took on a little water, spent a fair amount of time going backwards, but stayed in the boat all the way down the run. It wasn't pretty. Everyone realized that the only perspective that mattered was Petey's, and he was grinning ear to ear during the entire experience. With a minimum amount of assistance, and a maximum amount of encouragement, Petey came through it just fine.

Each of the boys was eager to tell his own tale when they arrived at the high bluffs around the bend. After everyone was finished sharing their exhilaration, and playfully jabbing Petey for his unorthodox style, Rufus laid down the law. They had arrived at one of the most perfect diving/jumping rock outcrops on the river. But no one was to do any jumping, much less diving, until at least two of the stronger swimmers had checked out what was below. Rufus knew that the water was plenty deep, but he wasn't going to miss an opportunity to teach river safety.

"Thomas and I are going to leave this one to you. We're going to cross the river and hike as far as we can up the bluff, so don't do anything stupid. Matthew, you're in charge."

The boys all started laughing, knowing that Matthew was the biggest daredevil among them.

Once Rufus and Thomas had changed into jeans and hiking boots, Rufus returned to his canoe one more time. He produced a Frisbee, and making a perfect toss to Andrew, he said nothing. He was absolutely certain the boys would figure out what to do with it. He had fond memories of mid-jump Frisbee catches on the river. How he had wowed the young ladies with each acrobatic catch. It was sweetly satisfying to achieve that perfect timing between the person throwing from the gravel bar and the person jumping off the rock.

After a half hour long circuitous journey up and around to the back of the steep hill that sported the magnificent bluff on its river side, the two older men finally reached a primo vantage point. Almost two hundred feet above the river, they could share the perspective of the turkey vultures, buzzards, and the occasional hawk soaring above the river gorge. They selected a shady perch that allowed them to enjoy the view, both up and down the river. After catching his breath and satisfying his thirst with some water, Rufus addressed his friend.

"Thomas, I'm really impressed with John."

"Rufus, you know I owe you. You know, for your advice. It really did turn out to be very helpful. I still can't get over how closely correlated those transits were with the problems that John was having a few years back. I remember feeling so bewildered in those days, so utterly powerless, as I watched my son deal with some really intense pressures."

"I wasn't looking for praise, Thomas, but I do appreciate your kind words. I think it was Kierkegaard who said: 'Life can only be understood backwards; but it must be lived forwards'. For over forty years, I've ratcheted up my appreciation for astrology each time a retrospective analysis revealed a truth. Kierkegaard and I probably would have gotten along really well. After all, he was a Christian and a philosopher, and he liked to approach life as a process. His emphasis on life as recurring experiences of crisis and re-evaluation offers an approach that is not so different from that of many astrologers."

"I have actually read some of his work, Rufus. You've had some good mentors. Kierkegaard and St. Augustine were not astrologers, but wouldn't they be fun to meet? You could have given them a copy of Heaven."

Thomas was really enjoying being alone with Rufus, and the two friends could not have imagined a better environment for their little heart to heart talk. From Rufus's perspective, it was not only the best location, but the best time, for what he wanted to pursue.

"Thomas, you are so right. That would be a hoot."

He turned his attention from the river vista and addressed Thomas directly.

"We can't interview Kierkegaard today, but there's something I need to ask you. I will preface it this way. Please base your decision solely on your own honest appraisal, preserving your own self-interest above all things. I don't want you to feel obliged to me."

"Rufus, you seem so serious. What are you saying?"

"I'll just come out with it."

He paused for only a few seconds.

"I've met some people, Thomas, very powerful people. They represent my chance to move forward on something I have dreamed of for a very long time. If there is one idea that I can never get out of my mind, it's the idea of proving or disproving astrological theory. Thomas, you see, what I want to do is match up a hundred million lives with a hundred million horoscopes and see what I get. Thanks to technology, not only does the necessary data exist, but we have the ability to analyze it."

Rufus waited to gauge the impact of what sounded shocking, even to him.

"You have hinted at this kind of thing before, but I thought it was just a fantasy."

"It was, in a way. But then I finally met this credible group of individuals who believe as I do   I have met with them twice, and they are dead serious."

"I'm afraid to ask where I come in."

"I want you consider helping us access census data. We would like to use census data as our starting point. Name, address, and birthday for everyone who participated in the census in 1960, '70, '80, '90, 2000, and 2010."

Thomas wanted to laugh, but thought better of it. He knew Rufus was serious. Dumbfounded, he just let Rufus go on.

"I know it's a lot of data, but it's relatively basic, low sensitivity data. I'm sure the same kinds of files we need have been provided to people in academia more than a few times. Remember, we're not after phone numbers, social security numbers, IP addresses, or credit card numbers. It's just name, address and birthday."

When Rufus was finished, Thomas delivered a barrage of healthy skepticism.

"Number one, I could lose my job. Number two, even if I were willing to risk my job, I wouldn't have the foggiest idea how to get that much data out of the building. Number three, how do you know you can trust these people?"

"Thomas, at this point, I'm just asking you to think about it. These people, with whom I have made my pact, have assured me, that compared to the computer hacking we will be doing later on, this is a relatively low risk operation. They are confident that it can be done without being detected. If you decide to participate, your part will involve creating the necessary files over the next three months or so, and then facilitating physical access to the building on a given day. We're thinking late September."

Noticing how Thomas's mood was changing, Rufus decided to wrap it up. He didn't want to push it, and ruin Thomas's float trip.

"These are just files full of data. We're not spying on people in real time. We just need to start with some base set of data, and we thought census data would be perfect. We have alternative ways of obtaining the necessary data, so don't worry about it. In fact, let's not speak of it anymore on this trip. Just give it some thought over the next couple of weeks, and let me know if you would even consider helping us. There are many questions to answer before you could be expected to make a final decision."

The two men descended the bluff to rejoin the boys. One thing was as clear as the June sky. No matter what happened with the census data, Rufus and Thomas knew they would always be friends.

When the hungry swimmers had finished their lunch,

Rufus gathered them around for a preview of the next river challenge.

"There's an old saying that paraphrases a line in a Shakespeare play: 'discretion is the better part of valor'. I want you to think about that as you see your life pass before you on this next run, when you're pointed squarely at a sheer wall of dolomite. Worse yet, you will have no choice but to approach with significant velocity, due to the fast current. About the time you realize you're not on some ride at the water park, you will execute a ninety degree turn to the left to avoid crashing into solid rock."

The young men's faces silently screamed that he had their attention.

"This is where the discretion part comes in. It is possible for the dare devil amongst us to stay in this fast current and steer his canoe so skillfully that he dazzles the crowd with a perfectly timed sharp turn, within inches of the stone face. However, I strongly recommend a more conservative approach. At just the right moment, you can make several strong left-side backpaddles and throw yourself across the huge bubbling eddy, thereby keeping a safe distance from the rock face. Experienced paddlers make this maneuver all the time without thinking. In this case, not only are you inexperienced, but it will happen so fast that you won't have time to think. You're in danger, and out of danger, in about ten seconds."

"That doesn't sound too bad."

Once again it was smart ass Matthew. Rufus ignored him.

"That was the easy part. Now, let's say you hit the eddy just right and you think you're fine, because it will really slow you down. This is a huge, up-swelling eddy. If you are complacent, when you slow down as you go into it, and celebrate too soon, your stern will get caught by the current behind you. Spun around in a heartbeat, you'll be going down the second part of the run backwards, in which case you will probably poop your britches."

This time Matthew kept quiet and waited for Rufus to tell them the secret.

"As soon as you hit the eddy, you have to switch your paddle to the right and start paddling like hell. You had to slow down to avert disaster, but now you have to pick up speed quickly, so you can regain directional control. Once you get pointed forward, and re-enter the current, you'll finish the rest of the run whooping and hollering with joy. I promise."

They followed the same order and spacing as before, only this time Rufus beached his canoe as he came out of the eddy, so he could be there to coach the boys through the challenge. Just modeling appropriate paddling technique was not enough this time, because only the person coming immediately after him would be able to observe his moves.

Robert made it through in perfect fashion, but Petey wasn't able to give the power paddling enough "oomph" when he tried to re-enter the current. His boat quickly did a 'one-eighty' and stalled in the eddy. Thomas, adrenalin flowing, in full collision avoidance mode, made some super strong moves. At the precise time, following Rufus's command, the two of them grabbed on to each other's canoe and held tight. While Petey held on to Thomas's boat, and Thomas to Petey's, facing each other, Thomas was able to muster the strength to power paddle them out of the eddy with one arm. There they went, down the second part of the run, together. Backwards again, this time Petey wasn't grinning. Luckily, John's decision to delay his run by just a few seconds had given them the time they needed to clear out.

Chapter 30: Hacker's Hole

Their second gravel bar camp was a jubilant circus. Once again, Petey got some good natured ribbing about his canoeing technique, or lack thereof. But this time, the real emphasis was on celebrating Thomas as hero, and he really seemed to enjoy the attention. This mid-level bureaucrat's life had not exactly been a bold adventure, so he felt empowered by his success on the water. The merry band enjoyed touting his strong instincts and his considerable physical strength.

Not only had each of them arrived dry, but they were feeling that extreme freedom and relaxation that came with spending an entire day on the river. No cell phones, no streets, no vehicles, no human beings except the ones that had chosen to be there.

Rufus felt really lucky to have a second primo camp spot. It was so wonderfully suited for swimming, fishing, and camping, that many floaters actually stopped there as early as mid-afternoon.

Thomas directed John, Matthew, and Andrew on firewood detail. Having made no secret of their desire to have a big fire that night, the boys were willing to range out far and wide to find enough drift wood. Rufus requested that Robert and Petey stay behind with him, supposedly to help him get things ready for the evening meal. The truth be known, he was using them to help pull off a couple of surprises.

Left alone with Rufus, the boys discovered that it was really about the mysterious cargo. Robert had been asked to carry a tightly bungeed cooler in the front of his canoe. No one seemed to notice that it had not been accessed. Rufus asked Robert to help him carry it up to the campsite, about forty feet from the water's edge. Then it was about the container that Petey had in the front of his canoe.

Noticing that the others were returning with their first delivery of driftwood for the night's campfire, Rufus suddenly turned his attention away from the cargo, and began directing Robert and Petey to help him locate large stones with which to line the fire pit.

As soon as Thomas and his crew had left to gather more firewood, Rufus turned his attention back to the containers.

"Here, let me show you something really sweet." Rufus removed the lid from cooler number one. Digging down through the ice, he revealed a large stash of cold beer.

"Happy Graduation boys! I thought you might enjoy a little buzz. No parents, no need for a ride home, and it's all free."

Robert voiced his approval, excited not so much for himself, but for Matthew, who had been the one most openly envious of the older men's beer drinking. Petey, the precocious one, having been raised with way too much personal freedom, gave Rufus a surprise of his own when he snatched one of the beers and was about to pop the top.

"Not so fast, little man. I'll let you know when it's time. Besides, you've got work to do. C'mon, hurry, before they get back."

Walking the second mysterious container towards the

woods, about thirty feet beyond the campfire spot, Rufus revealed surprise number two.   It was a CD player, an amplifier, a couple of speakers, and a twelve volt battery.

"OK, techno boy, get me some music going. Start with this."

Rufus opened the box of CD's and handed one to Petey: "Float Trip Mix #1".

"Wire up the sound, and let's go. Turn it up loud. Let's have a beer, sit back, and wait for the looks on their faces as they approach with their heavy burdens. It will be classic."

Rufus was right. The expressions on their faces were priceless, alternating between satisfaction, approval, anticipation, and disdain. Willing victims of an innocent practical joke, all was instantly forgiven with the first sip of beer.

Predictably, Petey's next move was to light one up. No better way to accentuate the pleasure of Bob Marley. In that moment, they were indeed a cohesive band of soul rebels, "living good".

The firewood crew took their sweaty bodies to the river, while Rufus and Thomas set about making a fire. There was plenty of daylight left, but Rufus needed coals to cook his famous pre-prepared, triple-foil-wrapped, Boy Scout inspired, campfire dinner. His river bank special was comprised of hamburger, sliced potatoes, onions, carrots, red pepper, herbs, and spices. One package per man, eat it whenever you please.

Robert was the first one of the boys to leave swimming behind for the day and change into some dry clothes. This worked out good for Rufus. With Thomas comfortable as deputy camp cook, Rufus asked Robert to go for a walk. Having already spoken with Thomas, he had decided it was time to tell his nephew about the DCG.

"Thomas, if the boys get hungry before we get back, let 'em have their dinner. I'd say about twenty minutes more on those coals and they'll be done. Just keep flippin' em."

Rufus and Robert walked down along the gravel bar to a place where a bank of pure sand had collected during the last river rise. They were far enough down the bar that they had a clear view of the moon at the edge of the bluff. Rising early and setting soon after, the new moon was one of Rufus's favorite things. They plopped their jean covered butts down on the pristine sand.

"Robert, on several occasions, I have left you with the impression that I was up to something. Several times, I have gone away, promising to tell you all about it when I return. You have been more than patient with me."

"That's OK, Uncle Rufus. I know you have a lot going on."

"Robert, now there's an understatement."

Rufus offered one of the beers he had brought along, but Robert declined.

"Remember the time I gave you a ride to the City? We talked about the idea of collecting enough data to take astrology to the next level, to kind of prove whether there was anything to it or not? But when I picked you up at Andrew's to take you home, I didn't want to talk about it?"

"Yeah, I remember."

"Well, things are different now. I have discovered that there are people who think like I do. I've met with them several times, and I've decided to join up with them."

"That's great Rufus."

"There's just one thing, Robert. I'm not just telling you this because I love you, or because I promised I would keep you informed, or because I think you have a lot of potential as an astrologer."

"What do you mean, Rufus?"

"What I mean is, it's time for me to ask for your help.

In fact, I remember my exact words that night by the pool bar, 'I will definitely need to tell you all about my project because I think I may need your help to pull it off'."

"Yeah, you did say that, but what could I possibly do?"

"Give me your permission to involve your friends."

Rufus chose to lay it right out there, and knowing full well that Robert deserved a complete explanation, he continued before Robert could say anything.

"The work of the data collection group, as we have named ourselves, the DCG for short, will involve a lot of computer hacking. The data sources, like the census department, the IRS, internet search companies, dating sites, social media sites, aren't just going to turn the data over to us. We will have to take it."

Robert looked bewildered. He reached for one of the beers Rufus had brought along, and without speaking, opened it and took a long drink. During his yearlong exposure to this crazy astrological zealot, Robert had grown comfortable with Rufus's advice to not take it too seriously. Suddenly, things were quite different. Robert felt like someone who had just survived a bomb blast, feeling around to see if every part of him was still there. What was he feeling, mistrust, suspicion, betrayal, surprise, caution?

Choosing to support an effort that reeked of "the end justifying the means" would imply a deeper commitment to Rufus than he had ever considered. For goodness sake, he was eighteen and a half! There would be no going back, for him, or for his friends. But strangely, one thing the shock wave did not induce was fear.

"I was going to say, 'are you serious?', but I know you are. All I'm concerned about is that my friends don't get in trouble. I assume you're talking about Petey, and maybe Matthew?"

"First, I swear on my life that I will not ask them to

do anything without working every angle to eliminate the risk. They will not be on their own. The technical people in the DCG will be helping us with every move we make. Trust me when I say, these are very powerful, very capable people with connections and deep pockets."

"Second, don't let your imagination run away with you. Everyone will be going on about their normal life. I'm not asking Petey and Matthew to drop what they're doing and join some 'mission impossible' cyber force. The hacks will occur at discrete intervals over the next couple of years. No one is in a hurry, but there is a lot of resolve to do this."

"Third, even though we realize that stealing the data is a crime, we have no intention of committing any crimes with the data we're going to steal. Unlike identity theft, all of the 'participants', shall we say, will be nameless. It will be a research project, not a criminal enterprise. All we hope to gain is knowledge."

"Are you asking me to talk to Petey and Matthew?"

"No, I just want your blessing. I plan on talking to them in the morning. But there is one thing. I think you should leave Andrew out of the loop for now. Thomas is in. John is not. We'll decide on Andrew later."

"I think that's a good idea."

Rufus showed Robert all the respect he deserved. After swearing him to secrecy, he told him all about the night in the desert, the meeting in New York, and the Institute for Humanistic Innovation. Rufus answered all Robert's questions, but he didn't volunteer anything about his plans for Thomas.

Lingering for a while, they savored the vivid glory of the new moon, now perched at the downstream edge of the bluff. There was no longer any competing light from sunset, and with her exit imminent, her beauty was lustrous, and enticing. The sky was so wonderfully dark that they could see the outline of the entire sphere, not just the silvery crescent. Robert knew that this was the beginning of something big, and could not completely stifle his worry. He was painfully aware, in that moment, that he was only able to glimpse a little sliver of what the project really entailed.

Over their shoulders, they could see another source of light was ready to compete. Finished with the dinner prep, Thomas had sanctioned the bonfire phase.

As the two of them walked toward the fire, they could hear Petey switch the music. Robert may have kept Rufus's plan to provide the sound system secret, but that didn't keep him from bringing his own music. After all, the float trip was his graduation gift.

Chapter 31. New Recruits

The next morning, Robert was awakened by the sound of Thomas and Rufus conversing as they worked to resuscitate the fire. Light banter about the wonders of morning tea on the river soon gave way to a much heavier conversation about Rufus's Heaven. Having read the book, Robert had no trouble following the discussion. The men were not exactly whispering, but they were speaking softly, as if to respect their young friends' need for sleep after a raucous night.

"Does God just give you the tools, or does He actively intervene on your behalf? If he does intervene, is it directly related to prayer, or not? If he does not intervene, a possibility that many Christians do not want to consider, does He at least provide us with clues? These are the seeds that your book planted in my mind, Rufus."

Robert stuck his head out from under the dewy sleeping bag and adjusted his pillow so he could hear better.

"God as purely Creator or God as active guide. That is one of the many issues I tried to address. You seem to have read the book, and me, very carefully."

Rufus poured Thomas some more hot water from the pot.

"Each of us is a divine work of art. But unlike a painting, or a sculpture, or even a book, we exist on a dynamic level. We change and evolve. We're God's performance art! But really, the sixty-four dollar question for me is, how much does God interact with us as individuals? Are we really, as some would propose, his little interactive programs, constantly being updated, as long as we continue to pray for His help, or could it be that we are really on our own?"

"Hey Rufus, prayer could be like On Star. When we get lost, you know, we can just ask for directions. That's actually the way most Christians believe, and I can understand why."

Thomas was enjoying his tea, playfully following Rufus's line of reasoning, all the while assuming that Rufus didn't really believe in the interactive God/man relationship thing at all. It didn't take long for Rufus to confirm his suspicion.

"I do not subscribe to the model that implies a God that is actively assisting us along the way, the proverbial father who is always there to pick us up when we stumble and fall. I do believe that He gave each of us the tools we need, as well as an individualized plan to follow to construct our future. From the moment we take our first breath, our promise to God is to use His gifts to build ourselves up, according to the design in the blueprint, one unique for each of us. The guidance comes only from our ability and willingness to pay attention to the forces inherent in the movements of the celestial bodies. It's up to us to follow the map and pay attention to the signs. There is no On Star. God 'loves you', and wants you to fulfill your promise, but He does not actively intervene to help you."

Robert figured it was about time he let them know he was listening. He made a little racket and crawled out of his bag to join them. The morning sun was doing its best to warm the riverside camp, but he couldn't help but seek out the small breakfast fire to dry his dampish body.

With one of their young comrades up and going, Rufus and Thomas raised the volume a bit, now unconcerned about waking the others.

"Good morning, Robert."

Rufus got him a cup.

"Good morning. You guys sure don't waste any time in the morning, you know, getting all philosophical and everything."

"Now Robert, how do you know that wasn't just for your benefit? Not only did we expect that you'd be the first one peekin' out of your sleeping bag, but you're the only other person on this river that has read my book. Maybe we were just testing you."

"OK, Uncle Rufus, I get it. But you're wrong about one thing."

"What's that?"

"Matthew has read the book too. I gave him my copy as soon as I was finished."

"Well I'll be a ding dang doodle. I'm happy to hear that. I can't wait to hear what he thinks."

Gruntin' and groanin', pissin' and moanin', worn down by the hard gravel bar and too much to drink, the other boys wandered up to the fire one at a time. Rufus fixed them a hot beverage, and accepted their hoarse statements of appreciation for the previous night's beer. It was clear that the second morning waking up on the river had a different kind of special feeling.

Last up was Petey. Declining the offer of coffee or tea, he walked over to the sound system, and removed the heavy tarp that had protected it from the dew. Looking squarely at Rufus, he silently signaled his fervent desire to play some music. He looked like a little boy who just wanted to know if it was OK to have the last piece of cake.

"Petey, I share your love of music, but we really need

to focus on getting out of here. Today we start on the river, but end up back home by nightfall. So I'll make you a deal. You pick a song, and I'll pick a song, and then we pack it up."

"Deal" was all Petey said as he connected to the battery's last volts.

The other boys took the hint about having to break camp. They laid their sleeping stuff out to dry in the sun while Rufus and Thomas began to prepare breakfast.

Petey didn't waste any time. Lou Reed's "Rock n Roll" stopped everyone in their tracks. Here he was, blasting out one of Rufus's favorites.

"How do you know about this music?"

"My Dad."

He brushed back his red mop of hair and began to sway with the music. He reached down and turned it up loud.

With one eye on Petey and one eye on what they were doing, the men tried to carry on. But watching Petey dance to Lou Reed, and play air guitar to the momentous rifts was just too much. Pretty soon, all the boys were down at the water's edge with Petey dancing up a storm. It was such a beautiful moment that Rufus actually had a hard time staying with his idea of Petey playing only one song. But Petey was satisfied. When the song was over, he dove into the river, and his friends couldn't' help but strip down and follow him.

Rufus cued up his own response just as they exited the water, Lou Reed's "I'm so free". It was right on the mark.

As they settled into their bacon and eggs, the sound system safely packed away, they heard a different sound. It was the sweet sound of female voices, bouncing off the bluff, expressing a desire to pull their canoes over so they could take a moment to appreciate this very special place on the river. Their boyfriends peered over at Rufus's ramshackle group as if to say, "is it OK?"

For an instant, no one knew what to do. The sight of a female froze all seven men in their places. The four boyfriends in the canoes, reluctant to share their feminine treasure, didn't know what to do either, because it was clear that they were screwed either way. If they pulled over, they had to deal with seven males ogling their girlfriends, but if they didn't pull over, they'd have four girls calling them wimps. Rufus was the only one who knew what to do. He stood up, waved, and hollered in a steady, confident voice.

"Hey guys, don't miss this swimmin' hole. We'll be gone in about ten minutes."

That's all the newcomers needed. The boyfriends skillfully beached the canoes a little ways down the gravel bar. As if Petey's dance moves weren't enough of a morning distraction, now there were pretty girls in bikinis. Robert and his friends had one eye on their packing and one eye on a stimulating reminder of the world to which they would be returning soon.

The rest of the float was peaceful, almost solemn. They caravanned down the river, each man quietly appreciating his communion with the water. Mindful of trying to generate an opportunity to be alone with Petey, Rufus paddled up alongside Robert's canoe to remind him of the plan to make one last stop before the takeout. It was a spring branch on the left. Robert paddled ahead to catch up with his old friends while Rufus hung back to float a while with Thomas and John.

The spring branch flowed clear and cold. It was one of the larger ones, making a 24/7 contribution to the volume of the river. Rufus explained that there wasn't enough time to hike all the way up to where it flowed out of the mountain. But they had almost an hour to marvel at the bountiful aquatic vegetation and mossy woodland at the mouth of the branch.

As they returned to the canoes, their feet still in the ice cold spring water, Thomas suggested that they join hands and offer a blessing of thanks. Within the hour, they would be loading their stuff into their vehicles and hoping that the experience would sustain them upon their return to civilization. The men felt triumph and sadness, all at the same time.

Knowing what was about to happen, Robert quietly encouraged everyone but Petey to hurry up. Rufus struck up a conversation with Petey just as he was getting ready to get into his canoe.

When they were finally alone, Rufus presented his plea to Petey in a most straightforward manner. Presuming that Petey could care less about his quest, from an ideological standpoint, Rufus appealed directly to the young man's talents and sense of adventure.

"I have been impressed with you on this trip Mr. Petey. Assumed to be the least likely to enjoy canoeing, because of your physical stature and your usual preoccupations, you seem to have had the time of your life. Am I reading you?"

"I guess. You're a little over-analytical about it, but, yeah, I've had a good time. You remind me of my Dad. He was never afraid to show me that he liked to party. A lot of kids' Dads try to hide it. I like your style."

"Interesting. I wouldn't know about keeping things from my children, because I've never had any. But I'll take what you're saying as a compliment."

"It is. But there is something you want from me. That's what I'm reading from you now."

"As a matter of fact, there is something I want, actually something I need. I need someone skilled at hacking into a server to retrieve some data. The target is a large governmental entity. The sensitivity of the information is low, and I think I have someone on the inside. Time frame, the end of September."

"How much data?"

"I'm not absolutely sure yet. That's one of my problems right now. We're right on the front end of this."

"When will you know?"

"Let's say you agree to help me, and my guy on the inside gets started preparing the files, I can probably let you know more in July."

"You sound like you've thought this through, and I like a challenge. So just let Robert know when you want me to take a closer look at your problem."

"Sounds fair, Petey. I'll let Robert know."

"I was going to ask you, does he even know about this?"

"Robert knows what I'm trying to do, but he won't be involved in the day to day. I asked for his permission to involve you, and I may use him to get a message to you. That's it."

"OK, just let me know."

Petey hesitated as he was about to push off.

"This has something to do with all that astrology stuff, doesn't it?"

"Yes Petey, it does."

By the time the two of them caught up with the rest of the group, they were almost at the take out. It was about noon, meaning they were right on schedule for packing up, changing clothes, and enjoying a country café lunch.

The young men's weathered, sunburned faces told a story of growth, the kind that happens only when you get out and do something in the natural world. As he guided them off the river, and watched them eagerly embrace their smart phones, Rufus felt proud. He wondered. Had he just instilled a new sense of appreciation in some young men, or had he actually witnessed the genesis of a canoe club?

Chapter 32. Farm Sitters

By the time Rufus and Katie were ready to leave for the northwest book tour, Thomas was on board. He had sent Rufus a handwritten letter stating that he would begin the process of assembling the desired data into files, under the guise of an academic request from a state university. Rufus wrote him back, promising to get him the technical advice he had requested, and confirming his agreement with their current form of communication. He exhorted Thomas to avoid texts, phone calls, and emails.

Rufus selected an evening when Katie would be at work for Robert to bring Matthew out to the farm. He couldn't put it off any longer. He had to get Matthew vetted before he left. There simply had been no opportunity to speak privately with Matthew since the river. What elicited his new sense of urgency was a letter he had received, presumably from Monique. It was a handbill from the book store in Minneapolis. Neatly printed on the back were these words: "We have a computer project. Get your best man ready." There was no return address on the envelope, postmarked Queens, New York.

When he was sufficiently refreshed by the shower of gratitude for his gift of the float trip, Rufus pursued his reasons for his calling the boys out to the farm. First, he needed to instruct Robert on the farm and house chores. Second, he wanted to lay down some rules about entertaining guests.

"Robert, I have everything written down, who's who and who's where. It will mostly be about keeping water and mineral supplied, but there will be a few lambs to feed. The dogs will help you with external threats. I'll have all the flashlights ready to go, and you can use that little 20 gauge if you need a varmint gun or need to fire a warning shot for the coyotes."

"I can handle it."

Matthew couldn't help his impulsive self.

"Yeah, we can handle it."

"I don't have any problem with people staying over. Katie is counting on Robert to stay every night, with the option of going home or to Grandpa Samuel's during the day. You and your guests may use the wireless signal for personal use, but you may not use any of my computers. If you do use the wireless signal, keep it clean. In other words, nothing shady, and avoid anything to do with astrology. Matthew, you'll find out in a minute what I mean by that."

Rufus got up and walked over to the pool bar. He opened the mini frig and took out a beer.

"There will be no alcohol of any kind allowed at the pool or out on the farm. If there is any alcohol consumed at all, it will be only by people who are spending the night, and it will be consumed only in the house. You and your friends are underage. I have no problem with you drinking. In fact, I've been your drunk uncle a few times, and thoroughly enjoyed it. But I can't risk any trouble out here. I have too much at stake."

"I understand Rufus. We'll be responsible, don't worry."

"If you can abide by the alcohol rules, I probably

don't have to say anything about other contraband, but I will, just to be clear. Weed only! If anyone shows up with anything but reefer, run 'em off immediately. Do I have your word?"

"Yes. Don't worry. We don't intend to have any wild parties while you're gone."

"Robert, do you think it's cooled off enough for you to trade that swimming suit in for some boots and jeans, and take a little tour of the farm?"

"I sure do. In fact, I've been looking forward to a sheep walk."

Robert knew it was time for him to leave Rufus and Matthew alone. He gave Matthew a supportive glance and headed for the house. Rufus didn't waste any time.

"Matthew, there's something I want to talk to you about. In fact, since you're not driving, and I'm still here, would you like a beer?"

"I'd love to have a beer. What do you want to talk to me about?"

"I want to hire you."

"Hire me? But I'm starting school next month, and the college is a long way from here."

"Yes. Hire you. I have a project I'm working on that requires computer research, and I have come to find out that you have skills."

"Sounds good. When do I start?"

"Whoa, not so fast. First I have to know whether I can trust you, and second, the project needs a little more definition before you can start."

"What do you mean, trust me?"
Matthew sat back in the lounge chair as if to say, "I'm all ears".

"I understand you have read my book. You know I'm involved in things other than nursing and sheep farming. You know that I have a keen interest in astrology. Let's just say, I've met some people who want to perfect the process of interpreting horoscopes, but they think they need more data, more analysis, more study."

"Sounds reasonable, but what could you possibly need me for. I'm a total novice when it comes to astrology."

"OK, let's see how much of a novice you are. What is the importance of birth time?"

"Without the birth time, you can't determine the Ascendant sign and degree. Without that, you don't know the person's first house from their last house."

"Very good, Matthew. You'd have no orientation, no compass, no key. A treasure map doesn't do you a whole lot of good if you don't know which direction is north, south, east, and west."

Matthew's expression, for a moment positive and proud, gradually reverted back to curious, and then quickly headed for confused. He thought for a minute, and then offered an observation.

"You can only find a birth time on a birth certificate. How am I supposed to access birth certificates?"

"You're not. I simply want to know if you are interested in doing some research. I will know more details when I return from my trip. I will pay you fifteen dollars an hour, cash, to do research that I direct, with two stipulations: First, you agree to keep it strictly confidential. Second, you may not use your home computer or any device that can be traced to you, or me. My associates will be able to help you with that."

"Oh, don't worry. I already know how to remain anonymous when I'm online. So, yes, I'm interested. What do I have to swear?"

"It's just between you and me, and the information stays off of hard drives, and I pay you in cash."

"Sounds good."

"Oh, I almost forgot. I will only contact you in person, or through Robert, and vice versa. No emails, texts, or phone calls."

"Fine."

They shook hands firmly, looking each other right in the eye. Matthew liked Rufus, and wasn't at all apprehensive about accepting his proposal. Besides, fifteen dollars an hour for a college freshman, and flexible hours on top of that, sounded pretty good. They swam and reminisced about the float trip while they waited for Robert.

Chapter 33. Robert's Farm

When Robert arrived at the farm the following Wednesday, he reveled in the sensation of being alone and in charge. He wasn't even answering his texts. Everyone, including Jane, persisted with questions about his plans for the long weekend.

After reading Katie's long dog note, Robert was energized. He felt like he needed to do something right away, so he walked down to the county road and gazed out over the fields. It didn't take him long to realize that there was no point in taking a sheep walk on a hot July afternoon. He knew full well that venturing too close to the sheep's shady hiding place under the big trees at the gap would be nothing more than an aggravation for everyone. Any sight or sound of Robert would immediately make them think of grain, and it was not on the menu in the middle of the afternoon on a sweltering summer day. Unable to suppress their instinct for protein, no matter how hot and humid the weather, Robert knew the sheep would involuntarily leave the shade and follow him toward the nearest feeder. They would be left standing in the field, expectations dashed. With only an apology they could not comprehend, the flock would make the long frustrating walk back to the shade. When he looked around and saw that neither of the dogs had interrupted their own shady naps to follow him, Robert really felt silly. The swimming pool was the place to be, for God's sake. It was way too hot for chores.

After supper, he did call Ginny and Jane, but everyone else would have to wait. He texted Andrew, Petey, and Matthew the same message: "Will call you tomorrow about the weekend". He didn't want TV, or music, or conversation. He didn't even want to read. Robert just wanted to sit and think. He mused about such things as the Sun being conjunct his natal Moon in Cancer, the significance of Neptune in his twelfth house as it approached his Ascendant, about Rufus's crazy plans, and about going away to college in less than a month. What would happen with Jane? Would Petey and Matthew benefit from, or get caught in, the bizarre secretive web that Rufus was spinning? He fell asleep in the warm star light, and remained asleep until he was awakened after midnight by the incessant mating call of a large owl that had perched itself high in the largest oak tree behind the pool.

By Thursday afternoon, having completed all his chores and satisfied that he had absorbed all he could from Rufus's astrology library, Robert was ready to plan for human contact. His first invitation went to Ginny, Angela, and two of her friends for Friday lunch and a swim. Matthew would be coming by on Friday evening with a couple of girls. Petey would try to make it down on Saturday, with or without Andrew, and Jane would get her chance on Sunday after church. So much for alone time.

The Friday visit from Ginny and company meant a really great lunch and lots of yummy supplies to augment the already vast store left by Katie. It made being invaded by a pubescent sister and her friends worthwhile. Besides, they didn't stay long.

Matthew's visit turned out to be much more provocative. Since graduation, the fire of Matthew's Aires rising and Leo Sun were burning hot. He was having no problem attracting girls. Robert was used to such a friend, having witnessed Andrew's easy ways with the ladies many times. But he was a little worried about Matthew's reckless drive to get in their pants. His ego was running just a bit too hot for the sensitive Robert.

Mathew's current flame was a girl named Laura. She was delicious fresh fruit, having just moved to the area from down south. Meeting by accident, they quickly established common ground, with a strong physical attraction, and the knowledge that they would be freshmen together at the state college. Matthew had all the advantages, his current heat, his knowledge of the area and its people, and now a friend with a pool.

The girls actually showed up in their bathing suits. As if the company of two skimpily clad females was not enough, Matthew had the pleasure of driving the sleek new sports car Laura had borrowed from her Daddy. Laura's face exuded sexy. But even the wavy blond-streaked, caramel colored hair, and the delectably vibrant smile, could not begin to compete with breasts that didn't need a bikini top to show them off. Smitten by this not so shy princess, who was more giddy than "goody two shoes", Matthew appeared to be getting in deep.

Laura's friend, ostensibly Robert's date, was the loyal friend type. She projected calm as her eyes darted around this unique, strangely appealing, yet scarily isolated, country environment that was Rufus's back yard. When Robert looked at another girl, he had trouble fending off thoughts of Jane. But this little ballerina named Staci definitely had his attention. Dark hair pulled tightly back in a bun, she had the body of a gymnast. She moved with so little effort, comfortably skinny, poised, and ultra healthy. Although she obviously wanted to be there, Staci telegraphed the message loud and clear that it was about swimming and supporting her friend. She was not available.

Robert was surprised by her ambivalence, when after only about a half an hour, Matthew and Laura disappeared into the house, their rather overt sexual behavior in the pool offering a clue to their intentions.

"They can't keep their hands off each other. I've been there, done that. I hope she knows what she's doing."

Robert's spirit was buoyed by her genuine concern for her friend, but it didn't last long. He didn't appear comfortable at all. He kept looking over at the house, as if he was checking to see if it was on fire.

"Oh, I get it. You haven't been there, done that. Am I right?"

She got up from the side of the pool where she had been dangling her legs in the water, and approached Robert, who was sitting in a chair in the shade of the pool bar. She beckoned him to get up, and then gave him a warm hug, a hug like you'd give your cousin when it was your turn at the casket at the funeral of your aunt. As she backed away from Robert, she smiled and offered this assurance.

"I don't even know you, but I know you are a good person, and you're very cute. You'll have your shot. Don't worry. Besides, it's not all it's cracked up to be. You check in the hotel with no baggage and you leave with tons."

Robert surely had never met such a girl. He was about to ask her where she was from because he sensed a mysterious worldliness about her. Instead, what came out of his mouth was a question that surprised even him.

"When's your birthday?"

"I'm an Aquarius, if that's what you're getting at, and my Moon's in Scorpio."

She seemed a little upset that Robert had asked.

"I'm so sorry. You've been so kind to me. I didn't mean to upset you."

"It's OK, but no, I don't want to do the astrology thing. My Dad thought astrology was the answer to everything, and then left me and my Mom high and dry. Let me tell you something that he told me when we used to fight. He told me that I was no good, and that I was manipulative, because my Moon was in Scorpio. It turned out that he was the one who was the manipulator. He lied to me and my Mom for years, and then screwed us over. Between him and some of the guys I've dated, I've got some issues with men."

She started to tear up, then sucked it up, turned around and dove into the pool. Robert followed her without thinking. By the time they climbed the stairs out of the pool at the shallow end, she was in the process of a valiant attempt to regain her composure, as if nothing had happened.

Robert sensed a deep dark feminine pool of pain. He was intrigued and humbled. How dare he play the pouty boy, envious of Matthew the horndog. He was the one who was getting lucky. Witnessing such a raw release of emotion from this girl he had just met was the only kind of roll in the hay that Robert needed.

Matthew and the girls didn't stay long after he and Laura emerged from their hour long tryst. The awkward after-mood of fresh sex induced a superficiality that compelled a desire to keep moving. None of the four of them had any regrets that the get-together was over.

Robert spent the rest of the evening alone. A call from Katie got him re-oriented to farm sitting. He even got a chance to speak with Rufus. He called Jane with a report, careful to leave out the part about Matthew's sexcapades.

Saturday morning brought confirmation that Andrew had decided not to make the trip. He would have come along with Petey if he had been able to interest Cindy, but Rufus's farm just wasn't enough for her. She was used to a much more complex social scene. Driving a couple of hours to hang out with a bunch of guys was not exactly Cindy's idea of a good time.

Matthew got his Mom's permission to spend Saturday night at the farm, on the promise that he would stay there the whole time, no "running around". Petey went out of his way to pick him up.

The threesome worked out well. Petey and Matthew did not share Robert's enthusiasm for the farm, and that was OK, because the sheep chores offered Robert much needed breaks from his friend's relentless fascination with all things cyber.

Petey spent most of the afternoon perfecting Matthew's skills concerning the anonymous use of wireless signals. They practiced the MAC spoofing technique using the signal from Rufus's wireless router.

Petey explained that computing using a WiFi signal in a public place seemed anonymous, but it was not. If the operator of the wireless network wanted to, he or she could identify the actual hardware device that was using the signal. Every device, be it laptop, smart phone, or tablet, had its own unique media access control identity, or MAC address. It was attached by the manufacturer. According to Petey, not only was it possible to spoof the physical hardware address to protect your identity, but operations could be carried out using programs on remote drives, ensuring that no trace of the activity would be detectable on the hard drive of the spoofer's device. Completely anonymous hacking was Petey's passion, and Matthew was a more than eager student.

As far as Robert could tell, his two friends were keeping the individual promises they had made to Rufus not to discuss anything about their involvement with activities related to the DCG. At least he really hoped that was the case. He couldn't exactly come out and ask them, lest he violate his own promise.

The whole thing made Robert a bit nervous because he remembered Rufus's instructions to be really careful about using the internet at the farm. Finally, reluctantly, Robert accepted Petey's assurances that Rufus, even if he knew how to track his own router history, still would have no way of knowing that it was Petey's device that had used the signal. Besides, they were not actually hacking anything or anybody. They were just practicing techniques to remain anonymous. Nevertheless, Robert was really glad when they gave up their laptops for a bass guitar and keyboard. Petey had learned guitar from his father, and Mathew had been a standout in the high school band's brass section. Adapting to Rufus's electronic keyboard was no problem. He made it scream.

The next morning, it was time for everyone to hit the road. Petey back to the City, Matthew home to play the dutiful son, having taken advantage of his mother's good graces enough during the previous week, and Robert back to his own home for a trip to Sunday Mass with his family.

After church, Robert brought Jane out to the farm. They swam and talked and cuddled and walked, neither one mentioning anything about their impending separation. It was a worry free afternoon. Robert was so thankful for Jane's affection. He often pinched himself, wondering if he were about to awaken from a dream, and find himself reverted to the stark reality of the insecure boy he had been before Jane came into his life. He knew he felt more loyalty than love, and more love than lust, but that was OK.

Jane's ticket to spend the afternoon with Robert was underwritten by his invitation to have Sarah and Jane's brothers and sisters out for dinner. The kids had never been swimming in an "in ground" pool, and Robert had never taken on the task of preparing a barbeque dinner for guests, but there was a first time for everything. Jane felt really good about herself that day. She cleverly concealed the intense love she felt for Robert because she didn't want him to feel any pressure as he prepared to depart for college in less than a month. Her mother had advised her well. True love was often obliged to stand the test of time and turbulence.

Chapter 34. Cyber Brunch

While pensive Robert was marveling at the serenity of his poolside isolation on Wednesday evening, Rufus and Katie were heading out to a romantic dinner near the hotel. They would stay only one night in Minneapolis, Rufus having agreed with Liz's suggestion to get Katie out to Seattle as soon as possible. There was more to see there, more to do, captivating topography, along with a unique climate. Katie had spent her entire life in the Midwest, and would be intrigued by the Emerald City. They were to have three full days in Seattle, only one devoted to business.

The Thursday book signing happened to be at a book store in the mall, which worked out perfect for Katie. She stayed with Rufus just long enough to witness his awkward embrace of celebrity, and then went shopping. Having arranged for a late checkout at the hotel, Rufus would meet Katie there when he was finished at the book signing.

About mid-morning, Rufus's hope of seeing Monique was dashed by the arrival of a very different looking DCG operative. He was a slender intellectual type, soft spoken, extremely polite, in his mid-thirties. When he presented his Heaven copy to Rufus, he exposed a small envelope.

On the outside of the envelope, in those same block letters Rufus had seen on the back of the flyer that was mailed to his home, were these words:

"I am the extropian that Lukas told you about. We will meet with you during Katie's spa time on Sunday morning."

In the process of thanking the man for his interest in Heaven, Rufus verified the name of the Seattle hotel where he and Katie would be staying, and stashed the envelope in his pocket.

During the plane ride to Seattle that evening, Rufus reviewed the contents of the envelope while Katie enjoyed a Dramamine-induced snooze.

"It has come to our attention that the credit card industry lobby orchestrated the inclusion of certain provisions in the post 9/11 homeland security legislation that may greatly facilitate our efforts to obtain birth time data. One section of the classified part of the legislation authorized the Department of Homeland Protection to require the states to create a backup data base of certain personal information on the citizens of their state, including but not limited to, birth certificate information. The lobby argued that it would help thwart identity theft. The rationale presented for such a provision was that law enforcement and security agencies, as well as credit card companies with proper clearance, could use the data base to quickly ascertain the authenticity of credit card, passport, and driver's license application information. Still classified, the law authorizes the states to store the birth certificate data in condensed form for easy reference. Actual copies of birth certificates are not stored, only the data on the birth certificates."

Rufus closed his eyes, put his head back against the headrest, and let out a holy sigh, as if his stress level had just dropped several notches. The entire task before them would be a daunting one, but there was nothing more confounding than how to obtain birth certificates on large numbers of people. It had been generally assumed that only some states had centralized repositories of birth certificates, and that most of the data would have to be obtained piece by piece from local jurisdictions. Having to obtain data from so many decentralized sources could easily threaten the entire project. Anything that severely limited the ultimate sample size would have a major impact on the validity of the conclusions. But this was huge news. Before they had even landed in Seattle, Rufus had some ideas about how this new information would inform Matthew's research.

Friday morning, they were awakened by a call from Liz. She wanted to make sure that they were happy with the accommodations, and asked if it would be alright if the concierge contacted them with some sightseeing recommendations. She went ahead and gave Rufus an update on the book signing details for Saturday, in the interest of having all business out of the way for the day. Liz didn't have to remind them that they had the whole day Friday to live it up.

By Saturday morning, Katie was acclimated to downtown Seattle and felt comfortable with her plans to shop solo. She gave Rufus her blessing as he got into the car with Liz's assistant, who would ferry the author between three different locations during the day and deliver him back to the hotel in time for dinner.

The composition of Rufus's book tour groupies was more eclectic in Seattle. He found this hotbed of intellectual chic quite amusing, and strangely refreshing. His Heaven had apparently touched a new age spiritual nerve. The tofu and yoga crowd was quite enchanted with his eccentric take on religious values.

What fascinated Rufus the most was the significant number of fans of the Far East persuasion. He was, after all, on the Pacific coast. Many were impressed with his treatment of traditional Chinese folk religions like Taoism and Shenism, specifically his respect for their bias for multiple gods and multiple souls. They also congratulated Rufus for capturing their religions' important emphasis on daily interaction with the gods. For many of the religions of the Far East, life after death issues took a backseat to daily ritual. The practitioners were much more focused on religious observances in the present time than they were on eventual outcomes in the distant future. Accustomed to multivariate systems like astrology, Rufus found the polytheistic, secular humanism character of Asian religions quite fascinating.

Rufus had the pleasure of meeting many Asians who appreciated his book for its comprehensive treatment of all world religions. One man thanked Rufus for his inclusion of traditional Chinese religious expressions, such as "if there is an entreaty, there will be a response" and "if the heart is sincere, god will reveal his power", because they portray the interactive nature of their relationship with their gods. There were few Chinese who practiced modern scientific astrology, but Rufus wondered if that might someday change. He didn't see an incompatibility there, any more than he did with Christianity.

Islam was another story. Much to Rufus's surprise, considering the strong "reward in heaven" emphasis of most of the Christian denominations, and the fact that they made up such a great percentage of his American audience, it was the Muslims, and not the Christians, who were his most vocal critics. They were clearly the smallest minority at the book signings, but they made up for it. The vehemence of their opposition to some of Rufus's unorthodox views was admittedly a little scary.

There were people of all religions who waited in line to denounce his belief that heaven was not an actual place. Rufus was beginning to realize that his theory of the unification of all afterlife concepts under the umbrella of astrology was not what made people nervous. It was his implicit denial of the restoration of the physical body in heaven. Apparently, neither Christians nor Muslims minded waiting for the Day of Judgment. What they could not tolerate was the thought that their essential individuality died with them, and that they might not be re-united with their physical body in heaven. The survival of their soul alone, as a purely spiritual component part of the Supreme Soul of a Universal God was apparently not enough to satisfy them.

Rufus didn't really feel threatened by his Muslim detractors. He had been careful to avoid secular references to Jihad or such things as suicide bombings. He treated Islam and the prophet Mohammed with great respect, making it very clear that his emphasis was on balance, ecumenism, and unification. One of Rufus's prime directives was to avoid picking a fight with any particular religion or promote one belief system as better than another.

The next morning, he was glad that Katie was enthusiastic about the spa appointment that Liz had made for her. He prepared her for the possibility that he would not be at the hotel when she was finished. He told her he needed to check out the rental car that they would be using for their excursion to Deception Pass.

Within minutes of Katie checking in at the spa, Rufus received a call. The voice was that of the man at the bookstore. A taxi would pick Rufus up at his hotel and deliver him to the marina.

It wasn't until he was safely on the yacht that the identity of his young extropian guide was revealed to him. The young man from the Minneapolis bookstore, who had facilitated his transport to the marina, was none other than Walter's son, Jacob.

Walter greeted Rufus with his customary long, hard handshake.

"Rufus, it's so good to see you again. Please forgive our fascination with the clandestine, but it's actually kind of fun, don't you think? I've told Jacob nothing but good things. Hell, I even insisted that he read your book."

"Walter, if it's good for the cause, I'm OK with it. Besides, this old sheep farmer needs a little intrigue once in a while. Thanks to my publisher, and my agent, my wife and I are having a fantastic time in Seattle. From the looks of this boat, you're not exactly suffering, eh?

"Well, looks like you caught me. We have a home in San Francisco, and we decided to sail up here, to meet with you and some of the other DCG members. You'll be pleased to know, that not only my wonderful wife Erica, but the great Lukas himself, will be joining us. They went to the market to get us brunch. It'll probably be mostly fruit, but what the hell."

As it turned out, the brunch was absolutely extraordinary. It was clear that Erica knew her way around the Pike Place Market. But the private one on one meeting with Lukas, deep down in the hold of the yacht, was even more remarkable. Rufus was proud to report Thomas's offer to help, and he did his best to describe Petey and Matthew's technical abilities.

Lukas was impressed, and offered congratulations. Having assumed Rufus would be successful in delivering his people, Lukas had prepared detailed instructions for Thomas to follow as he packaged the data into files. He even proposed a possible plan for actually accomplishing the data capture. Once he knew a little more about the types of servers, the cyber security, and the specific MAC address of the computer Thomas would provide for Petey's use, Lukas would be able to prepare malware that could successfully cover their tracks. Using nothing more than a flash drive, Petey would be able to download a virus that would mask the inevitable spike above normal usage levels when such a large download was executed.

Once the data was on the external drive, the virus would self-destruct, leaving no trace of a security breach. Lukas emphasized that without the malware and perfect timing, the census bureau's security software would detect a huge spike, and the resulting investigation could leave Thomas in jeopardy.

It was sounding too good to be true, so Rufus didn't mince words when he expressed his skepticism. Lukas just laughed.

"Rufus, this is an easy one, because we have someone on the inside, and these are just census files. Later on, bigger challenges will come. There will be times when we can't be absolutely certain of the security that awaits us. There will be times when we won't have the opportunity to pre-package the files for quick extraction. There will be times when having someone on the inside will not even be possible. You see?"

Feeling way too much like the sheep farmer/dreamer that he really was, Rufus reconsidered his momentary descent into the pit of insecurity. He thought to himself, "If you can't run with the big dogs, you better stay on the porch".

'I'm sorry, Lukas. I admit that it's all just a bit intimidating."

"It's all going to be fine. I know how these security people operate. Most of them operate like sleeping security guards on night shift, waiting for an alarm to wake them up. The actual hacks are not so difficult to accomplish. All we have to do is keep the alarms from going off."

Lukas handed him a list of all the information that Thomas would need to provide. Once collected, Rufus would then send it by regular mail to the New York PO Box provided. Lukas would need it by the end of August.

Back on the deck, Rufus had a relatively easy time declining Walter and Erica's invitation for him and Katie to go sailing that afternoon. Not only did he want to avoid having to explain to Katie who all these people were, but he really was looking forward to their sunset hike on the cliffs west of Deception Pass. The deception he was living in those days didn't bother him, but it did make him think of Monique. Even though he wanted to ask about her, he thought better of it.

In order to clear his head of thoughts of Monique, he imagined his beautiful Katie fresh from the spa, and he was fine. As he prepared to make his exit, he remembered the note that Jacob had given him. Walter was reading his mind.

"Rufus, old boy. Before you go, I'd like to have my turn with you."

He invited Rufus down into the cabin, and closed the hatch behind them.

"Let's talk about this all important birth time data, and how we might get started getting our hands on it."

Rufus pulled the note from his pocket and began to unfold it, believing he was impressing Walter.

"Rufus, tear that up into a million pieces, or, better yet, burn it, when you get a chance."

Walter reached into his pocket and handed Rufus a flash drive.

"Here's what I want you to do. You've got some hungry little computer guys, right? Well, take some of that money I gave you and buy a nice laptop. This flash drive contains a crash course on server technology, as well as data storage in the cloud. Use only the new laptop to access this information. Once you and your boy have mastered the information, destroy the flash drive. You understand so far?"

Walter checked his authoritative tone.

"I'm sorry. I shouldn't have said it like that. I'm getting in a hurry because we're due at a party up the coast. Erica wants to get going."

"It's fine Walter. I'm totally with you. I want you to know, one of my boys is a true hacker, and the other one is a worthy apprentice. The hacker doesn't need the money. He's just doing it for the thrill, and the chance to be part of something spectacular. The apprentice is ready to go to work right now, mostly for the money."

"Good. Purchase a new 256 gig flash drive, and have your guy accumulate all the information he can about the likely data storage approaches of each of the fifty state governments. It's pure research, long hours. No hacking into anything, just research. Have your guy store it on the flash drive, not on the laptop hard drive. This is very important. If these guys are any good at all, they'll know exactly what you mean when you tell them to conduct the research anonymously. There are lots of wireless networks to spoof, and there are other ways."

"Spoof?"

"Yeah. If you say spoof, and they don't know what you mean, you have the wrong guys. Don't worry about it."

"Ok, so the idea is to find out how each state stores the data, as a first step in getting ready to access it. Right?"

"Exactly right. As questions arise, make a list. Purchase a throwaway phone sometime in early September. On September 15, at 6 PM central time, use it to call that number I gave you in New York. That way you can ask all your questions about the birth time stuff. Better yet, you'll be able to finalize that deal you're working on with Lukas, you know, the census data. Of course, be sure to smash the phone when you're done."

"OK."

"Rufus, relax, and enjoy your stay in Seattle. Make some great memories with your wife. Lukas and I are the first ones to admit that we don't really have the vaguest idea how we're going to get our hands on that birth time data, but we will. Mark my words."

Rufus enjoyed the cab ride back to the hotel. Walter's remarks had restored his confidence, and reminded him that a project so huge and so important was going to take a while. He sat back, closed his eyes, and renewed his focus on the immediate future. He was about to take his wife to one of his favorite places in the whole world.

Chapter 35. College Boys

The crook in Robert's road was just about straightened out, and he had gained a lot of ground in the process. Fifteen months earlier, circumstances had forced him onto a new path. Having laid solid foundations during his time in the country, he was excited about the rest of the plan, to build an even stronger Robert, in an environment where he felt quite comfortable, academia.

Thanks to his many workdays with his grandfather, and a new approach to play that he learned from Matthew, Robert's body was strong. He almost allowed himself to feel handsome. Thanks to his many school days with learning-disabled kids, and a new approach to counseling he had learned from Rufus, his mental orientation was now in sync with his true personality. He thought he might really have something to contribute to the world. Thanks to his many intimate days with Jane, and a more honest embrace of his vulnerability, his emotions no longer seemed at odds with his brain. He was beginning to understand. The whole truly was greater than the sum of the parts.

During the first two weeks of August, it was easy to feel confident. The summer was hot and dry, and his work load was minimal. He split his time between helping his Mom look after Grandpa Samuel, running around with Matthew, and quiet times with Jane, usually at her place, but sometimes at Mindy's.

The day he and Jane drove to the City for pre-registration and orientation, the first cracks of relationship insecurity started to appear. Jane was not prepared for the experience. At home, she never wavered in her support of Robert. It was easy for her to say that she wanted him to chase his dreams, no matter what. But the reality of hundreds of young people, half of them female, all of them older than her, leaping into their futures right before her eyes, left her reaching down deep for all the positive spin she could find. A moment of weakness was inevitable.

"I shouldn't have come here."

"Why do you say that?"

He pulled her aside, motioning to the person behind him in the line to go ahead.

"I'm really happy for you, Robert. As I've told you many times, you're the best boy I've ever known."

Understandably self-conscious in the middle of a crowd of people, she suddenly got quiet. Robert decided it was time to head for the nearest exit.

"I'm sorry I'm being such a big baby, but this just makes me think . . . ., well . . . . . . , it makes me think I need to let you go."

In an instant, Robert's primordial masculine instinct to solve each and every problem immediately, combined with the sickening irrational fear of losing his "one and only", and propelled him swiftly toward the border of awkward land. Taking everything way too seriously, he launched into a series of melodramatic promises about their future, how he would call every day, how he would come home as often as he could, how he would . . . .

Ironically, this creepy boyfriend behavior, which could have made things worse, if Robert were dealing with a person of less inner strength than Jane, actually led to a quick resolution. Jane started laughing hysterically, realizing how pathetic and ridiculous Robert looked, as he desperately pledged his undying devotion there on the sidewalk. As suddenly as it had begun, her moment of insecurity was over. When she finally stopped laughing, she took Robert by the hand, and guided him back to the registration line, like she was taking her little brother to class for the first day of kindergarten.

The rest of the day was actually a lot of fun. Jane got to meet Andrew and Cindy for the first time. Projecting the scrappy little Virgo chick that she could be when she needed to be, she was able to hide how absolutely, incredibly, intimidated she really was. It wasn't her clothes, or her age, or her small town education. It was the glimpse into Robert's world, the one that he knew so much better than hers. She couldn't avoid the thought of how easily he would slide right back into it.

On the ride home, Robert got to do a lot of listening. Jane returned to the topic of their future. Even though she had probably never heard of the term "long distance relationship", she made a spirited argument against one.

Neither of them had a sense of anything being "over". It was more an acceptance of change coming, like when a person notices the first hint of a change in the wind's direction before a storm. Before Robert dropped her off, they made plans for the upcoming weekend, their last before school was to start. On Sunday, they would have a private picnic at their favorite spot on the river that ran through the State Park just west of Rufus and Katie's farm.

Before he could get to his Sunday with Jane, Robert would have to make it through Saturday, which would turn out to be quite a different experience. Matthew had been pushing him to ask Rufus if he could bring his girlfriend out to the farm. Matthew claimed that he and Rufus had been meeting about some computer project, and that he was pretty sure it would be cool, but he wanted Robert to secure the invitation, because after all, Rufus was his uncle.   Robert thought it was a little strange, but he did as his friend asked.

When Matthew showed up in Robert's driveway to pick him up on Saturday morning, Robert was ready to go. He noticed Staci in the backseat of Laura's sports car. No big surprise. But when he recognized the second backseat occupant, he was both happy, and perturbed with Matthew, at the same time. There was Petey, sporting a sheepish grin, pleasantly stoned out of his mind. Robert got in on Staci's side, and they headed west.

Rufus was waiting for them on the pool deck. Luckily, it was a work day for Katie, because she would have been mighty uncomfortable in the presence of the young girls. Naturally protective of Robert, she was the typical aunt, wary of any girl that may draw his attention away from Jane, of whom she enthusiastically approved.

"Welcome, welcome. Make yourselves at home."

Rufus turned his attention immediately to Petey, perhaps because he hadn't expected him.

"Petey, I'm pleasantly surprised to see you."

He looked right at Matthew when he said it, confirming for Robert that there was something going on.

After everyone was comfortably in pool mode, refreshments in hand, Matthew made his move. He asked Rufus if they could talk, and then invited Petey to come along. Leaving Robert to entertain the ladies, Rufus and the two young men disappeared into the house.

Obviously desirous of privacy, once in the house, they didn't stop until they had reached the basement. Matthew came right out with it.

"Rufus, I need Petey. I can't do this by myself. I've looked at all the stuff on that drive you gave me, and I can do the research you asked me to do. But if you really want to come up with a plan to get the birth time data, you should let me and Petey work together."

Rufus didn't know whether to be mad or sad. His decision that it would be better to keep each of boys working on separate projects was already being called into question. Should he be upset with Matthew for having already told Petey more than he should have, or should he be congratulating him for having the gumption to be so forthright about it? Relatively certain that the cow was already out of the barn, he opted for blind trust.

"Less than a year ago, my idea of gathering enough data to test the astrological theory was nothing more than a pipe dream. Now, I have incredibly powerful connections, and guys like you that want to help. Maybe I do need to rethink my approach. I just assumed that if we worked independently, we would be able to protect one another if something goes wrong. On the other hand, if we work too independently, we may be sacrificing the advantages that collaboration can bring."

Petey was ready to make it easy for Rufus.

"Mr. Rufus, with all due respect, even if Matthew can get you all the information you want about where the data is hiding in each of the fifty states, you still won't have any kind of realistic plan to actually get your hands on it. At this point, all we're asking is if it's OK for Matthew to keep me informed about what he finds. I am not proposing to go after any of the data. We won't do anything that even remotely looks like hacking, without running it by you first."

"Petey, you know more about it than I do, and frankly, it seems that you two have already made up your mind that you are going to work together, so what can I say?"

"Good. It may take a while for Matthew and I to figure out where the data is, what kind of security systems are guarding it, and who currently has access. But I promise, that by the time we have all that mapped out, I will be able to propose several possible ways to snatch it. Right now there's just too much that we don't know."

"How can I compensate you for your time?"

"Just pay Matthew like you said, and I'll do my part just for the challenge. If I need anything, I'll let you know."

Rufus sent Matthew to the car to retrieve the laptop. Those few minutes provided him sufficient time to update Petey on Lukas's plans to go for the census data in late September. Petey would accept an invitation from Thomas to tour the facility with his son John on a Saturday afternoon. Lukas would provide the external hard drives and the malware necessary to cover up the theft. Petey repeated his willingness to do the deed, on one condition. He wanted the opportunity to examine Lukas's actual anti-detection script. If he was going to do the deed, he wanted some input. Chances are he would be impressed with the malware program Lukas would produce to ensure that such a huge download would not be detected, but he still wanted to examine the program ahead of time.

When Matthew returned with the laptop, Petey demonstrated MAC spoofing for Rufus, assuring him that he and Matthew would be really careful not to leave any cyber trails. He also proudly reported that his father had called in a favor from the dean of the computer science department. Petey was to be one the monitors of the main student computer lab at the college. His father was adamant about him having a part-time job to keep him out of trouble.

"Sounds like the fox is gonna' be guardin' the chicken coup."

Rufus had summed up the sentiment in the room.

"So, you boys are confident that you can do what you need to do on the sly?"

"Yes sir, Mr. Rufus, we are. Let's just say that by the end of the first semester, our extra credit project will be completed."

Petey went to high-five Matthew, but he missed because Matthew wasn't ready for him. Matthew was apparently pre-occupied with thoughts of Laura by the swimming pool. But Rufus wanted to address one more important issue before giving Matthew the green light. He asked the boys to promise to leave Robert out of the loop. It was OK for him to know that they were working on cyber projects for Rufus, but he was not to know the details. When they asked him why, he adopted an emphatic tone, stating very plainly that it wasn't negotiable. Sensing his unshakeable resolve, and realizing that it wasn't that big of a deal, they agreed. The three of them shook on it.

Using the laptop, Rufus accessed Walter's flash drive. Matthew and Rufus left Petey in the basement to take as much time as he needed with Walter's crash course on server technology and cloud data storage. As he followed Matthew up the stairs to rejoin the others at the pool, Rufus couldn't help but wonder if there was anything on the flash drive that Petey didn't already know.

Matthew apologized to Laura for leaving her alone so long. She looked up at him, surprised by his concern, as if to say, "no worries, man, Robert is great!" So he laughed it off, and went about his business, which meant a few minutes alone with Robert.

"Rufus is OK with me and Petey working together on the astro-espionage, but he doesn't want you involved in the details. I'm thinking it's because he wants you to have one less distraction when you start school, but you can ask him."

"Matthew, I know Petey a lot better than you do, and I can honestly tell you, I don't want to know the details."

After they had a few laughs at Petey's expense, Robert was as anxious to get back to Staci as Matthew was to get back to Laura. While the boys were in the house with Rufus, he and Staci had gotten kind of deep. She knew just enough about astrology to be dangerous, but that wasn't what it was about. Robert was fascinated with the intensity of her life experiences. She had been kicked, bitten, and beaten up by life, but did not seem to be bitter. Her resilience was captivating for this "wanna be" psychologist.

When Matthew's crew was ready to depart, Rufus begged Robert to stay the night, so they could catch up. He promised to deliver him to his parent's house in time for Sunday breakfast. Robert agreed without much hesitation. He could never get enough of Rufus, and if he stayed with Matthew, he knew his only choices were being the fifth leg or an afternoon home alone.

Chapter 36. Clear Path

September was the month everyone had been waiting for. Robert loved living in the dormitory. He was making new friends fast. In pursuit of a degree in Educational and Counseling Psychology, Robert marveled at the amount of free time he had on campus. It didn't take him long to consider some kind of employment, and he ended up securing an evening job in the library system, about twenty hours a week.

Having decided that maintaining a car in the City was something he couldn't afford, Andrew the commuter was a true godsend. There were just enough trips to the suburbs to offer some relief from all the walking. Overall, Robert was intrigued with his first real taste of the urban lifestyle. He liked the constant contact with people.

By all reports, Matthew and Petey were also quite happy with their college experience. Matthew was pursuing a degree in Statistics, hopeful that his math skills would hold up, and Petey was bound and determined to be the wonder boy of Computer Security. If his parents were going to force him to go to college, he was going to have some fun with it.

Robert didn't tell either of his friends that Rufus was confiding everything about their activities related to the

DCG. He and Rufus decided it would be easier that way. Robert could appear clueless, pretending that Rufus was trying to shield him from all the horrible illegal endeavors they were undertaking, when in reality, Robert was his uncle's principal sounding board.

Rufus stopped by to see Robert for an early lunch on the 15th. He had met Petey early that morning, and was on his way to see Thomas. Rufus was ready to make the DCG help line phone call that had been arranged in Seattle. Petey didn't really have any concerns about the birth time data research that he and Matthew were doing, but he was concerned about Rufus asking all the right questions about the census bureau heist.

"Robert, you look good. How are you getting along?"

"Fine. I feel that I have made the right decision. I'm enjoying my classes, but mostly, I'm enjoying the people I meet in my classes. I wonder if I would feel that way in a Calculus or Physics class."

"Your Aunt Katie, and of course your Mom and Dad, send their best."

He made sure to give Robert the care package from his mother Ginny.

"So you're off to see Thomas. I bet he's getting a little nervous."

"I'll find out soon enough. Petey and I reviewed the plan this morning, and he gave me a list of questions he needs answered. Thomas will provide some of the answers, and the rest will have to come from the DCG tech guy. But enough of all that. I'm sure it will work out fine. Tell me more about how it feels to be living the college life. Have you run into any of your old flames?"

Robert filled him in. He expressed his confusion about not really missing Jane all that much, and freely admitted, with the obligatory dash of guilt, that he was really enjoying the constant supply of young women, even if he was just looking. He described running into Samantha a couple of times, and admitted that the girl he was most hoping to see was Kristin. Rufus wasn't surprised. Jane was reality and Kristin was fantasy.

When they had exhausted the subject of Robert's fascination with the fairer sex, predictably, the subject changed to astrology. This time Rufus was a bit surprised. Robert was almost gleeful as he reported the considerable number of encounters with students genuinely interested in astrology.

Rufus kidded Robert about staying true to the science and not using his considerable astrological savvy to seal the deal with potential dates. Robert laughed off the suggestion, as it reminded him of the ribbing he got from Andrew at the pool party the previous summer. Using astrology as a way to dazzle the mind of a young female? He would never.

Rufus told Robert that he was not sure when he would visit again. He gave his nephew a long hard hug, and prepared to get back on the road. It was four hours to Thomas's place, and he was invited for dinner.

It was an uneventful trip. Rufus arrived at Thomas's home right on time.

Apparently, the information that Thomas had provided about the servers and the security protocols at the census bureau was sufficient for Lukas. After verifying Rufus's identity, the voice on the other end of the line indicated that Rufus would be receiving a package very soon. It would contain, among other things, the viral code Petey would need to mask the huge one-time download. Rufus got the distinct impression from the tech support person that the security at the census bureau was relatively low grade, information he used to his advantage as he pursued the task of warming Thomas's cold feet.

Rufus and Thomas spent the bulk of the evening just catching up. They had not seen one another since the float trip. John was doing quite well, having met a girl who was helping him complete the transition away from some of his so-called friends from the drug and alcohol years.

"Rufus, you're really lucky to have a woman like Katie, someone who tolerates all your travel."

"You know Thomas, that tolerance you just referred to will be put the test this fall and winter. I'll be back here in ten days to rendezvous with Petey. When the deed is done, I will travel westward to the Rockies to deliver the goods, and get my first look at the Institute for Humanistic Innovation, something I'm sure I'll have to see to believe. In November, I fly to LA for a book fair. I'll make a detour up to San Francisco with Liz, my literary agent, to attend the World Ecumenical Conference. Apparently, I've been invited to participate in some kind of panel discussion, and the publisher won't let me say no. Then in January, I have my annual Saturn Conference in the desert, something I want to do more than ever, because now it means communion with the other members of the DCG. How agreeable do you think Katie will be with all that, especially without Robert nearby to help out?"

"I see what you mean. I wish we lived closer to you and Katie."

"Katie will be fine. She knew who I was when she married me. Besides, she likes the book money. You know she's been nursing for over thirty years, and I would like nothing more than to be able to tell her that she can retire."

"Maybe that will happen, Rufus. Book sales have been steady, haven't they?"

"Thomas, the weirdest part is that Liz thinks she can talk me into writing another book. What would it be about? I think I'm a one trick pony. Besides, once you've tackled heaven, what else is there to talk about?"

The two men stayed up late that night drinking beer and philosophizing, things that came naturally to each of them.

Chapter 37. Computer Mountain

Only ten days later, Rufus was back across the state, this time having caravanned with Petey. They couldn't ride together because Rufus was heading to the mountains, and Petey had to get back to school.

Avoiding all contact with Thomas, Rufus waited at a restaurant a couple of exits east of the Census Bureau regional office. Petey was introduced to the security guards as a friend of the family pursuing a degree in computer science who wanted to get a feel for a large government office. It wasn't difficult to sell the truth. John had no idea what Petey and his father were up to, which helped to promote an air of innocence. What could be more natural for a college age boy than showing off his Dad's workplace? No acting lessons required, because in John's mind, that's all he was doing.

Thomas needed to justify leaving Petey in his office alone. So he made up a story about how Petey had received a voice mail from home and needed to call right away about a private family matter. Thomas suggested to John that they visit the vending machines in the employee lounge.

Petey quickly targeted the census bureau security programs that Thomas had indicated were responsible for detecting and flagging a breach. He was cautiously optimistic that Lukas's custom malware would be effective. He uploaded the virus, connected the external hard drive, and executed the download. In less than twenty minutes, he emerged from the office with the files Thomas had prepared. Lukas would be able to start building the data base from these six sets of census data from 1960 through 2010, over 100 gigabytes of data.

Petey knew the data was safely on the drive. What he didn't know was whether the malware he had used to attack the security system would self-destruct as promised. He was confident that they had successfully masked the download, but he couldn't be absolutely certain that an investigation would not reveal traces of the virus. They were relying on the fact that it would be extremely unlikely for someone to look for a problem that they had no reason to suspect existed. Hackers often relied on this principle. No suspicion, no alert, no investigation.

Petey had travelled all morning to get there, and was anxious to return home. He met Rufus in the parking lot of the restaurant to deliver the hard drive.

"Mr. Rufus, I did my best to assure Mr. Thomas that we pulled it off, and that he shouldn't worry, but now I've got to go. Good luck with him. He'll probably be just a bit nervous when he arrives to work on Monday."

"Thanks Petey. The worst part is that I can't risk calling him or going to see him at this point. I'm on my way to the mountains with the data. He's got a cover story. Let's just hope he doesn't have to use it."

"This is the kind of hack they'd have to be looking for, and why would they be looking for it? We masked the download for sure. We didn't arouse any suspicion. Not only that, I made copies of the files and lost them in the server. If anyone asks Thomas why they were moved, he can just say he didn't need them anymore. If he is asked to retrieve them, I can show him where to find them. Bottom line, Thomas's computer looks just like it did before he started assembling the files."

Rufus thanked Petey one more time, and each of them settled in for a long drive, in opposite directions. Petey knew exactly where he was going, to spend the night at his parent's home before returning to college in the morning. Rufus, on the other hand, was entering unfamiliar territory. That night, he travelled as close to his destination as wakefulness would allow and grabbed a cheap motel.

The next morning, refreshed by a shower and copious amounts of hot tea, courtesy of his travel tea pot, Rufus continued toward the Institute. Walter's directions were as clear as the weather. He was more than anxious to see what Erica was building in the mountains.

Situated at about 4,600 feet above sea level on the eastern side of the Rockies, the Institute for Humanistic Innovation was being constructed on the site of Erica's father's old cattle ranch. Past the original ranch house and huge barn, there was nothing but ultra-modern.

Set into the concave base of the south-facing mountain were six identical rectangular three-story structures of steel and glass, arranged in a semi-circular pattern, and connected by enclosed elevated walkways to a dodecagon central building. Like spokes extending outward from the hub of a wagon wheel, the six hundred foot long, third floor walkways shimmered in the morning sunlight. They connected the third floor of the main building to the first floor of each of the six structures. The terrain sloped upward that much.

The ground floor of the hub building was mostly covered parking. There were tunnels from the parking area toward each of the six buildings, indicating that each building had a significant underground footprint. The roofs of each of the six buildings were beset with solar panels, and there were a series of wind turbines prominent beyond the complex.

Rufus was no stranger to construction. He could tell by the level of activity at the site that there was a concerted effort being made to finish the superstructure before the harsh mountain weather brought construction activity to a screeching halt.

He parked the vehicle and headed into the main building. At the central, circular reception counter, he followed the instruction to ask for Jacob. When he did, things happened quickly. A small four-person electric vehicle picked him up and carried him down the second tunnel from the right. It was marked "5".

He had never expected to get wherever he was going so quickly and so easily. Better yet, he was greeted by Walter!

"Rufus old boy, I'd say you're right on time. Did you have any trouble with my directions?"

"They were perfect. It's good to see you. The way you get around, I'd say you must have a private jet or something."

"As a matter of fact, I do, but we don't have the runway built here yet."

Smiling big, even with the cigar in his mouth, Walter entered a code to unlock a large steel door. Beaming with pride, he ushered Rufus inside.

"This is my baby."

The large space they entered was bustling with activity. Hard-hatted workmen were in the process of installing the electrical and cooling infrastructure for thousands of server clusters. The stainless steel piping and radiator-like manifold systems were the most prominent feature, covering the walls and ceiling, as well as forming huge partitions between each bank of servers.

"The key is optimizing the management of the thermal flux. Any centralized multi-core processor cluster like this, what you would call a supercomputer, puts off a tremendous amount of heat. This design will enable us to be centralized, and still dissipate the heat. It's all Linux operating system, with the emphasis on capability as opposed to capacity."

Rufus was a pretty good physicist. He understood the need for an efficient cooling system.

"Walter, this is going to take huge amounts of electrical power. What's your solution?"

"Rufus, you've just asked the sixty-four dollar question. So far, we've got enough juice run in here to get through the construction phase. The local utility has been great. But you're right. When she's up and running, she'll need power more than they can deliver. So we're installing a 2.4 megawatt molten carbonate fuel cell plant. It will convert natural gas to electricity. We can get the gas. The only thing is, the fuel cell modules won't arrive until spring. But that's OK. The weather's going to shut us down pretty soon anyway."

Walter held his hands up to his ears as if to say he was tired of the noise level, and motioned for Rufus to follow him. They walked toward the back and to the left, eventually passing down a short hallway and through a door.

"Ah, much better."

Walter removed his hard hat, offered Rufus a high-back office chair at the centrally located conference table, and sat down himself. He addressed the only other person in the room, a young woman who was working at a large bank of computer monitors.

"Stephanie. Get Lukas for me, will you, sweetie?"

Rufus looked around the room. He felt like he was in the control room of a major news network. There were monitors and computer interfaces available on every square foot of wall.

"Everything that's going to happen with my baby out

there, or at the entire Institute for that matter, will be controlled from here."

Within only a few minutes, Lukas appeared. When Rufus saw him come through the door, he reached to feel for the external hard drive in the pocket of his jacket. Walter had dazzled him so much with the tour of the facility that he had almost forgotten why he was there.

"Rufus, I offer you my congratulations."

Lukas left it at that, and the two men shook hands. Lukas turned towards Walter, and spoke to the assistant at the same time.

"Stephanie, we're plotting the overthrow of the US government here, and we don't want you to be an accessory. So, how about if you take the buggy back to the main building and bring us some lunch."

She smiled graciously and took off, as if it were not the first time that Lukas had politely asked her to make herself scarce.

"Let's see what you've got."

As Stephanie departed, Rufus removed the hardware from his pocket and placed it on the table. Lukas picked it up immediately and gave it a little victory squeeze. Hard drive in hand, Lukas led them to a secure-looking, side mini-office.

"This is my computer. I am the only one who can access this computer, and this room, for that matter. There is no internet connection. This is currently the home of our copy of the chart construction software, and the place where I write all my programs for the IHI."

He connected the external hard drive, and with the click of a mouse, uploaded Thomas's data. He opened the 1960 census file. In less than a minute, he found Walter, born November 19, 1945, and residing at 346 Jefferson Avenue in Hartford, Connecticut. They had name, address, and birthday on hundreds of millions of Americans. Data collection was no longer an idea. The baseline data was in the house.

"Now I have something to work on. I will assign my own encrypted identifier to each unique name, and construct a spread sheet to accept the data that we will be collecting in the future, like social security numbers, birth times, personal dossiers, browsing histories, and so on, and so on. This is a very exciting start."

Lukas disconnected the hard drive and handed it to Walter, who explained that it would find its way to the incinerator before the afternoon was over.

The next order of business was the lunch that Lukas had ordered. Ice tea and club sandwiches made for a simple, but adequate repast that would sustain them as they embarked on their afternoon activities. Walter wanted to get back to his "baby", and Lukas was anxious to begin configuring the data base. Uncertain what was planned for him, Rufus was pleasantly surprised to find out that Stephanie had been instructed to give him a full tour of the IHI grounds.

Each of the six satellite buildings was essentially identical, architecturally. Numbered one through six, from left to right on the base of the mountain, they would house each of the six divisions of Humanistic Innovation emphasis. Building number one was Biological Studies. Then came Environmental, Sociological, Economic, Technological, and finally, Spiritual. The first floor of each building boasted a central auditorium for presentations, multiple conference rooms, a computer lab, a lounge, and basic classrooms. The second floors were reserved for research labs, computer simulators, and library facilities, depending on the discipline. The third floors of each of the six buildings were identical. The small-windowed rooms along the sides facing toward the main building were the administrative offices. The rest of each third floor was designed as housing for guests and permanent staff. Staff members would occupy the small private rooms off the interior hallways. The guest suites, set up for multiple occupants, faced away from the center of the wheel toward the mountain, and were fitted with large windows and sliding doors to enable an intimate view of all things natural. Each structure was built on the model of a retreat, where guests could come for extended stays, able to work on their projects without the typical interruptions of the outside world.

Rufus was shown to a room in Building Five. He was tired from all the travel, and was very happy to have a quiet place to crash before heading back east. Overwhelmed by the potential he saw in the Institute for Humanistic Innovation facility, he couldn't help but recall Erica's inspiring speech that evening on Long Island. She was spending a fortune. If the work of the IHI was as innovative and bold as its architectural design, it would be a tremendous success.

Rufus's evening consisted of dinner and drinks with Walter, someone with whom he had a naturally competitive, but extremely satisfying relationship. He was surprised to learn that Lukas had already departed. Apparently he had come to the IHI for the exclusive purpose of taking delivery of the census data. He was the man that would write the software for the project, and he had just made it clear that he, and no one else, would be in control of the data.

Rufus was on his way the following morning, holding an invitation from Monique to meet in San Francisco during his west coast book tour, a promise from Walter that the DCG meeting in the desert in January would be awesome, and a fervent wish that the Thomas he would see on his way back home had not gone out of his mind with worry.

Chapter 38. Zodiac Psychology

By mid-October, Robert and Andrew had a
friendship routine going again. They met on campus
whenever they could. Trips to the suburbs, mostly to
Andrew's house, brought them right back to the kind of
relationship they had in high school. Andrew's parents
were thrilled to have their son so near. When the baseball
scholarship didn't materialize, there was a sympathetic
sigh of satisfaction with his choice to pursue a business
degree closer to home.

Cindy was back on the west coast, and Andrew was
staying true. He had a lot of encouragement to be faithful,
in the form of the numerous girls who had volunteered
their vigilance on Cindy's behalf. Andrew didn't mind the
attention. Not only was he hopelessly in love with Cindy,
but he was naturally the kind of guy who could be friends
with a lot of different girls.

Robert was excited about a second chance to hang out
with Andrew the chick magnet. But Robert soon found
out he didn't need Andrew to meet girls. His new persona
as astrologer prince was enabling him to call the tune. The
girls danced, and Andrew was more often the one playing
second fiddle.

Robert's references to astrology during class

discussions in psychology and sociology, as well as during social time, were beginning to elicit a fair amount of interest. He really took notice when people started contacting him outside of class with questions, and even requests for readings. More and more people, especially young ladies, wanted to know more, but many were notably self-conscious. They found it easier to approach him during his evenings in the library. They pretended to seek help with their research and then slyly confide their fascination with the mysteries of the zodiac.

Unfortunately, Robert had to learn the hard way. After wasting a considerable amount of time and effort constructing horoscopes and doing readings for people whose interest was little more than flattery, Robert learned to differentiate between the curiosity seeker and the fledgling disciple. He consulted Rufus several times, submitting to the older, wiser astrologer's humbling lectures about maintaining proper reverence for the art, and requiring more individual effort from people who claimed to be interested.

The discussions with Rufus led to Robert's decision to offer an astrology class on campus. The administration gave him permission to use a classroom in the evening as long as the class he offered was free. So he began making preparations for a weekly class that would begin after Christmas break.

Rufus didn't have a problem with Robert's pursuit, but he did make it clear that he couldn't be any part of it. He agreed to be Robert's silent partner and mentor, but he wasn't exactly volunteering to appear as a guest lecturer.

Robert's involvement with the student chapter of the American Psychology Association provided him a way of getting the word out about his upcoming astrology class, without resorting to flyers on student bulletin boards, or relying solely on word of mouth. Besides, wouldn't the typical psych student make a better astrology student?

Some of them might actually share Robert's belief that modern astrology, however unconventional, would someday be respected as a legitimate tool in the field of psychology.

Andrew wasn't crazy about the idea of the class, but he agreed to lend his support. Although he wasn't interested in becoming a student of astrology, he didn't want to be left out. He was aware that Robert's relationship with Petey and Matthew had an astrological component, so he felt he needed to at least maintain the appearance of interest. Besides, several of Cindy's friends were talking about signing up for the class.

The real reason that Robert decided to pursue the astrology class actually had little to do with meeting girls. Of course he liked the attention, and astrology provided him a way to control the dialogue. But more important, he was just plain bored. He found his introductory classes to be profoundly simplistic. To Robert, this theory and that theory, confirmed or debunked, refined or replaced, represented academic psychology at its worst, more confusing and conflicted than it was useful. He hoped that he would be able to maintain his interest and stick with the program, but in the meantime, he thought the astrology class would provide him a better avenue for exploring his own ideas.

One lonely night at the library, as most of the student population was more occupied with planning Halloween parties than doing research on their second quarter term papers, Robert was approached by a person who would significantly challenge his all too comfortable zone. At first he thought she was just another astro-groupie and treated her as such, only to quickly find out he was mistaken. He knew he had seen her before, but that wouldn't have been so unusual on a college campus.

"Robert, my name is Alexis. I understand you are planning to teach an astrology class."

"Yes, that's right. It's nice to meet you, Alexis. I don't have a sign-up sheet prepared, but you can find me here any time before the end of the semester, or I'll be at the next APA meeting."

"What qualifies you to teach an astrology class?"

With that question, she abruptly shed her jacket and scarf, laid them on the counter, and proceeded to run her fingers up underneath her long black hair on each side, fluffing it backward and upward, over and over, as she waited for a response to her question. Her frame was tall and supple, and she seemed to enjoy how her breasts rhythmically projected towards Robert each time her arms repeated the hair fluffing motion. Her eyes were closed, and her full lips seemed to be kissing the air as she confidently waited for Robert to break his stunned silence. "I've never really asked myself that question, and no one else has asked that question either. I guess it's a fair one."

"Well, then what qualifies you to teach an astrology class?"

Robert deftly stifled his urge to tell her all about Uncle Rufus, deciding instead to find out more about who was offering such a challenge and why. Having met few people with his depth of astrological knowledge, he had just assumed he was qualified, but couldn't help but admit that it was a very good question. He had yet to see his nineteenth birthday. This Alexis person appeared to be a very well-educated woman in her mid-twenties. He wasn't sure what to do, so at the risk of sounding like a smart ass, he came up with a question of his own.

"Why do my qualifications concern you?"

"Because about three years ago, I did the same thing, and it may have hurt my chances of getting my Doctoral Thesis topic approved. If you put the spotlight back on astrology, it could mess things up for me."

With that off her chest, and seemingly impressed with Robert's essential fearlessness, her body language

312

softened, as if she was inviting him to sympathize.

"Well, Miss Alexis, I would never want to do anything that would hurt you, or anyone. I had no idea."

Since there were no students who needed his assistance, and with the library about to close, Robert came out from behind the counter and invited Alexis to sit at a nearby table. She seemed to lighten up some more, like a person in the process of admitting that she had probably appeared a little defensive.

"I know you are a psychology student, because I have seen your name on the class rolls. I've probably graded a few of your papers. I'm one of the graduate assistants. Let me ask you a few questions, since you claim to know about astrology. You undoubtedly know who Carl Jung is, and the importance of his work. But do you know who Dane Rudhyar was?"

"Only because I've read Stephen Arroyo and Michael Meyer."

"Good. Rudhyar wrote too much anyway. It would take you the rest of your life to read everything he wrote. But his Astrology of Personality is undeniably a very significant work."

"What are you getting at?"

"Anyway, so far, you seem credible, and I already know from my snooping that you are very well versed in true scientific astrology. I really don't seriously question your ability to teach a beginner class. Here's my point. You may have come across this famous Carl Jung quote: 'Astrology represents the sum of all psychological knowledge of antiquity'. In other words, Jung acknowledged that astrology may have something to offer, correct?"

She graciously extended her hands across the table toward Robert as if to emphasize what she was about to say. Having just met her, Robert was pleasantly overwhelmed by her honest intellect and her confident femininity.

"Even as a freshmen, you know what personality assessments are. There's one called the Myers-Briggs Type Indicator, or MBTI, that is widely used. It was originally introduced in 1962, and is based on the four personality types proposed by Carl Jung in 1921. It's a widely used personality assessment, but I believe it is flawed. I believe I can improve it, you know, revamp it, using astrological data. But in academia, anything astrological spells controversy, if not heresy."

"So you're afraid of my astrology class because. . . . .? "

"I just about have the committee convinced. If you turn astrology into some kind of popular movement around here, like I tried to do a few years ago, then I might be in trouble."

"I understand. Let's see. Maybe I can just delay the class. Once they approve your thesis topic, you'll be OK, right."

"I guess so. I don't know. Robert, I'm sorry for the way I came off in the beginning. I can tell that you are a serious young man, and I believe you, that you intend the class to help people, and that you're not selling snake oil, or trying to profit."

The security guard was making his final round. The library was about to close. They exchanged contact information, with Robert promising he would continue his preparations for the class, but hold off on advertising any kind of start date. Alexis seemed relieved, and departed quickly.

Robert took several deliberate deep breaths as he considered the ramifications of meeting this woman. He couldn't help but think of Rufus, and wondered what his impression of Alexis would be. Would he admire her as a true disciple, or would he react with distrust because of the sensitive nature of his activities with the DCG?

As he walked home, his thoughts turned to Andrew's Halloween party. Robert smiled to himself as he considered how Andrew could always count on his mother to make a big deal out of Halloween. Having missed the party the previous year, Robert was actually looking forward to the affair, and wanted his costume to be a good one. He had borrowed scrubs and medical related paraphernalia from his Aunt Katie and Uncle Rufus, and planned to go as a brain surgeon.

When Petey and Matthew showed up at his dorm room that Friday night, it was the first time the three of them had been together since that August day at Rufus's place. Robert had seen Petey in the City and had occasion to see Matthew when he was home in mid-October, but this night would give them a chance to catch up as a threesome. Petey had talked Matthew out of bringing Laura, explaining that an Andrew Halloween event was not about couples. It was about giving Andrew's mom a chance to dote on her son. Robert wondered how many more years she would get Andrew to agree to celebrate Halloween in this way.

Matthew brought fresh greetings about Jane. She was still content with her role as dutiful daughter, was doing well in school, and was not "going out" with anyone. She didn't really talk much about Robert, at least to people who Matthew had checked with. Robert was looking forward to seeing her at Thanksgiving. The time apart had surely induced a better understanding of "absence makes the heart grow fonder".

Once they arrived at the party, all thoughts of Jane evaporated quickly. The place was packed. Invitation only, costume required, the party was a throwback to the days of trick or treating. Andrew's mom and Millie had gone all out, providing a bounty of food, drinks, games, contests, and prizes.

Although most of the activity was in the kitchen and

game room, with occasional forays outside to sip some spirits or puff on a joint, attendees were allowed, only on this occasion of Halloween, to venture into other areas of the house to accomplish their trick, or realize their treat. So Robert didn't think twice, during a scavenger hunt game, when a masked Cinderella took him by the hand and silently drug him upstairs. He hadn't seen her before that moment, but was not surprised considering how crowded the party was and the fact that he had been spending most of his time in a corner of the kitchen with Matthew.

He had a sense of déjà vu about half way up the stairs. Why him? Who was this person? Could it be?

When Cinderella headed straight for the plush guest room that overlooked the pool, Robert knew.

"Trick or treat", was all she said as she faced him, removing her mask to reveal her beautiful countenance. Robert was elated, but typically insecure.

"Kristin, I guess you thought I forgot all about you."

She hugged him warmly but briefly, and gestured toward the bed, where they sat down, next to one another.

"I never allowed myself to think, even for a second, that you would forget. But, mostly, I am impressed that you listened to what I told you that night. You have never tried to contact me, and that is what I wanted."

"I thought about it a thousand times."

"But you didn't. You have passed the test."

"Now that I have passed the test, can we get together?"

"Robert, we can most definitely get together. I would like that. I promise that I will soon tell you the whole story. But tonight, let's just have fun at the party. Do you remember how you felt when we walked out of this room the last time?"

Robert didn't have to answer.

Chapter 39. Astrotheologian

Rufus thoroughly enjoyed his time in Los Angeles with Liz, in spite of the fact that, as a Taurus, November was not his best month. He hadn't been to California for a very long time. He kept telling himself to relax and enjoy his time in Southern California because he knew full well that the stuffiness of the Northern California conference was surely going to make him nervous.

The book fair model was much easier to deal with. It wasn't about Rufus being held captive all day and obliged to sign books for people who were already fans. It was about Rufus and other authors of a similar stripe representing the publisher, and trying to market their work to potential readers. The relaxed atmosphere of the fair, along with the great diversity of offerings, reminded Rufus of the days when he attended science teacher conventions, only this time he was the one greeting the curious.

The most welcome news for Rufus was Liz's admission that she wanted to ride with him to San Francisco for reasons other than the interfaith conference. He was hoping to see Monique, and would have a difficult time explaining his rendezvous if it had to occur right under Liz's watchful eye. Her intention to spend an entire day with her son provided him the prospect of privacy.

The ride up the coast was actually fabulous, in spite of Liz's insistence that he consider writing a second book. Naturally straightforward, Rufus was uncomfortable with having to continually make excuses, but he couldn't possibly tell her the truth about the DCG, or the hopes he had for the ultimate prize. There could be no mention of the IHI, or Walter, or Lukas, and not one single word about his dream of the first ever astrological analysis of a large population? All he could do was repeat the same old BS about how he had already said everything he had to say about heaven and hell, and that he wanted to spend more time on the farm. Rufus was persistent with his evasive tactics. Liz had absolutely no inkling of his true intentions, and he wanted to keep it that way.

Rufus had been a little surprised that he received an invitation to the Interfaith Conference. He was hardly a religious leader. But his book had caused enough of a stir in the ranks of theologians that the publisher was able to goad them into an invitation. By clearly calling into question the significant divisions that exist amongst world religions regarding the afterlife, Rufus had become a force that could not be ignored. Was one religion more correct than another regarding what happens after death? Were they all right? Were they all wrong? Who's got the best explanation? If there were only one God, then it would follow that there had to be only one afterlife. Which religion was closest to the truth? Which representative on the panel would address the topic and which of them would try to avoid it?

Rufus had not tried to offer a definitive answer in this book Heaven, but he had raised some legitimate questions, especially for those who desired more cooperation between religions for the good of mankind. He would be participating in a panel discussion: "Sharing a World, Sharing a Heaven". It was as if Rufus had come up with the headline. He thought it was perfect.

There had been no word from Monique. For the first time, a book signing event had come and gone with no secret message being delivered. But Rufus had faith in Walter's assurance that he would be seeing Monique in San Francisco. His desire to see her was as inexplicable as it was overwhelming. She had called herself an operative, but the more time he spent with her, the more Rufus felt like she was operating on his heart. He yearned for the encouragement she offered. More than anyone else, she validated his passion for his mission.

Rufus and Liz arrived at the hotel in the city, ready for nothing more than a simple dinner and some rest. They retired to their respective rooms early. Rufus spoke with Katie by telephone for more than an hour. He described the drive up the coast, how Liz was working on him to write another book, and his apprehensions about the panel discussion on the following day. Katie emphasized that she was proud of him, and encouraged him to have a good time with it, reminding him that he had nothing to lose. If he made some good points, he would make friends. If he ruffled some feathers, part of the fallout would be selling more books. Katie admitted that she wasn't sure why he was so obsessed with something as unknowable as heaven, and God, but that it didn't matter. She loved him, and she would always support him. Rufus went to sleep that night wondering if he could have accomplished any of his goals without Katie.

The following afternoon, in front of an audience of thousands, the eight participants in the panel discussion assembled on stage. They were all clergy or academic theologians, except for Rufus. Each participant was to make an opening statement of no more than three minutes.

Rufus felt out of place from the beginning, but having

been invited, and having travelled so far, he was not about to be a wallflower. He looked over his notes and tried to maintain his composure as the illustrious members of the panel were introduced.

The panel's leader was a Catholic priest, renowned for his work in the ecumenical movement. His opening remarks clearly defined the agenda and set the tone. The other members of the panel included a Jewish Rabbi, a Methodist minister, a Baptist, a Muslim cleric, a Hindu, a Buddhist, and a non-denominational Christian. Rufus was introduced as the non-denominational Christian. Although he had never represented himself as such, he felt it was an acceptable description of his theological orientation for the purposes of the panel discussion.

For the first forty-five minutes of the ninety minutes, the discussion was dominated by the Catholic, the Muslim, and the Rabbi. Without being overtly political, the three of them expressed their views on the importance of better understanding amongst the faiths if there were ever going to be any meaningful resolution to the problems in the Middle East.

Finally, out of boredom, or a desperate desire to focus the discussion back on afterlife concepts, the Hindu courageously pointed out that the mono-theistic religions were the ones that were experiencing the most interfaith conflict. He skillfully broached the topic of re-incarnation, maintaining the kind of political correctness one might expect for a conference in the heart of the western world. He implied that the eastern religions were more open to different religious beliefs and that tolerance was the essential ingredient of world peace. Then he made a bold move. He contended that a belief in re-incarnation was inherently more tolerant than a belief in an exclusive physical heaven. He was playing the dreaded transcendental card.

As some of the panelists squirmed in their chairs,

either because they were uncomfortable with, or titillated by, the statements of the Hindu scholar, the Buddhist priest, notably passive up until that time, made a sign that he would like to speak. His English was more than adequate, and the cadence imposed by his accent immediately captivated the audience.

"Whether we transcend out current life by passing into another plane of existence, such as heaven, or hell, as many of the western religions espouse, or whether we embrace a new life through re-incarnation, we are still focused on right living during our current existence. The interfaith focus should be on how to promote right living. On this we probably agree. But progress is not possible if we are constantly adjudicating the mechanism for how some people will be rewarded and some people will be punished. We all agree that we should do good, but within each of our religions and cultures, there are distinctly different opinions as to how the quality of one's life after death is determined. Some believe that an entity will judge, and some believe that the actions of the person directly dictate the outcome. I have read this man's book, and I would ask him to speak to this dilemma."

He gestured toward Rufus, as if he were finished, but then continued.

"If a religion offers an uncompromising directive to the believer as to how he needs to behave to obtain his reward, or avoid his punishment, and it is clearly different than the direction offered by another faith, then how can they cooperate? The goals do not correspond. If we cannot foresee being united as human beings for eternity, in some kind of heaven, or through the eventual liberation inherent in re-incarnation, then how can we ever be truly united here in this mortal life?"

Now every eye in the auditorium was on Rufus, who up until that time had made only conciliatory remarks, focused primarily on his belief that Christianity offered the

clearest directions for right living, intimating occasionally
that the study of astrology, as an individualized endeavor
to perfect the human character, could possibly be an
important adjunct to Bible study. He reached out to adjust
the microphone and gallantly accepted the invitation to
speak.

"I have tended a sheep flock for twenty-five years. In
the field, the sheep run this way, and the sheep run that
way, sometimes toward the feed bucket, and sometimes to
escape the wolf. But as they run, they never really know
for sure what awaits them, because they cannot think."

Noting the hush that fell over the audience, induced
perhaps by his refreshingly plain speech, Rufus felt a tinge
of the self-conscious. He looked up at the crowd and
paused. In his mind's eye, he suddenly saw a room full of
parents anxious to see their child accept an accolade at
eighth grade graduation. Feeling spiritually renewed by
his illusion of presiding over yet another ceremony in the
gymnasium, he cleared his throat and continued, this time
with more conviction.

"The clergy of all religions have a very serious
responsibility. When to appeal to the individual's natural
desire for reward, and when to warn of punishment?
Sometimes we ring the dinner bell, and paint pretty
pictures of the "kingdom", and sometimes we do nothing
more than threaten the faithful with the high cost attached
to a life of sin. Anyone who takes on the tasks of the
shepherd knows of this paradox."

The priest made an effort to regain control of the
discussion, skillfully couched in a compliment.

"My friend, you rightfully acknowledge the dualism
of good and evil, right and wrong, charity and avarice that
we consider in the course of our ministry."

"Thank you, father, but my point has yet to be made.
My concern about the reward/punishment model is that it
may have unintended consequences over time.

Perpetuating the reward/punishment dualism over generations has essentially de-emphasized individual initiative to interpret life, and more importantly, it has de-emphasized man's essential nature as innately good. The truth of man's ultimate goodness has accidentally been trivialized and taken for granted, instead of being the focus."

Rufus let that heavy thought sink in for a few seconds.

"As human beings, capable of free will and thought, what we really need is a path to achieve our unique, maximum potential. Instead, we pay way too much attention to the dynamics of the group. Encouraged by our religious leaders, we react to issues that cause the flock to run in a certain direction, as if the threat perceived by one is really a threat for all. The more we listen to dogma of a particular faith, the less we are capable of the kind of individual effort necessary to reach our true potential."

His body language signaled he was about to wrap it up.

"My thesis rests in the following paradox. Only by exploring and embracing our individual differences can we discover our commonality as human beings. If we could just accept the idea that there may be only one outcome, only one afterlife, no matter what it is, and we could celebrate the fact that we have different paths to get there, then why would we ever have conflicts in this life? We are not divided by the subtle differences between our approaches to right living. We are divided by the extreme variations in our presumptions that we can actually know what God intends for us when we pass from this life!"

By this time, the Rabbi and the Muslim were looking very uncomfortable. Having agreed to participate in a conference known for its political correctness and lack of controversy, and hopefully spin a few headlines for back home, they were now concerned that this non-academic, this non-theologian, this Rufus person, was stealing the show, and maybe even making them look bad. The Rabbi became contentious.

"I'm not certain what qualifies you to call the traditions of the great religions of the world into question. Regardless of individual differences in people, we are all bound to adhere to religious law, as determined over many centuries by the leaders of our respective churches. What makes you so certain that individualizing the approach to God will not lead to religious anarchy?"

Rufus had a very difficult decision to make. Should he choose conciliation and offer a response like "point taken", or should he seize this opportunity to tell them what he really thought? Should he elaborate on his belief that astrology was the best path to maximize individual potential, and thereby fulfill the promise of God?

There was so much he would like to say. But with time running out, and the Buddhist and Hindu looking extremely satisfied, his behavior followed from the spontaneous appearance in his mind of one of his favorite expressions, that prudence was the better part of valor. He had been courageous to speak his mind in such a forum, but what would be gained by persisting?

"I respectfully acknowledge your concern, and I do not believe that our views are in conflict. It's a matter of emphasis, individual initiative versus adherence to the traditions and collective efforts of a group. We need to emphasize both approaches if we are going to succeed in bringing people together."

The Catholic priest clearly appreciated the way Rufus wrapped things up, taking it as a sign that the torch of control was being passed back to him. He proceeded to bring the panel to a close, returning to the kind of language with which he had begun. The audience as a whole seemed quite satisfied. No real fireworks, but plenty to talk about.

Rufus had only one thing on his mind when it was over. As he exchanged pleasantries with the panel members, he wondered how he was going to avoid the Heaven groupies. He had noticed them out there in the audience during the discussion. All he wanted to do was to meet up with Liz and get back to the hotel.

As Rufus and Liz waited for the elevator to their parking level, one person approached him from behind, a copy of Heaven in her hand.

"Monsieur, s'il vous plait, votre autographe? I have come a long way to hear you speak, and I adore your book."

Even before he turned to look, he knew it was Monique. Trying to manage his excitement, because he had no desire to explain anything to Liz, he removed a pen from his pocket and carefully signed the young woman's book. Instead of "best of luck", he wrote the name of the hotel, the room number, and the words "have all day tomorrow". With one little note on the inside cover of a book, Rufus was once again looking forward.

Chapter 40. Angels and Saints

Monique knocked on the door of his hotel room at 7 AM. Suggesting breakfast on Fisherman's Wharf followed by a hike to the Golden Gate Bridge, she admitted she had the whole day planned. For his part, having spent way too much time sitting, Rufus absolutely relished the idea of donning boots and jeans for some serious hiking along the Bay. When Monique began to share the rest of her plans, Rufus stopped her. It didn't matter to him. He was happy to do almost anything, as long as it meant he would be with his angel. They had not been together since that night in New York.

Over tea and pastries, they filled the gap. Monique wanted to hear every detail, about the float trip, the trip to Seattle, and most of all, Rufus's first impression of the IHI. When he felt he was doing too much of the talking, Rufus tried to get Monique to open up, but with no luck. She was as warm and tender and honest as he had always known her to be, but it was obvious that she was making a conscious choice to defer discussion of her life until a later time. She said things like, "we have all day" and "all in due time" when Rufus gently pressed.

Appealing to his ego, in order to divert attention from herself, Monique was very complimentary about Rufus's "performance" at the Interfaith Conference. She exhorted him to expound on some of the ideas he had explored during the panel discussion, but this time it was Rufus who did some deflecting.

During their hike to the Bridge, the wind was so extreme that it inhibited their ability to converse. It was so annoying, given that there was so much to say. So they cancelled their plan to walk out to the first tower. Monique suggested a cab ride to one of her favorite places, and before long they were at the Museum of Modern Art.

As they strolled through the exhibits, all Monique wanted to talk about was the DCG. Apparently, she had spent a considerable amount of time planning for the January meeting. She was proud that she had managed to rent a private home. They would be able to maintain secrecy without having to resort to camping out.

When they left the museum in mid-afternoon, Monique suggested a pub. She knew that Rufus had to have his beer. Only after several tall frosty mugs of designer beer, did Monique decide to spill the beans.

"Rufus, you have all day reserved for me, correct?"

"Yes, Liz will not be back until tonight. What do you have in mind?"

"I want to make you dinner, Monsieur. I haven't mentioned it, but I have an apartment just down the street where I am staying. Would you like to come?"

"I would be honored. I was assuming that I would return to my hotel at some point, change into different clothes and take you out for an elegant San Francisco night. Are you sure you wouldn't prefer that?"

"Monsieur Rufus, that does sound incredible, but I have my reasons. The best thing is, there will be no need to change. You can come as you are, and it is only a short walk from here."

Monique was seldom nervous. From the first time he met her, Rufus had been struck by her self-confidence. But at that moment, as she turned her bar stool toward him and gazed into his eyes, she was a trembling lamb who had lost sight of its mama. She reached for him, and touched him on the cheek, as if she was making sure that he was really there and was truly listening.

"Monsieur, I need for you to know . . . . , this will not be dinner for just two, and I want you to be OK with that."

"Monique, of course, it will be fine. It is your dinner, and your apartment. You are so emotional all of a sudden. Please tell me, what is going on?"

At that point, looking like she didn't know whether to laugh or cry, she blurted it out.

"Stephan and I are to be married. I want you to have dinner with me and Stephan. I need you to be OK with this, because I know that you are in love with me, and I know that I am in love with you."

He got up from his barstool and literally picked her up off the ground, practically crushing her with a huge hug of joy. When he put her down, and wiped away his own tears, he made her understand how happy he was.

"I feel like you have just asked my permission. From this moment forward, for the rest of my life, I will never have to say that I have no children, because I now have a daughter that respects me, and loves me, as if she has known me for an entire lifetime."

He kissed her on the lips briefly, and then on the cheek. As Rufus wiped away her tears, Monique began to breathe again. The vivid sensation of intense relief revived her beautiful smile. She turned and began pounding on the bar with her fist for another round of beer. Tension was about to give way to celebration.

"I know that you made a difficult choice in New York, Monsieur. You had me if you so desired. I think you know that. So please pardon me. I have dwelled on the fear that you would expect to have another chance.

Without Stephan, I would be that same little bird, unsure whether I should fly away or nest. Merci, mon pere, you have taught me a great lesson, and I will always love you."

The short walk to the high-rise included stops for wine and bread. They found Stephan in the midst of dinner preparations. He was as soft spoken and self-assured as ever. Rufus was very happy for him, as he sensed the sweet fulfillment Stephan derived from his quiet patience with Monique.

As Monique opened the wine, and defended Stephan's resistance to Rufus's offer to help with the dinner, she explained that the apartment was not theirs. The two of them had come to visit Walter and Erica, who had already escaped the San Francisco winter for the Miami sunshine. Considering the time they would be spending at the IHI, and their homes in New York and Miami, Walter had listed the apartment for sale. In the meantime, their son Jacob was the primary occupant. Stephan and Monique were simply fortunate travelers, taking advantage of the luxury digs while Jacob was away on business.

After a sumptuous dinner, the three of them settled into a most extraordinary conversation. Not about marriage, not about astrology, not about the DCG, but about God. Snuggling together in the same karass, Rufus and the young couple set about forging a spiritual bond that would provide them strength in the days to come. Having always known in his heart that he could survive on any kind of relationship with Monique, as long as she was in his life somehow, Rufus couldn't help but consider the expression, "not losing a daughter, but gaining a son".

Relentlessly topping off his wine glass, Stephan and Monique wanted to dig deeper and deeper into Rufus's theological psyche. Unbeknownst to Rufus, both of them were in attendance at the interfaith panel discussion, and had noticed his restraint. It appeared that they had enjoyed the appetizer, but were now ready for some theological tartar. Stephan went first.

"So Rufus, your years as a teacher were apparent today. You speak well. But Monique and I cannot help but wonder what you really think. What we heard today was, as you Americans say, 'sugar-coated'."

"Well I'll tell you right now. If you read between the lines in Heaven, what you may discover is this."

Rufus was quite drunk, but he wore it well.

"Work backwards from heaven. Make up your mind. Are you trying to do something here on earth to earn a ticket to somewhere else better? Or is this where you have arrived to make your mark? Make up your mind!"

He raised his glass, scooted forward on the sofa, and delivered the red meat they were craving.

"Man's mistake is that he presumes to know God. Out of one side of his mouth, he talks about God's unfathomable greatness and power, and then out of the other side of his mouth, he describes his personal relationship with God. Creating a personal God inevitably means attributing human characteristics to God. For the common man, who listens to his minister, once the personification of God starts, it cannot be mitigated. The effect is dangerous. People embrace the belief that God is infinitely great, and mysterious, and all-powerful, and unknowable, but then simultaneously attribute human qualities that make him totally relatable and available. That's having your cake and eating it too."

"Monsieur Rufus, this is why you say in your book that God is not an entity, but a force? If God is an entity that we can describe, we have a certain amount of control. But if God is merely a force. . . . . . . , well that is not so exciting for us, because we cannot make him our own personal confidant."

Monique seemed so proud of herself.

"Monique, you are such a good student. That is

exactly right. Each religious person, by presuming knowledge of their own unique God, ascribes certain powers and attributes, even a kind of personality. Ritually reinforced, generation after generation, these Deist characteristics cannot help but become proprietary. Even with the knowledge, on a rational level, that there can only be one God for all men, each religion markets its brand with an unbridled sense of exclusivity. With exclusivity comes competition."

"But Rufus, if God is not an entity at all, and merely a force, it's not so easy to present God to the masses."

Stephan had been trying to break in. He not only wanted Rufus to get back to the afterlife connection, but he was more than willing to bring astrology back into the discussion.

"Stephan, I think we need more wine. I'm so glad you two are helping me get this out of my system, so I can go on with what I really want to do with my life."

Laughing in the midst of the metaphysical, they opened yet another bottle. Rufus was ready to oblige Stephan on the astrology issue.

"May I remind you Stephan, that man always finds a way to personify, even when he is obviously dealing with a force. How about Father Time? Old Man Winter? Mother Nature? But let's get to the point, shall we."

"No matter how incomprehensible God is, man claims to know exactly what heaven is all about. It's something man gets out of the deal, something he deserves somehow. The Our Father says: 'Thy Kingdom come, Thy will be done, on Earth as it is in Heaven'. But most religions try to shift the focus away from our responsibility to perfect our collective lives here on earth, in the present time. Whether it's a newly re-incarnated body, an everlasting soul, or a physical body that lasts forever after Judgment Day, all religions are selling immortality. Who's going to argue with individuals achieving immortality, as individuals?   It's a very appealing notion!   However, it's a bit narcissistic for me!"

Stephan was ready to speak his mind about the idea of a personal God.   Like Rufus, he was a Christian existentialist, comfortable with placing the onus on men, to continually re-evaluate their approaches to accomplishing good works.

"Each of us benefits from the Sun's energy, more or less equally, without having to make any requests.   I believe it is the same for God's grace.   We spin through the beneficence of God's energy every twenty-four hours.   He has given us everything we need to save ourselves, without having to ask.   We know what we need to do and we have been given all the tools.   As we spin through our days, God's assistance is always present, in the form of the Heavenly Zodiac.   The Sun, the Moon, and the planets are our Angels and Saints.   There is no more need to pray for their intercession than there is to pray for God's."

Stephan's words inspired Rufus just when he thought the evening couldn't get any better.   He wasn't trying to have the last word, but it turned out that way.

"Only by celebrating our uniqueness can we find our common purpose, as we apply ourselves to the task of completing the beautiful jigsaw puzzle that is God."

Monique had gotten up to change the music. Suddenly, Bob Marley was part of the discussion:

>Preacher man, don't tell me,
>Heaven is under the earth.
>I know you don't know
>what life is really worth.
>Most people think,
>Great God will come from the skies,
>Take away everything
>And make everybody feel high.
>But if you know what life is worth,
>You will look for yours on earth:

And now you see the light,
You stand up for your rights. Jah!

By this time, they were all up dancing around the apartment. Monique had lightened the load with music. But after a few more carefully selected tunes, she shut it down. Rufus was visibly played out, even though he wouldn't admit it. He didn't want the day to be over.

When the doorman rang that the taxi was waiting, Monique and Stephan walked him all the way to the curb. Rufus made them promise that they would both attend the DCG meeting in the desert, and headed back to his hotel. He and Liz had early flights in the morning.

Chapter 41. Family Time

Robert was only a little surprised that Jane turned down his invitation to Thanksgiving dinner. Although they communicated almost every day, he had actually been with her only a couple of times since August. In spite of his constant lust for Kristin, Jane was still his girlfriend, and he looked forward to seeing her, but it surely didn't have to be at Thanksgiving dinner. She requested that he come over to see her as soon as he arrived home, and promised to reserve Friday for some date time.

Robert didn't know how homesick he really was until he got into the car with his father that Wednesday afternoon at the University. James's fatherly pride and devotion was coming through loud and clear, inducing a feeling of appreciation in Robert that was different than ever before. Having been on his own for a while, Robert was able to see his father in a different light. Here was this man, who he assumed to be conventional and thoroughly devoid of idealistic notions, openly discussing the difficult choices he had made when he was Robert's age.

Seeing his mother and his sister multiplied his already heightened emotions. This time, Robert was the guest of honor. He wasn't the brave soldier that his brother Gary was, but he was treated like a decorated warrior nonetheless. Their little Robert was on his way to becoming a man. Ginny was mother hen proud, and Angela was pleasantly envious.

Robert's celebrity status was short lived. When he pulled up in front of Jane's trailer, she came flying out of the front door, looking uncharacteristically flustered, still in the process of pulling on her jacket. Her mother Sarah was calling after her.

Robert didn't bother to get out. He shut off the engine and reached over to let her in the passenger side. Once inside, she put her hands in the pockets of her jacket and pulled it around her, as if she were trying to conceal how her tight red sweater was showing off her perfectly shaped breasts. She was wearing make-up and her hair was different. As if she was pre-empting Robert's affection, she looked straight ahead and started talking fast.

"Robert, I shouldn't have asked you to come over this evening, with me having plans and everything. It's just that when I told you I didn't want to come over to your folks tomorrow, I didn't think it would be good for us to wait until Friday before we even saw each other."

She gave him a brief gratuitous glance.

"How are you? You look good. My Lord, college has done you good."

He stopped her somehow, and for a few long seconds, did a little bit of his own staring straight ahead. He felt like the world was shifting under his feet, and that he was in the midst of a reality that he had only read about in books or seen in a movie. Here was Jane, fluffed and buffed, snuggled inside a push up bra and tight sweater, doing her best to clue him in. She was going out that night, but it wasn't going to be with him.

Robert didn't know what to say. Smothered by the knowledge that Jane was the one who had taught him

how to walk down the center of the sidewalk, and
overwhelmed by the feeling that he had taken more than
he had given, he wondered whether he had actually
forced her rebellion.

"You look so beautiful Jane. It's so good to see you.
You don't have to explain. I should have realized that you
would be going to the game tonight."

Without a word, she moved toward him in the seat
and hugged him around the neck. He could tell she was
having a lot of trouble and was trying hard not to cry. He
was struck by the sweetness of her smell. It wasn't her
perfume. It was simply Jane. As if she were trying to
squeeze the decision out of him, the decision to set her
free, she tightened her hold on his neck. She stayed like
that, saying nothing, only whimpering, and barely
breathing.

When he tried to re-position himself, in an attempt to
kiss her, she saved him the trouble. She rose to her knees
on the seat, kissed him on the mouth, and made her
escape. Her mother was waiting for her at the door.

On his way home, he couldn't help but wonder how
incredibly naïve and selfish he had been. He descended
into a vivid daydream while he drove, remembering that
April day on the way back from the creek when he walked
with Jane and thought of Kristin.

Believing that more information would help him
understand Jane's behavior, Robert contacted Matthew,
who agreed to do a little digging. Several sources,
including Mindy, verified that Jane was spending a lot of
time with a particular boy, and that the relationship
appeared to be turning in the direction of high school
romance, but of course, "nothing serious". This new
information left Robert conflicted. He was justifiably
jealous, a brand new feeling for him, but he was also
strangely happy for Jane, a person who he had always
reluctantly perceived as friend first, and girlfriend second.

Thanksgiving Day with the family may have been the perfect medicine for a heartsick boy. Without ever mentioning Jane, they masterfully massaged his sore spots. But, like any college boy about to turn nineteen, it took only until the end of the day Friday for Robert to exhaust his supply of things to talk about with his mother, father, and sister. So he and Matthew cooked up the idea of spending Saturday out at the farm. With everything on his college campus shut down for the holiday weekend, including access to his girlfriend Laura, Matthew insisted that Uncle Rufus was just what they needed. When the boys each sought parental approval, they made sure to include Rufus's standard promise that he would have them home in time for Church on Sunday morning.

For Robert, the time with Rufus and Matthew was almost as therapeutic as his time with family on Thanksgiving. But it was less about warm hugs and soothing statements, and more about good old-fashioned distraction. Three men, each with a thirst for beer, and tales to tell, were feeling free and easy. Matthew's girlfriend Laura was down south for the holiday. Rufus's Katie was heading to Grandpa Samuel's after her shift at the hospital, and Robert. . . . . . . .well, Robert needed all the distraction he could get, because he didn't want to consider, even for a minute, where Jane was or what she was doing.

Before the Sun had even set, with Rufus on his way to inebriation land, Matthew's marijuana provided the perfect catalyst for a little "come to Jesus". As they gathered around the wood stove in the basement, Robert and Matthew didn't have to ask about how the old man was feeling. As if he had been waiting for the proper audience and the perfect occasion, he unleashed a satirical tirade about religious exclusivity, American exceptionalism, and his profound belief that many who had read his book would never really understand what he was trying to say. Even at their young age, they knew that "high and drunk" guaranteed neither redemption nor destruction. But it was very entertaining.

"I didn't have the balls to tell them in plain English that their insistence on a personal God that can intervene to fix all their problems and save them from themselves was nothing more than a fantasy created by man to keep the pews full of the penitent. At the conference, I had the chance to tell them. To just come out and tell them, that when they presume to know God, they open Pandora's box. Flooding people's consciousness with promises that a powerful entity will answer their prayers, creates dependence. People will do as they are told simply to get their reward."

The boys couldn't tell at first if he was happy or sad. All they knew for sure was that he was smiling. Was it the maniacal smile of a man losing his mind, or the smile of a man who was feeling the ultimate satisfaction of having discovered a truth? Rufus took a long drink from his beer and explained his need to rant.

"I'm sorry guys. Thanks for listening. It's just that I've been doing a lot of thinking. No more book signings. No more conferences. I'm very proud that I wrote my book, but I have to move on. San Francisco made me see that. They invited me to participate, but they didn't really want to have an honest conversation."

"God is very real, but God is nothing more than a universal, collective consciousness of what is good. I have been hung up on trying to convince people that all they have to do is make a contribution. There is no test. But it's not my problem anymore. No more abstract notions. I'm done with all that. From now on, I will devote my precious time to proving that astrology is the individual's best path to discover how to optimize his contributions."

The boys applauded softly. Not only his final words, but his actions, indicated that Rufus had reached a triumphant climax. He fell back onto the couch, closed his eyes, and descending into a peaceful, rhythmic breathing pattern. Matthew, now feeling his beer, glibly re-directed the lofty discussion back to earth.

"Speaking of astrology, I've been doing a lot of research, which takes up a lot of my time, and you know what they say, time is money."

Rufus realized right away what he was getting at. It had been a while since Matthew had been paid. He headed upstairs on the excuse that he would check on dinner, and returned with an envelope for Matthew, who put on airs of being shocked.

"In front of Master Robert? How daring!"

"Yes Matthew, that's another thing that's going to change. You and Petey no longer have to withhold information from Robert. I was just testing you. He has known about everything all along."

"No problem. Why does that not surprise me? So that means it's OK for me to tell you what Petey and I have figured out so far? Right now?"

"It would not only be OK, but I would consider it the perfect answer to that ridiculous speech I just made about wanting to move forward with what I really care about. Please proceed."

"We have a pretty good idea where the birth time data is stored in each of the fifty states, and we have identified vulnerabilities. Long story short, if you give us the name of a person in just about any state, we can use a relatively simple form of identity masking to access the data base and get their birth time. We just pretend to be some sheriff's office or passport office to get in the front door. By the time anyone figures out that we spoofed the MAC address, we're long gone, and it would be almost impossible to find us. Obviously, the more often we do it, the more of a fingerprint we leave."

"Matthew, I think I know where this is going."

"Yeah, I bet you do. We can easily hack these state agencies to get a birth time here and a birth time there, but that wouldn't be much of an improvement over hacking the local jurisdictions. Either way, it would take a long time to get the data you say you need. If you want to extract a lot of data at one time, you'd have to either have someone on the inside, or you'd have to be willing to do it only once. You could hack all the data from one state data base, one time, from the outside, and get away with it, but good luck with the other forty-nine states, because then they're gonna be wise to what you're doing."

"I'll need to meet with you and Petey before I go to the desert. Remember, the little rascal promised he would come up with a solution. For now, just keep working. I appreciate everything you guys have done so far, and I've got plenty of cash."

Rufus signaled a departure from serious talk by getting each of them another beer and begging for another hit from Matthew's joint. He put on some music, and they each drifted pleasantly into la-la land.

They woke up to a cold, blustery Sunday morning. Robert was the first one up. He really wanted to talk to Rufus about Alexis. He had to make up his mind about the astrology class.

Knowing to fill the tea pot and get it steaming, Robert made a little noise and waited for Rufus in the kitchen. He hit up his uncle even before he could get his first cup of tea, a risky move. He described Alexis, their meeting, and his new doubts about the astrology class. While the bacon was frying, and after a few sips of tea, Rufus mustered the blunt response that only a hangover could enable.

"From everything you're telling me about this person, she sounds like she could be an asset, not only for you, but maybe even for the DCG. I would like to meet her myself, but not right now. Bottom line, do whatever she says. It's so rare to meet someone in psychology who is open to the idea that astrology may have something to contribute. The vast majority of them look down their noses at you, like you're some kind of heretic."

He paused just long enough to put a pan of biscuits in the oven.

"So, if she says she has misgivings about the astrology class ruffling the feathers of the higher ups, then listen to her. Even without her situation to consider, the astrology class is probably not a good idea. If you hadn't brought it up again, I wouldn't be telling you this. I respect your decisions. You know me, 'live and let live'. If you decide the class is something you really want to do, then, by all means, do it. But it has some potential downside, trust me."

Robert was relieved. Rufus had just helped him realize that he may be chasing the astrology class for the wrong reasons. Was he trying to help people, or was he trying to be a big man on campus? Was he being true to the science, or was he about to risk opening a door to an unworthy throng of thrill seekers? He had only been with Alexis on a few occasions, the time they met in the library, once at a meeting, and one time for lunch, but maybe she was right to question the wisdom of abruptly bringing astrology into the light of day.

For Robert, the early AM conversation over tea had the effect of reviving a more serious doubt. Why would he even consider introducing Alexis to Rufus? More and more, he wondered whether his tacit approval of Rufus's penchant for secrets and lies was such a good idea. Rufus was positioning himself on the top of a slippery slope. Was it really a good time for anyone to be holding his hand? Rufus had made a move for Petey and Matthew, and was now setting up a move for Alexis. His one over-riding concern was the ultimate success of his pet project. Robert appreciated his astrological enlightenment, but was beginning to think that he might be too inexperienced with life to seriously embrace all the implications of his uncle's passion.

Matthew ascended the basement stairs to join them. All the intellectual meanderings of the previous evening were relegated to nothing more than bacon and eggs. Robert kept his thoughts to himself. He was glad to serve the tea and orange juice, and he cheerfully did the dishes as they came. Robert knew all about Sundays.

Rufus rode with Matthew and Robert eastward toward their respective churches. Robert got dropped off first, at his home, so that he could attend the Catholic Mass with his family. Matthew took Rufus to Grandpa Samuel's to join Katie. Rufus genuinely liked going to church with Katie and Samuel. Not only did it make Katie extremely happy, but he appreciated and respected the preacher for his emphasis on "works". It wasn't clear whether Matthew was going to church with his mother or not. No one asked, and he didn't offer.

Chapter 42. Disequilibrium

When Robert sat down in the pew between his mother and father, he was philosophical about his losses and feeling good about his prospects. As the Mass progressed, he felt selfishly satisfied with how well he was adapting to the changes. But he wasn't prepared for how easily the priest would be able to exchange an attitude that bordered on smug, for a genuine crisis of confidence. Whether it was the rumbling of his own thoughts, the hypnotic breathing pattern of his father, or the occasional sound of his cold-stricken mother clearing her throat, Robert could not escape the impact of the priest's message about white lies and deception.

Did the end ever really justify the means? Wrong was wrong, wasn't it? Lies were lies, weren't they? When an individual invoked his own brand of rational self-absolution, was he actually being true to God, or even to his own fabrication of a God, or was it just convenience?

As the second reading from Colossians made its way through the sound system to Robert's ears, ". . . . . beware, lest any man spoil you through philosophy and vain deceit, after the tradition of men, after the rudiments of the world, and not after Christ. . . . . ", Robert could think only of how he wished Rufus were present to hear the sermon. As the priest developed his theme, Robert couldn't avoid thinking about how awful he would feel if Petey or Matthew got caught hacking data, or how catastrophic it would be for Katie to experience the embarrassment associated with the public downfall of her husband. She was an innocent Christian woman.

As the priest conducted the sacrament, Robert thought of Kristin. When that didn't work out so well, considering that thinking lustful thoughts during the consecration of the Body and Blood of Christ was just a bit too weird, he turned his thoughts to Jane. No relief there. He really needed to move forward, not backward. As the gentle reverberations of the altar bells faded, Robert closed his eyes and tried to focus on the future. Immersing himself in the solemnity of the religious experience, eyes still closed, he successfully navigated away from charts and quests, away from the glorification of the astrological hypothesis, and away from the lure of Rufus. All he could see in his mind's eye, as the Mass came to a close, was his own personal, individual future.

The family trip to the City after Sunday brunch was Angela's idea. They dropped Robert off at the dorm and headed for the suburbs, to visit old friends.

Robert was glad to be back at the University. His initial enthusiasm for his return to a free life prompted the desire to talk. But a quick phone call to Kristin yielded only voice mail. Texts to Petey and Matthew went answered. Andrew was tied up with Cindy. He didn't even consider calling Rufus. He lay down on the bed and tried to re-establish a connection to the path he had discovered in church. Instead, he became bewildered by a myriad of possible paths, with no present ability to set foot on them. He had no choice but to relieve his considerable frustration with a foray into the seductive world of solitary physical pleasure.

The run-up to finals was a piece of cake. His library

job afforded him plenty of tme to study. Jane was history, and Kristin was offering only vague notions about how they might soon be able to get together. "Maybe after Christmas" did little to bolster Robert's confidence. Even his birthday went largely unnoticed, except for a few cards, a quick call from Rufus, and a night of games at Andrew's house.

December turned out to be about Alexis. Happy with the news that Robert would not be pursuing his astrology class, she was actively trying to befriend him. She apparently saw him for the brilliant, honest intellectual that he was, and the timing couldn't have been better for young Robert. Alexis was the first female with whom Robert shared strictly cerebral interests. He graded papers for her, met her for lunch to discuss psychology department issues, and was careful to show his appreciation for her respectful attention. Whenever he felt himself slipping back towards awkward-ville, he could look up, and there was Alexis throwing him a line.

Just after his last final, as he was about to meet up with Petey and Matthew for the ride home to the country, Alexis came to his dorm room and asked him a favor. Committed to a New Year's weekend Caribbean cruise with a girlfriend, she wanted to know if Robert was willing to return to the City a little early, to watch her apartment, and feed her cat. Afraid of spending the whole holiday break in the country, he accepted the task with zero hesitation. Anything to avoid the Jane-related sentimental boyfriend weakness syndrome,

The hacker boys' last day of school before Christmas break was one day before Robert's. Petey brought Matthew home with him to spend the night, knowing that the next day he would use Robert's need for a ride home as an excuse to head right back south.

Petey and Matthew were obviously in "school's out" party-mode when they picked Robert up at his dorm

room. They were more than ready to rattle his cage. They
arrived just in time to witness Alexis leaving. Matthew let
her go without making a scene, but hit Robert up hard as
soon as she was gone.

"Robert, who was that tall babe we saw leaving your
dorm room? We thought you'd still be all teary-eyed
about Jane, and here you've got this sophisticated lady.
Are you going to the opposite extreme, or what? I wish
Jane could have seen that gal. Way to go, bro'."

"She's a colleague, Matthew."

"A colleague. . . . . Oh pardon me."

Happy to see his friends, and even happier to be
going home, Robert kind of enjoyed the good natured
ribbing that he got. He told them the truth about Alexis,
told them what they wanted to hear about Jane, and told
them absolutely nothing about Kristin. He was about to
make a move and he didn't want to risk entertaining even
the most friendly advice.

It became clear on the way home to the country that
each of them had different agendas for their holiday break.
Petey's decision to travel with his parents was a bit of a
surprise, but even he couldn't turn down the Virgin
Islands. Every other remark from Matthew was about
Laura, while Robert stuck to the only story he had. He
would spend as much time as he could with Rufus,
because it was the best way to steer clear of Jane.

They spent a considerable amount of time during the
two-hour drive to Robert's house talking about Rufus and
the DCG. They no longer had to be careful about what
they said. Petey could discuss his cyber sleuth
recommendations openly in front of Robert, and Robert
could offer clarifications about what Rufus's plan really
entailed. Petey and Matthew hadn't really minded being
treated more like hired hands than premier club members,
but at least now they could be free with their opinions.
Stopping short of calling Robert's uncle a lunatic, because

they sincerely liked Rufus on a personal level, they simply suggested that he was ridiculously heavy on goals and woefully light on expertise to achieve them. In it mostly for the cyber-challenge, Petey and Matthew admitted that they were not true disciples.

Given the new "one for all and all for one" arrangement, and uncertain about the next time he would see Rufus, Petey appointed Robert as the official spokesman for how they might acquire the birth time data.

"Tell Rufus that there are only two possible approaches to getting large amounts of birth time data. I know what Matthew has already told him, and I know he just said to keep working on it. Here are two approaches he can present to his people. If he decides he needs to talk to me about it, that's on him. He can come and find me before he leaves in January."

"Number one approach involves using a variety of hacking strategies to accumulate access codes for the fifty state data bases. When we have accumulated enough combinations to enough vaults, we will strike them all simultaneously, accept detection, cover our tracks, and try to hide the data quickly. You won't be able to send it right to this Lukas guy, you know. They'll know they got penetrated. They just won't know by whom, or where the data is headed. This approach is extremely risky, but it could work."

"What do you mean, where the data is headed?"

"Obtaining the access codes will require a lot of patience, some stealth, some payoffs, and some luck, but it can be done. Whacking all the data bases at the same time, given that we have reliable access codes, will not exactly be easy, but Rufus says these guys have resources. The problem is, that when the upload of the data begins, many, if not all, of the agencies will detect it right away, and will be able to trace it to a physical location faster than you can imagine, even with a sophisticated bot-network in play. I wouldn't want to be at the physical location where the data is going."

"Petey, why not send it to the cloud?"

Matthew knew that Petey had considered the cloud, but he wanted to solidify his position as the official cyber sidekick, so he took the liberty of providing the answer.

"Risky. We're thinking that the cloud is only as secure as the people who control the cloud want it to be. Besides, we're talking about unencrypted data that can be quickly discovered to have been transferred at a certain time. Alarms are going to be going off at fifty state offices. The big boys can surely track a data transfer of that size, believe me. If they do find it, even if they can't trace the account to you, they'll just sit on it and see who retrieves it, and you'll be right back where you started from, worrying about them identifying you."

Robert was starting to pick up on what they were getting at.

"Petey, what I hear you saying is that you can do the hack, and upload all the data at one time, but wherever the data goes is gonna get really hot, really fast, and whoever accepts the data, would have to disappear very quickly or get nabbed."

"Yeah, like they'll be hearing sirens. Like, 'c'mon let's go'. Like, 'load the damn computers in the truck. We gotta' go now'."

"So we're talking rented storefront, assumed names? All that stuff?"

"Right."

"What about having the physical destination in a foreign country, or some obscure location?"

"That would help, but then you would still have to find a way to get the data to Rufus's people."

"So what's the other idea?"

"Number two is better, but it can only work if Rufus's group has the kind of connections they say they do."

Petey exited the four-lane and pulled into the gas station. He asked Matthew to drive the rest of the way to Robert's house. Mathew graciously obliged. He knew Petey didn't like driving the hilly, winding, two-lane country roads.

Once on their way again, Petey lit up a joint from the back seat and offered plan number two.

"Here's my idea. Provoke a crisis of vulnerability. A hundred people like me and Matthew execute a bunch of random hacks on the system over a short period of time, stealing birth certificate data on people we don't even care about. Like Matthew has already told Rufus, we can easily mask identities and steal data without them knowing, just small amounts of it. But we'll do it to the extreme, and get them worrying about the possibility that their security is not what it's cracked up to be."

"What good would that do?"

"You know damn well that the feds will be watching, especially when it comes to data that they have mandated that the states keep secure. So we get a guy in cyber security that works for the feds to come in and check things out. While he's investigating, he copies the data and parks it wherever he wants. In the meantime, everyone is impressed, because it will appear that the measures the guy puts in place to stop the security breaches are super-effective. No more hacks are detected. Everyone feels good. No one ever knows the system was compromised. In fact, just the opposite, they will think that it's all fixed."

The joy of discussing a common interest with his friends was not sufficient to override Robert's skepticism. He didn't share their enthusiasm, and he felt he needed to go on the record.

"I truly hope it all works out for Rufus, and that you guys don't end up in jail, but the DCG having those kinds of connections is a little far-fetched, don't you think?"

Overpowered by expanding reefer smoke, Petey coughed up a muffled answer.

"You never know."

"I hope you guys know what you're doing. You know how I feel about my uncle. But sincerely, bottom liine, sometimes I think you all just smoke too much weed."

Chapter 43. Converging Disciplines

The slower pace of life at home afforded Robert time for rest and reflection. Ginny was busy with holiday preparations and James had an electrical substation project that had to be completed before Christmas. For the first several days of his break, a Thursday and a Friday, with mother and father suitably occupied, Robert could sleep late, laze around the house, resist the temptation to call Jane, and daydream about Kristin. The most strenuous thing he engaged in was retrieving wood from the woodpile to feed the fire in the fireplace.

Robert desperately wanted to trust what Kristin seemed to be telling him, that they would be spending time together soon.   But he also had to admit, that when it came to this girl he adored, yet barely knew, he was having some difficulty reconciling fantasy with reality. The more she re-assured him, the more he was reminded of how long it had been since she first lit his flame of passion. Was she his grade school crush, his supreme erotic nexus, or was she just another college girl who liked to date a lot of boys? Robert was certain of only one thing. If there were one person on the planet that he wanted to spend more time with, it was Kristin.

Family dinners and evenings around the Christmas

tree were satisfying, but by Saturday night, Robert could
no longer hide his desire to visit Rufus and Katie. He
proposed that after Sunday Mass, James drop him off at
Grandpa Samuel's. He would catch a ride to the farm
with Rufus and Katie, and be back home by Christmas Eve
on Wednesday. It would be his longest stay at the farm
since Rufus and Katie had trusted him to watch the place
when they travelled to Seattle.

A winter solstice walk on that first afternoon gave
Rufus and Robert the perfect opportunity to take stock of
their futures. There was nothing like a sheep walk to
throw the door of speculation wide open.

"Uncle Rufus, when I'm not obsessed with thoughts
of Kristin, I'm thinking about how incredibly long four
years of studying psychology is going to be. I want to
help people find their true path, but I'm beginning to
wonder if this is the way. I've got my little four point
average and my honorary appointment to the student
Society for Personality and Social Psychology, but I'm
already feeling like it's too much about credentials and not
enough about effective, practical methods."

"It's about all those things Robert, but those letters
you will have behind your name are a big part of it.
You're right. Your heart doesn't need a college degree to
care."

"So what are you saying?"

Rufus started to laugh at his young nephew, but only
to lighten the mood.

"I'm saying that life's too mysterious. Don't take it so
serious. Enjoy your time in college. There are many
exceptional individuals who have tried to bypass the
traditional road to influence, which is, like it or not, formal
education. In some fields, it is possible to do that. But in
your case, you have to get the degree. However 'right'
you may be about your approach to counseling, the
parents of that child you so earnestly want to help will

absolutely demand to see those letters behind your name. Besides, there are many practical, effective methodologies that you will learn in the coming years. You may be too quick to judge. It's not all about theories espoused fifty to a hundred years ago. You will soon learn that there really is a discipline called modern psychology."

"Sometimes I wonder if it was such a good idea for you to teach me astrology. When I study modern psychology's supposed 'person-centered' approach, I'm skeptical. Astrology seems to do a better job. Psychology's methods are really 'one size fits all'."

"I understand."

They lingered by the beaver pond for a while. The sun was bright, but low in the sky, so it was fortunate that they were dressed for winter Rufus always managed to have some junk lawn chairs available at the water's edge, so they sat down and gazed out over the still water as they talked. Rufus didn't have much to say when Robert mentioned Kristin, or Jane, even though it was obvious that Robert was fishing for advice. It was only when Robert mentioned Alexis that Rufus came alive.

"This girl sounds like the real deal. Now that you've decided you're not going to be so public about your astrology, I think I'd like to meet her. Anyone as far along as she is in academia who is still trying to meld astrology with psychology has to be both courageous and capable. Most who have tried have failed. I already admire Alexis and I've never even met her."

"Uncle Rufus, speaking of astrology and psychology, there's something that I have to ask you, and it didn't come from Alexis. This is my idea. She's totally hung up on Jung, and Rudhyar, and Meyer."

He paused because Rufus was shaking the arm of his chair and giving the "ssshhhh" sign to be quiet, and pointing across the pond, all in rapid sequence. There were two large beavers exiting the water to forage, a rare sight in the middle of winter. When they were out of sight, Rufus urged Robert to return to his question.

"Freud proposed Superego, Ego, and Id, right? Don't you think there's a strange resemblance to Ascendant, Sun, and Moon? The Ascendant is how we express ourselves to the world. Just like Freud's Superego, it's our approach mode. The Sun is our individuality, our essential sense of self, very much like our Ego. The Moon is our subconscious pre-disposition, and for me, looks a lot like Freud's Id, more instinctual, and far less accessible than the Ego. Do you get what I'm saying?"

"Robert, I'm so proud of you. You are making some intriguing observations. Let me tell you what I know. First, there is no evidence that Freud dabbled in astrology. Unlike Carl Jung, he probably dismissed it out of hand. Second, amongst astrology nuts like me, the idea has been proposed before, although not in any formal way. For some reason, great thinkers are prone to construct three-legged stools. Pascal deals with the question of the existence of God with his famous triangle. Astrologers can't say much about a person without knowing the location of their Rising Sign, Sun, and Moon. Freud chose a three-layered model to present his psychoanalytic theory. There's the shell, then the white, then the yolk. I love your idea, but I would have to say the resemblance is mostly a weird coincidence."

Robert was beaming with pride. The only thing that mattered to him was that Rufus believe he had come up with the idea all by himself.

"Whether it was intentional or not, isn't important. I just couldn't read Freud's model of human consciousness without being reminded of Ascendant, Sun, and Moon."

Rufus was totally supportive.

"Carl Jung actually broke with Freud because he felt that Freud was merely saying 'this is why you are the way you are', instead of offering a dynamic approach that would help the individual to re-invent himself. Jung believed that psychologists had a responsibility to do more than analyze a person's shortcomings. He believed they had an obligation to show the individual the best way forward."

"Uncle Rufus, I'd say you've got it right. It's funny. This conversation took off when we mentioned Alexis, and now you're sounding just like her. She's convinced that she can make the Myers-Briggs Type Indicator a more useful personality inventory."

"I'd say she has her work cut out for her. But then again, so do I, and so do you."

Rufus got up from his chair as if to signal it was time to depart. As his nephew rose to join him, Rufus offered his final analysis.

"Robert, you mark my words. In a world where people want answers from apps, you will be needed. Whether you become a traditional counselor, a psychologist, or the greatest astrologer who ever lived, you will be needed. You have what it takes, an intense desire to help."

They set out for the house as the sun was setting. The chilly wind and falling temperature induced a steadily increasing pace. But it wasn't just the weather. There was something about the promise of homemade wine and lamb chops that helped to spur them on.

The weather deteriorated over the next several days. Intermittent snow showers and blustery winds kept them indoors. With more than ample time for conversation, the two men enjoyed exploring every angle of their prisms. Rufus was committed to helping Robert renew his commitment to counseling. He stressed that Robert's pursuit of traditional psychology didn't mean he had to sacrifice his love of astrology, any more than it meant he had to question his Christian faith.

The younger man's agenda was different. Concerned

about Rufus's increasingly radical rhetoric regarding the DCG, he played the devil's advocate, proposing that Rufus may very well be a on a dangerous path. How could he be claiming to help people while invading their privacy in such an extreme way?   How could he be sure that the answers gleaned from "taking astrology to the next level" would only be used for good?

"Rufus, I know you have the best of intentions, and I know you sincerely believe that the knowledge you seek will benefit mankind. But how do you know that all the people in the DCG are going to stay on the righteous path? What if this noble quest becomes a dirty can of worms? This may not turn out the way you think."

"You know, young man, I have anguished over all of this. You are very brave to challenge me. Because it is coming from you, I will consider it a sign of respect. All I can say is that I have to take the chance."

Robert had obviously given it a lot of thought. He was in the mood to persist.

"OK, regardless of how successful the project, or how reliable the conclusions, how are you going to account for the fact that people are really so much more than what their horoscopes portray them to be? There are social and economic and political factors, not to mention plain old biological factors, like disease, that affect a person as much as their natal chart or current-time planetary transits. How are you going to account for those things? With a third of the world going to bed hungry every night, what good is improved chart interpretation, really?"

"For such a young man, you sure have a way of asking hard questions. I have considered all of this, and I'm not saying that I have all the answers, or even some of the answers. But I do know that I'm asking the right questions. Robert, I must go on. If I'm tilting at windmills, or if I'm trying to slay the wrong dragon, so be it. I can bear the consequences."

"That's my point. YOU can. I know you've considered every angle, and I respect the integrity of your beliefs, your motivations, your rationalizations. But what about Aunt Katie?"

"I'm not sure what you mean."

"This isn't just about white lies. She is subject to more and more risk factors going forward, but she doesn't have a say about it. Are you going to just hope for the best, and never tell her about the illegal activities of the DCG that could affect her? And don't you dare say you're afraid she'll worry. That's not enough."

"Well young man, let me tell you. When I returned from the Saturn Conference eleven months ago, I told her I was making a conscious effort to put astrology on the back burner. Recently I told her I was going to cut back on the book tours. I was surprised how happy that made her."

Rufus got up and started pacing around the basement.

"Every once in a while, I feed her bits of information about the DCG. Of course, I leave out the parts about Monique, and I make it sound like we can get the data just by filing freedom of information act requests. We're just conducting a little experiment to see if we can improve the accuracy of astrological interpretation."

"Wasn't she surprised, or suspicious, that you had never mentioned it before?"

"No. To Katie, it didn't sound much different than any other astrology-related project I've talked about when I come home from a conference. In a way, she's conditioned to never be surprised about anything that comes out of my mouth, especially things that have to do with astrology."

Rufus appeared to like the sound of his own justifications. The shakiness of his initial defense was replaced by a weird bravado.

"Justifying my future involvement with the Institute

for Humanistic Innovation without telling her the whole story was actually very tricky. I told her about Walter and the supercomputer, but not exactly about how we planned to use it. I claimed I was introduced to Walter and Erica by Liz, my literary agent, and that the thrust of my involvement with the IHI had everything to do with my theological leanings. I'm sure you won't approve of this part, but I also promised Katie that my work with the IHI had little to do with astrology, and that I would be working with people I had met while promoting my writing. I admit, it felt a little naughty when I threw her the bone. You see, I speculated that my work at the Institute might lead to another book. She really likes the money that Heaven has brought her, you know."

Reluctant to push Rufus any further, but in need of closure, Robert decided on one final brash barrage.

"Sounds like Katie's buying your bullshit this time, but what about the next time, when you need even bigger lies. I know you're between a rock and a hard place, Rufus. I know the sense of anxiety that the truth would induce in Aunt Katie, but I also want you to know how ridiculous it feels to see her being treated just like any member of the general public that the DCG is trying to fool."

"The shock I am feeling right now, as you unleash the resolve of your Capricorn Mars on me, is something I can tolerate. What I cannot tolerate is losing you. You and I are metaphysically intertwined, and I am bound by that fact to process your concerns. I'm going to go for a walk now, and I want you to stay here."

Rufus donned his warm weather gear without saying another word. As he was about to exit, he turned to his young nephew and bowed.

Robert knew that his uncle didn't have to be reminded about how absolutely crazy the whole DCG enterprise appeared. But he had asked his questions, and made his challenges. He wanted to believe that his only intention was to show his love and support. He knew that Rufus could have taught him astrology for fun, and left it at that. Instead, he had let Robert in on the mission of his life. Intimacy was not too strong a word to describe their relationship during those days leading up to the celebration of the birth of Jesus.

But even in his youth, Robert understood that familiarity really could breed contempt. However much he tried to approve of Rufus's right to take a risk, he was still saddled with the struggle to balance his respect for his uncle with his fears of losing him.

CHAPTER 44. CHRISTMAS CALL

A Christmas card from Jane awaited Robert when he arrived home on Christmas Eve. It was essentially a peace offering, coupled with a humble request to get together on one of the days after Christmas. At first, he felt flattered, and fulfilled, over what appeared to be a resurrection of continuity in his life. The gesture was re-assuring, like an unexpected signal from a ship previously thought lost at sea. But at Christmas dinner, talk of Jane's communication made him feel alone with his own family. With all the best intentions, they politely probed his soul, suggesting that his fate was somehow tied to his old girlfriend. It was the last thing he wanted to hear.

Robert's parents had always done a fantastic job of balancing the sacred and the secular of Christmas, and this year was no exception. Yes, he received gifts from Santa Claus that any freshman in college would have to brag about. But more importantly, having become lazy about religion while he was away at college, Robert made a fierce effort to generate a genuine spiritual appreciation for the observances of Christmas. Drawing on the traditional strengths of his Catholic upbringing during the solemn times with his parents was the only thing that induced a feeling of warm and fuzzy. Rufus's metaphysical waling against the idea of a personal God was very unconvincing for a person who was actually immersed in the celebration of the true meaning of Christmas.

Alone in his room on Christmas night, Robert finally received the flash of forward movement that he had been praying for. It only took one phone call to inject a much needed dose of future. Kristin's voice was soft and sexy, as she alternated between caring questions about Robert's Christmas and sad intimations that hers wasn't going so well.

Robert was mesmerized by the sound of her voice. As they talked, it became clear that this young woman, normally the instigator, the leader, the supremely confident force, was engaged in a serious struggle with her own emotions. What he was reading between the lines was that she needed him. She said she couldn't explain, that she couldn't talk about it over the phone, and all he knew to say, with words that felt inadequate, was that he understood.

Any sense of exhilaration over Kristin reaching out to him was obviously unsustainable. She started to cry. As she fought to untangle a chain of "I shouldn't have called" and "what the hell am I doing", her whimpers would have made anyone uncomfortable. Robert managed to keep her on the phone, gently begging her to reveal the true cause of her sadness. But after nursing her to the point of regaining her composure, he finally accepted her desperate plea. She couldn't bear him forcing her to pursue the truth over the phone.

Realizing his persistence was counter-productive, Robert re-focused the conversation on the future. When he was finished detailing his plan to feed Alexis's cat, he could hear the old Kristin come back to life for the first time during the call. Tears drying, voice more confident, she made him swear that he would not worry about her, and that he would not call her. She just kept repeating her promise that she would call him on Sunday morning.

He could barely sleep that night. All that mattered was how he could get to the City on Sunday. There was nothing he could do until morning. Not only was it Christmas night, but it was getting late. The only bright spot was a return text from Matthew. Laura was staying with her parents for the duration of her Christmas break, so he was available to help him with Jane.

The next afternoon, Matthew showed up at Robert's house with Mindy and her little boy. Much to Mindy's chagrin, Ginny was the first to notice their arrival and insisted that they come in the house to see the Christmas tree and have some candy. Mindy managed to survive her time in the spotlight, Matthew scored chocolate cake, while Robert reveled at the thought that Matthew was willing to help him out. He was deathly afraid to meet Jane by himself.

Matthew had borrowed his Mom's car, which provided Robert and Jane with a back seat. The physical closeness the back seat enabled was buffered nicely by the supposed disinterested curiosity from the front seat audience, relieving them of the intensity of a purely private moment. They were able to catch up, in a light and lively way, never actually alone together and therefore never really on the spot. It was the epitome of the obligation experience, and everyone involved was soon anxious for it to be over.

Robert and Jane truly cared for one another. There was absolutely no doubt about that. But Jane now had a boyfriend that could give her what she deserved, fun times and lots of attention. The long distance attachment to Robert had done nothing but starve this beautiful flower of the light it so desperately needed to fully bloom.

Lacking interest in the details of Jane's life, and feeling intensely private about his own prospects, Robert spent much of the time expressing his gratitude for how much of a positive influence Jane had always been. It bordered on patronizing. Intellectually, he knew that Jane's influence was primordial, profound, and life changing. But psychically, and emotionally, as he spoke with her in the back seat of the car, he was already embracing Kristin.

Jane had come a long way in a very short time, but none of what she revealed was a surprise to Robert. She had a new boyfriend, someone who she had known all her life, and she was not having sex with him. With great pride, she professed her plan to enroll in nursing school after high school. That was that. Robert would always be special, and of course, she wanted them to be friends.

When Robert tried to confess his feelings to Jane, he didn't sound very sure of himself. Jane had no trouble perceiving how hollow his claims of happiness really were. But it didn't matter. In the midst of the back seat exaggerations, Robert suddenly realized that he didn't really care whether Jane found him convincing. Their encounter made him realize that he had reverted to the place where he was on the day they had met, yearning for acceptance, still desiring some kind of transformation, acutely aware that Jane had taken him as far as she was meant to take him. Once again, he found himself thanking her for all she had done. He felt appreciation, but nothing else.

By the time they dropped Jane off at her home, Robert perceived the change. As if to set him free, Jane had abandoned her pretense of concern. When she kissed him on the cheek, the look on Robert's face was solemn testimony to the fact that Jane could not help him anymore.

The young man's thoughts immediately returned to how he would get to the City. His parents couldn't help. They were leaving on Friday afternoon to spend the weekend with Thomas and his family. He could catch a ride north with them, but with Andrew and Petey both out of town, Robert would have no place to stay until Sunday when Alexis was due to leave on her cruise. Rufus was working. Desperate, Robert had no choice but to pay the bribe.   Matthew would give him a lift on one simple condition, that he agree to confess the details of his desperate desire for this girl named Kristin.

Chapter 45. Robert's Redemption

Only in retrospect would Robert realize how perfectly aligned the heavenly bodies were on that last day of December. He was reminded of what Rufus had taught him during the first two lessons, that free will is paramount, and that any attempt to predict the influence of the planets is futile. Only present time emotive responses to circumstance and experience were real. Only the choices made by the heart and guided by the brain were real. During that day with Kristin, Robert never one time thought about the fact that Jupiter was on his natal Moon, or that Venus and the Sun were simultaneously conjunct his natal Mars, or that Mercury was retrograde in Capricorn, or that the Moon was New.

Kristin's call came as Matthew and Robert approached the City on Sunday morning. Matthew tried very hard to contain himself as he listened to Robert speak to her. But when Robert was off the phone, it was time for the turkey to strut. Matthew smooched at the air incessantly, and repeated "Ooh baby" so many times that even non-violent Robert was about to whack him one. In a way, Robert deserved everything he was getting. He never protested when Matthew shared the juicy details of his romantic encounters. He now had to pay the piper, even if all he had was what he vividly imagined.

Alexis's apartment was on the third floor of a brick four-story walk up. Robert had managed to get rid of Matthew before Kristin arrived. She knocked softly and then walked right in. She was wearing jeans and calf length boots, very sensible for such a cold blustery day. But when the coat came off, it was anything but winter gear underneath. A lacy top, over a low cut tank, over a silky chartreuse, strapless bra somehow instantly warmed up the room. The lavish layering accentuated Kristin's tanned athletic arms and shoulders, as it slyly distracted Robert from her perky breasts. For a split second, Robert felt like he was the one going on a cruise. After a brief but sensuous hug, Kristin sat down on the couch and pulled off her boots.

"I'm ready for the tour."

She knew it wasn't Robert's place, but she made him oblige. When they reached the kitchen, her face lit up and she became very excited.

"Oh, this is perfect. If you let me stay that long, I'm going to make you dinner. Is that OK, Robert?"

He could not answer. Robert was so mystified by Kristin's air that his speaking function had become temporarily de-activated.

When they reached the bedroom, she took him by the hand and made him sit down next to her on the bed. She looked around the room and took a deep breath.

"Oh, this is marvelous. Don't you think so, Robert?"

He was beginning to think that either Kristin had lost her marbles, or that he was dreaming. Kristin was acting like they were shopping for an apartment. This was just a place where they had decided to meet, and what was this about cooking dinner? Robert had reservations at the German restaurant in mid-town. What was going on?

But there he was, a young man with the age old dilemma. Time had stopped, leaving pure desire to burn like an eternal flame. He was sitting on a bed with a girl who was closer to his perfect fantasy than he had ever imagined, and he had to make a choice. Strangely, he was struck by one of Rufus's favorite quandaries. If you don't know what to do, do something, or, if you don't know what to do, don't do anything. For Robert, the "do something" was to lay Kristin back on the bed and smother her with kisses, just for being so damn cute, and so damn genuine, and making him feel so valuable. The "do nothing" was to passively marvel at the incredible confidence and happiness that Kristin portrayed, to silently appreciate each of her words, her smile, her smell, and to simply soak up the divine sense of titillation suggested by the circumstances.

Although he was only lost in the Rufus quandary for a second, it was plenty of time for Kristin to make the decision for him.

"Robert, isn't there a grocery store near here? Could we walk there? I'm so happy to see you. I want to tell you everything. You have been such a good boy. I'm ready to tell you everything. But I have to cook for you, and I don't want to get back in that car. I want to walk to the store with you, and I want to talk, and . . . . "

"That sounds perfect, Kristin. I cannot tell you how happy you are making me right now. I have waited so long for this moment. Now that we're here, I agree, we should take our time. But what do you mean, tell me everything?"

"Robert, from that very first night we got together at Andrew's, and ever since, don't you think maybe I've been hiding something?"

It was like she reached over and ripped the rose-colored glasses right off his face. As they stood up and started walking toward the living room, he shyly, gently, almost fearfully, stopped her. He kissed her on the lips, as if to proclaim that whatever she was about to tell him wouldn't matter. He was full of optimism for the first time in a long while. As Robert slowly backed away, not letting go of her hands, they smiled at one another, and locked in a stare that lasted for at least a count of ten.

The heat was building in the wires that connected their spirits. Robert's circuit breaker was about to trip. He finally let go of her hands.

"I am really happy that you finally want to tell me everything. Whatever you need to do, that's what I'm down for. I can still hear you crying on the phone on Christmas night, and I'm not having any more of that, no matter what we have to do."

His statement made her pause for a moment. Realizing that she may have gotten ahead of herself, she tried to cool things off.

"Let's go to the store first."

All bundled up, they walked to the store. As they shopped, Robert began to wonder why Kristin was buying so enthusiastically. It wasn't that he was worried about carrying the groceries back to the apartment, but really, why so much food? When he questioned her, she just laughed and said that she was really hungry, or that Robert was a "growing boy", or that she was sure Alexis wouldn't mind. When they checked out, she wouldn't even let him pay. She swiped her credit card and that was that.

Back at the apartment, Kristin wasted no time embarking on her culinary escapade. She opened a bottle of wine that she had stolen from her father, poured Robert a glass, made him sit on a stool at the opposite end of the center island, and commenced the peeling and slicing and chopping. Robert was growing more and more comfortable with Kristin's penchant for wanting to run the show. She operated like a seasoned chef, and offered her personal take on the nutritional advantages of each of the items.

Every once in a while, Kristin would leave the kitchen. Robert didn't notice anything different the first time she returned, as she had just removed her boots. The next time it was her lacy top. He asked her if it was too warm in the apartment, and she just smiled and said "no, just right". The third time she returned, she waited until Robert was distracted before stepping back into the room and snuggling up close to the counter. That way, he couldn't see that she was minus her jeans.

When she was ready, she asked him to pour her another glass of wine. He dutifully got up from his stool and came around the corner, still not noticing that the girl was down to her panties. As he returned to his stool, she called to him.

"One more thing Robert."

When he turned back around, he saw a goddess in the process of removing her top and stepping out from behind the counter, all in one motion. Barefooted, silky little panties, strapless bra, enticing smile, neither brash nor shy. Just Kristin.

Like the night in the guest room at Andrew's, she was in complete control. Robert was just a drooling boy. But this time, she was ready to give him the reigns. She gently stripped him down to his underwear right there in the kitchen. Then, as equals, hand in hand, they slowly walked to the bedroom. She pulled back the covers, laid out flat in the center of the bed, motioned for Robert to drop his drawers, and began to softly moan.

When Robert tried to lie down beside her, without stopping the soft, constant, melodic moan, she motioned for him to take a position between her legs. There was nothing tentative about Robert's moves from that moment on. He removed the last few articles of clothing from the young woman's body, and proceeded to satisfy a longing like no other he had ever felt.

Eventually the dinner was made. The truth would be

told, and the groceries, as Kristin intended, were to last all week. It was premeditated romance, with Robert as the willing victim. Needing desperately to play hooky from her life, Kristin had run away from home, away from everything and everybody, to a place where she could not be found. Holing up with Robert at Alexis's apartment was the culmination of a perfect plan. But why did she need to escape?

Making love with Robert helped her peel back the layers of a deception that she had not been so proud of. After dinner that Sunday evening, the young lovers returned to the bed, where Kristin offered her long overdue confession.

"Robert, please don't judge me too harshly for the things I've done. I have prayed that if anyone would ever be able to understand me, it would be you."

Cuddled up to his naked body with the sheet pulled up around them, Kristin purposely avoided eye contact while she told her story.

"When I was fifteen, my parents were divorced. It was probably a good thing overall because they used to drink and fight so much that there was seldom a sense of peace in our household. At about the same time, we got new neighbors. That's how I got involved with Damion. He was older, he was handsome, he was fun, and I thought I knew what it meant to be in love. All it really amounted to was me letting him write the script for the part of the nubile young wench in the school uniform. For a long time, I thrived on playing that role."

"My Mom played the part of the wealthy divorcee who enjoyed going out with a lot of men. She didn't seem to care that I was spending a lot of time with Damion, because after all, he was such a 'nice', 'polite' young man, and his parents were stinking rich. According to my Mom, if I knew what was good for me, by god, I'd be lucky to marry someone like Damion. Oh yeah, I thought for sure I loved him, and in a way I did. But eventually I realized that Damion was just an addiction. The drug seemed so safe and effective that I overlooked how habit forming it really was."

Robert listened and held her close. For a moment, he thought of Jane. Kristin's vulnerability was taking him back to that overwhelming appreciation of femininity that he known so little about before he met his sweet country girlfriend.

"It wasn't until the night of the pool party, when I had the sense to listen to my girlfriend, and come to find you, that I ever considered I could gain the strength to get away from him. It took me over a year, after that night with you, to convince myself I would actually someday be able to summon the strength to reject Damion, once and for all. The experience with you that night was the first time I realized that freedom was possible.

Robert relished the realization that he had lost more than his virginity. He had also lost his naiveté. Rufus had prepared him well. Robert's existentialist eyes were now wide open. He could plainly see Kristin's pain, and was able to comprehend the courage she needed to finally find relief.

That first night, as he fell asleep next to this gorgeous young woman, he couldn't help but sense the irony. He always had Kristin on a pedestal. Having broken up with Jane, he desperately, consciously tried to avoid making Kristin his rebound. Now it was clear that his worry had been for nothing. He was the rebound, and he didn't mind at all.

Chapter 46. Respectful Resolve

On the face of it, almost ten days of no contact with Rufus seemed to be fine for Robert, but Kristin could tell something wasn't quite right. During the evening of the next day, she unintentionally struck a nerve.

"You have barely mentioned your uncle Rufus. Is everything OK?"

Robert rolled off of his back toward her and snuggled his way up against her welcoming shoulder.

"I think I hurt his feelings the last time we spoke, and it's hard to repress my guilt, you know, with us getting so close. When the impulse to call him energizes, it's more like a flare than a flame, but I still manage to put it out."

"So he hasn't reached out to you in any way?"

"No, and I haven't made any effort either. He's going to be leaving for a conference pretty soon. I guess I've just been a coward. I was hoping that he'd call to say goodbye, or maybe even stop by here on his way to the airport."

"I know he is really important to you. I don't want to come between you two. So if this has anything to do with me. . . . . "

He stopped her in midsentence with a sudden slide of his hand down her belly to her inner thigh.

"Don't you worry pretty girl. Rufus and I are good, and we will always be good."

Robert knew that Kristin was not, in any way, the cause of his problems with Rufus, and so did she. They also knew that the pressure was building, and that it was only a matter of time before Robert would have to deal with his feelings. But it was just too easy for him to escape during those days. All he had to do was lower himself into the ever present steaming cauldron of sexual sustenance.

As Robert prepared for class the next morning, he couldn't get their conversation out of his mind. He summoned the courage to call Rufus. Voice mail, didn't leave a message. He called his Aunt Katie at the farm.

"Hello."

"Aunt Katie. I'm trying to get ahold of Rufus."

"Oh honey, I thought you knew. He left this morning for that astrology thing."

"A little stunned, Robert involuntarily voiced his feelings.

"Oh no!"

"Robert, is there something the matter?"

"Aunt Katie, please. . . . . just tell him I called."

After apologizing for bothering her, and a bit of small talk, Robert claimed he had to get to class. Overcome by the feeling that he had let his uncle down, he started to panic. He called Katie again, this time he asked for the flight number and departure time.

Hearing Kristin exit the shower, Robert called out to her.

"Hurry. Get dressed. We're going to the airport."

Speeding westward on the interstate, Kristin struggled to concentrate on her driving as she sought to calm him down. Robert was babbling about needing to see Rufus, and how he couldn't explain right then, and how he'd made a big mistake.

They had reason to believe that Rufus would use the airport's long-term parking, so they paced the sidewalk where the shuttles dropped off the passengers. Rufus's flight wouldn't depart for another two hours, so they were optimistic. There was a chance that he had already passed through security, but they tried not to think about it.

Suddenly, there he was, the blue-jean clad pony-tailed sheep farmer looking surprised, but otherwise absolutely thrilled. Rufus threw his bags to the side, and his arms wide open.

"A sight for sore eyes, nephew, and sportin' a pretty girl to boot. I bet you just wanted to show her off."

Kristin offered a polite hello, but given the tears running down Robert's cheeks, she thought it no time to socialize.

Rufus put his arm around his nephew and brought him in close and secure. With his other arm, he reached down and picked up both of his bags at one time. Kristin followed them into the building. The two men sub-consciously side-stepped their way into a vacant corner by the entry doors. Kristin stayed back to watch the bags.

Robert composed himself and asked Rufus if they could go back outside. Kristin could see only the bright light-glared vision of what was happening outside the window. She couldn't hear their conversation.

"You taught me that 'people do what they want', and sometimes I have a heck of a time figuring out exactly what it is I want. But I know now. God Damn it, I know now."

Rufus didn't figure it was time to speak, not quite yet. He offered only devoted attention.

"I shouldn't have questioned you, and I'm sorry if I hurt your feelings, or if I made you think I didn't care about your dream. But this is my time. I'm not worried about personal Gods, or theories of Heaven, or beneficent transits. I don't need any retrospective analyses. I need it raw, and real, and present time . . . . , not explained, not programmed, not predicted, not justified, not expected, not legitimized, not virtualized. I need to live it right now, like there's only one direction. Forward!"

Rufus stepped back from his nephew and threw his hands up in the air, as if he were stopping traffic to help people avoid an accident.

"I respect that Robert. You poor boy. It's going to be OK."

The cat was out of the bag, and the look on Rufus's face was strong encouragement to let it run.

"I want to feel everything. I don't want to spend any time analyzing anything. How did you feel, when you were armed with this knowledge, and only nineteen?"

"Just like you do now, but I didn't have anyone like me, screwing with my head. I was allowed to pursue astrology for fun, on my own terms, without the knowledge of someone's crazy quest, and without the burden of allegiance. I have asked too much of you."

Robert started to cry again, tears of reluctant joy, like someone who had gotten the last seat on the lifeboat. Respectful resolve was clear on the face of this young man, who felt he had no other choice, but to hit the one he loved with blunt force truth.

"You're right to pursue your dream, but it's not my dream."

Rufus didn't say anything. He merely smiled a sad smile, one that attempted to portray his love and support, restrained, reluctant to preach or teach. Only when Robert started to bite his lip, and beckoned with his eyes for Rufus to speak, did the older man offer his absolution.

"Robert, remember when I told you that your incredible strength and intelligence would always have to be tempered by the sensitivity of your Moon? Well now you know it. You have arrived."

Rufus hugged him with a manly hug and shoved him back quickly, as if to remind him to stand firmly on his own two feet.

"This is not your fight, and I think you know that. But you have learned how to love, and I humbly acknowledge your love for me. I understand why you cannot be a part of my mission, but that doesn't mean I'm sorry that I have shared it with you."

Rufus's voice started to crack a little, but his meager tears dried rapidly in the dry winter air.

"Forty-two years ago, I was where you are now, at the beginning. Uranus offered me a great gift in the form of transformative knowledge, and you're right, I was 'happy go lucky' about what I learned. But now astrology is something different. It is pulling me along with a relentless force of curious fascination. It is now nothing less than serious obsession. How close can I get to the edge of the volcano without burning up? How near can I fly to the sun? Can I even consider dying before I reach the top of the mountain, considering how long I've been climbing?"

"But, Rufus, I don't want you to get hurt, and I don't want Aunt Katie to get hurt, or Petey, or Matthew, or anyone!"

"Robert, I'm going back to the desert, that'll all. Right now it's all talk. Sure, this time there is an expectation that we can get down to business. Of course, the DCG is committed to seeing this through no matter how long it takes. You can bet there will be risks along the way, but we will evaluate each one when we come to it."

"Well, I wish you luck, and I love you."

"Monique has rented a home in the desert near the conference. We will have several days to concentrate our efforts on a practical approach to data collection before the Conference starts. That's why I'm leaving a little early.

I'm sorry I didn't call you, but I wanted you to have. . . . . .
. . . . . .well, just what you've got done telling me you
wanted. Now let's get back in there before that doll baby
of yours loses patience with us."

As they walked back into the terminal, Rufus tried to
encourage Robert not to worry.

"All of the members of the DCG have lives they
cherish. They all have families and people they love. We
will make every effort to achieve our goal without
jeopardizing our futures. Try to relax."

Once inside, Rufus concentrated on schmoozing
Kristin. As a creature of deception for the good of the
cause, he knew that Robert was going to be hard pressed
to explain what could have been so important. He hoped
Robert would not be forced to spill the beans about the
astrology project to a girl he had known for only short
time, but he also saw no reason to hold back on his own
obfuscation contribution.

As the clock ticked on, and Rufus nervously
considered his entry into the security checkpoint line,
Kristin thought it wise to give the boys another private
moment. When she was out of earshot, Rufus made his
confession.

"I know that it is very possible that I have been
caught in a trap of my own making. I realize that much of
my life has been characterized by the supreme assumption
that what is implied to be true may actually be true. I
know astrology so well that I have willingly danced a
madman's dance on the border of the retrospective and
the prospective. I have sinfully allowed myself the
predictive attitude all too often, leaving myself open to
criticism for embracing self-fulfilling illusions of truth.
But I don't care! I don't care, because if I am right,
whether I have led a virtual life, or a real one, it has been,
and will be, my life."